Wynanda

A STATE OF GRACE
DAILY MEDITATIONS

The Augustine Fellowship,
Sex and Love Addicts Anonymous,
Fellowship-Wide Services, Inc.

A STATE OF GRACE

DAILY MEDITATIONS

1550 NE Loop 410, Suite 118, San Antonio, Texas 78209

First Edition, 2019

Grateful Acknowledgement is made for the permission to reprint and adapt the following:
The Twelve Steps and the Twelve Traditions of Alcoholics Anonymous are copyrighted by Alcoholics Anonymous World Services, Inc., reprinted for adaptation by permission of the publisher.

This book is S.L.A.A. Fellowship-Wide Services Conference-approved literature.

Library of Congress Control Number: 2019918493

ISBN 978-1-7342265-0-8 (Hardcover)
ISBN 978-1-7342265-1-5 (Paperback)
ISBN 978-1-7342265-2-2 (ePub)
ISBN 978-1-7342265-3-9 (Mobi)

Cover Art; axllll / DigitalVision Vectors / 479362635 / Getty Images

This book was compiled by S.L.A.A.'s theJournal magazine staff and Volunteers. It contains various S.L.A.A.-related topics for each day of the year for the reader to contemplate. Each entry has a quote from S.L.A.A. Conference-approved literature, a share from an S.L.A.A. member and an affirmation.

The S.L.A.A. theJournal magazine disclaimer applies to the shares contained in this book: Stories, interviews, personal testimony, and other content contained herein are authored by members of Sex and Love Addicts Anonymous. The opinions expressed in theJournal shares are not necessarily the opinions of the Augustine Fellowship, S.L.A.A., Fellowship-Wide Services, Inc., F.W.S office, Annual Business Conference or any other Conference committee including the Conference Journal Committee or theJournal production staff.

Conference Literature Committee (CLC)

January 1

GRACE

As we contemplated our changing lives, we actually felt longing for a future time in which we might once again come to experience the magnificence of our own solitude, and come again to know directly that well-spring of inner dignity and wholeness which was filling us, and which was now to flow, through us, on into our lives in the world outside. We knew we had experienced a Grace. – S.L.A.A. Basic Text, Page 115

For me, Grace was hearing the Characteristics of Sex and Love Addiction for the first time. It was the calm that settled deep within me as I realized that I had this thing. Not only did I have it, but that it could be defined, that I was not alone, and that others were recovering from the pain of withdrawal, which was excruciating. Grace came to me in many forms, in finding a sponsor, in relating to literature, in helping others once I was out of withdrawal. It was the realization that I could be emptied out and rebuilt into the design my Creator had originally envisioned, which had become warped and damaged into unrecognizability by my love and fantasy addiction. My whole life strategy had created a miserable human being. Here, in these S.L.A.A. meetings, I was told I could empty that cup of misery and find recovery, solace and healing. This was truly grace.

The Grace of recovery is fully available to me. I ask my Higher Power for the willingness to be honest and open-minded.

January 2

ABUNDANT LIFE

Today I have hope that I can have a life as full and free as I've always wanted. – S.L.A.A. Basic Text, Page 189

It's not that I don't lack things in my life. I just try to avoid focusing on and complaining about it. I am grateful for what sobriety has given me. Addiction had backed me into a corner. I had a lonely life of going back and forth between my apartment and work and nightclubs. Some might think nightclubs are glamorous but not when you're trapped in your own addictive thoughts. Living a free life means that I am free (one day or one minute at a time) from the negativity and obsession that used to plague me. A full life, to me, means taking risks for healthy intimacy. I go on double dates and to parties where I connect with people, usually other S.L.A.A. members. It means meditation, fellowship, long walks in nature, going to the theatre, advancing my career; I could add to the list infinitely. So that's my focus in sobriety: Getting to know and take care of me instead of focusing all my energy on the object of my affection. It's much better to live in this world.

I am happy to be alive and look for ways to enhance my life.

January 3

IDENTIFICATION

I spent much time comparing rather than identifying. But then I began to get in touch with my emotions and feelings. Listening to others share their experiences brought up many feelings and memories. I could no longer avoid them through acting out...I found a tremendous amount of support in the fellowship, from people who were going through the same pain and from those who had gone through the same feelings. – S.L.A.A. Basic Text, Page 175

A member of S.L.A.A. regularly advises me to get out of judgment and to identify with people's shares. It can be transporting and transformative. Identifying with people's shares has brought me into contact with my deepest inner self. Often, the people I would judge or wouldn't relate to ended up giving me the skills I needed to look at the parts of myself that I've been avoiding. Once I heard an S.L.A.A. member share that he wished he could tell his grown children he was sorry for not being present. I've waited my whole life for my dad to say these very words to me. It felt like it was my dad talking directly to me and a shiver ran down my spine. It was so healing. I have heard many times from other members that they have had similar experiences. When I concentrate on the feelings being shared I usually realize that I've felt that way before. I look for the similarities and forget about the differences. I find intimacy in the rooms when I do this. We are all fighting a battle together.

I identify with others today, knowing that I battle this disease with the support of others.

January 4

WITHDRAWAL

Despite the grueling qualities of dealing with outer temptations and inner insecurities, we began to experience withdrawal not as deprivation, but as self-enrichment* – *S.L.A.A. Basic Text, Page 113

Withdrawal is a painful process. It is disorienting and confusing to transition from a life spent indulging every addictive impulse to one in which we reject these impulses and feel our feelings. Our entire system of living can be cast away to gain the gift of sobriety For some, the process is every bit as painful, if not more so, than withdrawing from drugs or alcohol. As we struggle through this period of abstaining, it seems that opportunities begin to pop up everywhere for us to slip back into addiction. It would be so much easier than facing the gut-wrenching experience of withdrawal. We listen to the experience of our fellows at S.L.A.A. meetings and hear them describe the pain they endured as they withdrew from sex and love addiction. Some even acted out on their bottom-line behaviors during the process and had to start again. Not everyone gets through withdrawal without acting out once or twice. But when we do make it through to the other side, we realize it is possible to abstain from acting out.

I ask my Higher Power to help me stay sober throughout my withdrawal and develop a healthy support system during this difficult time.

January 5

THE FIRST STEP

We admitted we were powerless over sex and love addiction – that our lives had become unmanageable. – S.L.A.A. Core Documents, "The Twelve Steps"

To admit that we are powerless over our sex and love addiction is a difficult and humbling process. Many of us have not been willing to admit that we lack power in any aspect of our lives. We believe that admitting this is tantamount to failure. Our perfectionism tells us that if we can't do something then we are deficient, unworthy or broken. True freedom comes from surrender, a paradox that is difficult to wrap our brains around. If we give up, we are taking the first step toward success in arresting our addictive behavior. It is okay to be imperfect. Addiction is not a personal failing. It is a spiritual "dis-ease" that may only be overcome with a spiritual solution. Have our lives become unmanageable? Are we sick and tired of being sick and tired? Recovery is possible if we are willing to open our minds to new possibilities and give up on living life on our own terms. Only we can make this decision for ourselves. No one else can force us to let go.

I am ready to surrender my strategy of the pursuit of and obsession with sex and love. I am willing to try a new way of living.

January 6

SHARING

First, we had to remember that even if our sex and love addiction stories fell on deaf ears, recounting them continued to put us in touch with our own experience, which in turn deepened our resolve. – S.L.A.A. Basic Text, Page 118

When I first arrived in S.L.A.A., full of pain and hopelessness, sharing my experiences for the benefit of others was the furthest thing from my mind. I desperately needed relief and felt I had so little, perhaps nothing, to give. Later, it gave me relief to think that all my pain might have value if it was to prove useful someday in some way to help another. Plus getting current often helped me find an answer to some troublesome problems. Sometimes people came up to me after the meeting and gave me insight or shared their experience, strength and hope. I found much-needed support. Sometimes just hearing myself say something out loud gave me insight into what I should do. Now I know in sharing the story of my life of sex and love addiction, with all its painful consequences, I'm the one who benefits. I am humbled and grateful for the miracle my Higher Power has given to me—a life transformed.

My Higher Power works through me to help others as I am helped. By serving others I strengthen my sobriety, ever grateful for my progress.

January 7

RESOLVE

"Success" in handling temptation was measured only by the outcome. The fact that I did not succumb, rather than the gracefulness (or lack of same) with which I resisted temptation, was the payoff. – S.L.A.A. Basic Text, Page 32

Once again, my hand rests upon the phone, that overwhelming urge to call my unhealthy ex-lover eating away at my resolve. We've all felt that way. We forget that we are calling someone who isn't capable of being there for us emotionally. We are aware that this is all a part of our sex and love addiction, but still cannot rid ourselves of that urge to call and don't have the strength to stop ourselves. What are some recovery tools that we could use during times like this? We could choose to phone or e-mail a program friend instead. We could pray to have the strength not to call. We could, at that very moment, write about the urge in our journals. We could take a walk, go for a drive, get involved in something we are interested in. We could do some service work and help someone else.

Higher Power, help me to remember the recovery tools I have available to me and to use them when I struggle.

January 8

LEAVING A RELATIONSHIP

A prospective partner's inability to accept us as we were would confront us with a choice. Either we would have to tailor ourselves to meet our prospective partner's expectations, or we would have to recognize that the raw material for partnership was not to be found with this particular person. – S.L.A.A. Basic Text, Page 154

For many of us, choosing whether to leave an unhealthy relationship or not can feel like one of the most excruciating decisions we've ever had to make in our lives. We may point to healthy aspects of the relationship and inflate them into reasons to stay. But, for our recovery, we need to leave. We fear and dread the loneliness. Will our self-esteem be able to endure the feelings of rejection when they don't call and beg us to come back? Many sex and love addicts are also fearful of doing without sex during the abstinence period. These issues can be a part of making a choice to end an unhealthy relationship and they can be painful. But the most difficult experience is making that decision. After the decision is made, the pain eases somewhat and a calmness washes over us in its place. Many of us have found that a no-contact rule helps bring us to this place of serenity. We give ourselves a chance to grieve the relationship without the chance of scheming to manipulate the person back into our lives. We can make better decisions when we're not face to face with our previous partner.

I pray for my Higher Power to provide me with the strength to get through that first wave of healthy pain that will lead to the calm, still waters of recovery.

January 9

THE FIFTH CHARACTERISTIC

We feel empty and incomplete when we are alone. Even though we fear intimacy and commitment, we continually search for relationships and sexual contacts. – S.L.A.A. Core Documents, "Characteristics of Sex and Love Addiction"

Society often tells us that we are incomplete if we are alone. We have a big hole of emptiness that only Higher Power can fill. Being alone in my apartment with my insane thoughts was intolerable in my first year of sobriety, but we don't have to be alone when we have a meeting and fellowship to go to or even outreach calls. We may fear intimacy and commitment. After all, being vulnerable in intimacy usually got us into painful situations in the past. Further, commitment sounds like prison to a sex and love addict. But interaction with fellows and our sponsors and service commitments can help us practice and get more comfortable with both. In S.L.A.A. we have come to find that a continual search for relationships and sexual contacts yields nothing but insanity, while a search for conscious contact with a Higher Power yields serenity.

I embrace intimacy and solitude. Today, I will pray and meditate when I feel lonely and know that I will be fine with my Higher Power by my side.

January 10

SEXUAL PREFERENCE

What we were increasingly "hearing" was the pulse of our common humanity, transcending all lines of gender, gender preference, or specific sexual aims. We were all fish in the same ocean. – S.L.A.A. Basic Text, Page 146

Those of us who were gay, lesbian, bisexual or transgendered were so isolated in our disease. Not only did we feel bad due to our out-of-control acting out, but we were also told we were bad by the society we lived in. It was a terrifying realization that we needed help and the ones who were likely to help us were part of that same society. So, with great trepidation we went to our first S.L.A.A. meeting. When it came time for us to share, we were in so much pain that we let it all out, including our sexual preference, as it is such an undeniable part of who we are. We expected to be doubly rejected, both for the terrible deeds we had done and for whom we loved. But others nodded in agreement and understood us. They accepted us. After the meeting, they came up to us and welcomed us. Meeting after meeting, we shared who we were and found unconditional acceptance. Finally, we have found the family we always wanted that loves us no matter our sexual preference or the color of our skin. We no longer need to hide who we love. We are all in this together, loving and helping each other recover. We have come home.

I courageously work this program, holding nothing back.

January 11

HIGHER POWER

Our relationship with God was indeed a personal one. It did not need to be consistent with the definition of any religious institution or the experience of any other person. In fact, we didn't have to define our Higher Power even for ourselves.
- S.L.A.A. Basic Text, Page 100

To some of us it may seem that spirituality is out of reach. Maybe we never knew a Higher Power. Many of us grow up with an idea of God imposed upon us. This world is filled with so many different interpretations of a Higher Power. There is no reason why each of us cannot have our own concept. I realized part of my resistance to turning over my life and my will was that I had superimposed my father onto God. I did not want a version of a Higher Power that I could never live up to or never please. When I could separate my view of my father from my concept of God, I got a sense that there is a more loving, giving and tolerant Power in the universe; that's the God that I build a relationship with today.

Today, I continue working on my conscious contact with my Higher Power.

January 12

REGRET

The guilt of prior deeds and passions or missed opportunities gave way to the deepest, most pervasive guilt of all: that of having left life unlived, of having turned our backs on the possibility of fulfilling a meaningful destiny. – S.L.A.A. Basic Text, Page 70

I'm sad today as I reflect on the high body count I left behind in my addiction; so many failed marriages, so many broken hearts Yet to stay stuck in regrets of the past is a waste of the life I can have Recovery for me today is not lingering too long in the regret, for that would defeat the very purpose of working the Steps. I need to be watchful, for these feelings can turn into shameful remorse Instead, I can genuinely feel the sorrow, and join with my Higher Power in the sacred act of letting go. I can learn to be loved and to love. I can learn to make wise and loving choices for myself. S.L.A.A promises me a different life if I am willing to do what is suggested I've had so many years of feeling unlovable, lonely, desperate and hopeless. I'd like the rest of my life to be different. With God and S.L.A.A. all things are possible, even a life of emotional sobriety.

Today, I can embrace sorrow, recognizing that my healing occurs in my Higher Power's will and time.

January 13

"WE" PROGRAM

A fellowship of others who can truly say, "Yes, I understand—I felt that way too" is a vital part of what makes recovery possible in each avenue of addiction. - S.L.A.A. Basic Text, Preface, Page viii

When we reach out to others we realize that we are not alone. We are so situated to be extremely helpful to another addict when we have gone through the same experiences and found our way to sobriety. The Steps say "we" for a reason. Many have recovered before us by using the tools of the program. When we hear our story in a meeting, we can usually identify. Even if we don't, we can know that the speaker is going through struggles as we are or have experienced. We can identify with the pain of the addiction and see others who have found a way out. They usually are of service and give us a hand in climbing out of a dark pit of despair. There is hope in the rooms and much-needed support. Instead of living in a closed relationship, relying only on one person to fulfill our needs, we have fellows. Speaking our truths in a meeting full of people and hearing others share on the same topic can be a relief and can bring about healing. Watching someone do service work for the meeting for fun and for free shows us that we are in a caring, helpful environment. Everyone pitches in to keep our "we" program alive and thriving.

I go to meetings, am of service and listen when others share. I remember that I am not alone.

January 14

SOBRIETY

We were living in the immediate present, and discovering that we could indeed make it through an hour, or a morning (mourning!), or a day. And we were discovering that there was a joy to be had in successfully negotiating our way through each twenty-four hour period. – S.L.A.A. Basic Text, Page 109

Some of us began our journey in S.L.A.A. by going cold turkey. We weathered our way through the storm of withdrawal, turning to our sponsors when we needed directions. Some of us had to hit one pothole after another, picking up desire chips on a regular basis until we were finally able to stay on a straight and sober course. No matter which path we take, it is important that we keep our eyes on the road, be open to asking for help and be gentle with ourselves. A long road trip must be made one mile at a time just as sobriety can only be obtained one day at a time. We need not worry ourselves by wondering why we haven't gotten as far as others have, comparing our insides to their flashy, sports car exteriors. Recovery is not a race. The more bumpy, slow-going and rougher the road we trudge in maintaining our sobriety, the more fulfilling the breakthrough to smooth cruise control when we finally turn the corner. Persevering in open connection with our Higher Power means that while our journey may be difficult there will also be some pleasant surprises around the bend.

I am sober today by the grace of God and continue to do my Twelve Step work and reach out to others.

January 15

HITTING BOTTOM

I had reached the point which is the prelude to change for most addicts: I was at my bottom. – S.L.A.A. Basic Text, Page 217

Why is it only by experiencing devastating pain that we begin to see clearly that change must come? Wouldn't it be more pleasant if we could simply act on the fleeting thought that perhaps this sexual encounter, or this emotional intrigue, could have disastrous results? Once we truly hit bottom, we are confronted with two choices: we either keep digging to self-destruction or we surrender. If we are able to surrender and fully accept our powerlessness, we are able to push ego and self-will out of the way and make room for our Higher Power. As we work each Step in our recovery process we begin to see we have choices. With help from our Higher Power, others in the program, our sponsor and the Steps, we begin to steer clear of our bottom-line behavior and the pain of finding yet another, deeper, bottom. We find it difficult to go through this ego-puncturing, but know that the alternative is worse. We may not survive another acting-out episode.

Today, I choose to use the tools of the program to help me stay free from the pain of my bottom-line behaviors.

January 16

CHARACTER DEFECTS

What would our lives be like, we wondered, if we were really to empty our chalice of disease and refrain from refilling it again ourselves, and instead let it be filled eventually through God's grace? – S.L.A.A. Basic Text, Page 76

Sometimes we may go to a meeting and find ourselves face to face with a mirror. She's talking about the way she beats herself up or he's talking about putting off talking to his sponsor. We may recoil. We may judge them. We might even find ourselves asking "How could they do that?" With a little self-reflection, we may find that the faults we point out in others are the very faults we despise in ourselves. As the old saying goes, "You spot it, you got it." Taking someone else's inventory keeps us from having to look at ourselves. But if we are rigorously honest and fearless in our Fourth Step, we may come to realize the inherent imperfection in everyone. Knowing that we don't have to be perfect opens the door to self-acceptance. Slowly but surely, we come to love ourselves and others, "warts and all." The Fifth Step allows us to be vulnerable with another human being without being judged. When we work Steps Six and Seven, we take an active role in letting go of those character defects that have gotten in the way of our usefulness to God and others. We ask our Higher Power to remove our shortcomings with the knowledge that it may be a long and painful process. It is only when we become willing to let them go that God can take them away.

I ask and become willing to have my Higher Power heal my character defects.

January 17

STATUS

In relationships with others we let go of self-serving power and prestige as driving motives. – S.L.A.A. Basic Text, Page 102

Before S.L.A.A., I wasn't really in relationships with others, they were objects to be manipulated to meet my needs. They didn't have thoughts and feelings. Self-serving power and prestige were the point of the relationship. Why would I want to let that go? When I listened to others share, I saw how pointless and dramatic it had all been. Most people sought power by going after the powerful partner, but I sought power by having control over my partner. My driving motives were to seek out attractive partners and do all kinds of crazy things to get them. I needed good-looking partners to validate my self-worth. I remember a friend saying, "How did you get him? He's so good looking, even I'd go out with him." I was so proud of myself. In sobriety, I've learned to be myself and see if I am compatible with another person. Today my partner and I are equals. I no longer feel the insecurity that leads to the need to control.

As I think about status today, I humbly seek opportunities to be of service to others.

January 18

THE SEVENTH TRADITION

Every S.L.A.A. group ought to be fully self-supporting declining outside contributions. – S.L.A.A. Core Documents "The Twelve Traditions"

Being self-supporting can be a struggle for addicts. We wasted so much money and time on our addiction. I never got the college degree that would have given me my dream high-paying career It can be a badge of honor to a sex and love addict when they ensnare the rich rescuer who makes all their money fears disappear Why struggle with dead-end jobs and dingy apartments when my addiction could give me world-wide travel and mansions? The one in charge of the checkbook has control. Being self-supporting brings self-esteem because we don't have to answer to anyone but God and ourselves. That goes for S.L.A.A. groups as well. This is the reason we decline outside contributions. We have a prudent reserve and running expenses from our own members and we don't accept donations over $20,000 per year from individuals Following these principles helps S.L.A.A. focus on its primary purpose: to help the addict who still suffers.

I am grateful for the ability to support myself today. I am not alone.

January 19

WISDOM

The time-honored Serenity Prayer became a part of our daily repertoire for handling challenging and potentially dangerous situations: God, grant me the serenity to accept the things I cannot change, courage to change the things I can, and wisdom to know the difference. Thy will, not mine, be done. – S.L.A.A. Basic Text, Page 77

Growing up, my dad always told me I was very intelligent but had no street smarts. I thought, ***If he only knew about my secret life***. He was right. I had no experience handling challenging situations because I always ran from them into mind-numbing addiction. I had no knowledge because if I could use sex to escape the consequences of my mistakes, I did. Good judgment eluded me. The Twelve Steps and my spiritual experience changed that for me. I no longer had to rely on myself to make decisions. Prayer and meditation often showed me the correct path to take with challenges. I learned to avoid potentially dangerous situations and practice self-care instead. The difficult part is having the wisdom to know the difference between the things I can change and those I cannot. Hearing people's stories in the room, being in contact with my feelings and listening for my Higher Power's will have all helped give me wisdom. We can't battle this disease without it.

I grow in wisdom and strength daily by saying the Serenity Prayer.

January 20

DENIAL

***If we were able to manage the maze of intrigue without discovery, or could keep the one we were dependent on from knowing our true feelings, then we apparently never had to deal with the consequences of our actions. We could even deny to ourselves that there were such things as "consequences."* – S.L.A.A. Basic Text, Pages 81-2**

The word "denial" has so many meanings and I suffered from all of them. I like the acronym D.E.N.I.A.L.—Don't even know I am lying. That's what it was for me in my first few years of working the Steps. I either hid behind my character defects or didn't know I was engaging in them. When sponsors pointed them out in my Fifth Steps, initially I got angry and believed they were wrong. But after careful consideration, I realized I was in denial. Relationships before S.L.A.A. were all about assigning others magical qualities. I wanted the perfect partner but was usually with an abusive or disinterested partner. So, the only possible way to stay in that situation was by living in denial. This character defect was also a large part of my infidelities. When in danger of getting caught, I would deny, deny, deny. This usually left me juggling all sorts of untruths and patting myself on the back for being intelligent enough to keep my stories straight. But this was a high-anxiety way to live. I also denied my needs in bad relationships. Before finding healing in S.L.A.A., I believed my only choices were to continue living this confusing life full of all sorts of denial, or to kill myself. Thank God the program gave me another way of life.

I live in reality today, rather than denial. I keep conscious contact with my Higher Power and check my motives with S.L.A.A. members.

January 21

HIDING OUT IN MEETINGS

[We had] tremendous incentive...to stay closed and not reveal our true selves to anyone! But in continuing to "go it alone" we were suffering from emotional and spiritual constipation, unable to make constructive use of our experiences and emotions. - S.L.A.A. Basic Text, Page 82

I will often go to meetings and refuse to share. I sit in the back of the room at large meetings and run out the door as soon as the meeting ends. I don't allow people to get to know me. I fear they won't like me because I'm different or they can't relate to me because I'm a porn addict and they are love addicts. But I see people share all the time who are unique and they get a lot of love and support from the fellowship. My sponsor told me, "If you feel isolated, it's because you're not taking contrary action: outreach calls, sharing and greeting people." I had to get to the meeting twenty minutes early and talk to someone new. I had to get the phone list and call people. I needed to take every opportunity to share, even if my addict voices were telling me not to. The voices would say, "You don't have anything good to share. People will dislike you. You shared last week, so just be quiet this week." Those are just old tapes from childhood, trying to keep me sick and alone. When I participate in my recovery, I reap the rewards. I'm surrounded by a supportive community even during difficult times.

I stay open and reveal my true self today, letting people into my life.

January 22

HUMILITY

In humility, we understood that we were only being asked to get out of God's way, so that, with our cooperation, God's work could be done in our lives. – S.L.A.A. Basic Text, Page 87

I thought humility meant putting myself down in front of others even if I didn't really believe it. Fellows in the program said that it's an honest appraisal of oneself and our place in life—being a worker among workers—not being below the ground underneath everyone else or high up in the sky above everyone. When we put ourselves down, we're saying Higher Power made a mistake and when we're grabbing for the brass ring we're ignoring our purpose (to be of service). Before my Twelve-Step-induced spiritual experience, I thought God was out to get me, or at least just inept when it came to my life. He wasn't doing it right, so I had to take over. I couldn't get out of God's way. I wanted what I wanted, when I wanted it. All Twelve Steps, done in order, showed me how to cooperate and do God's work. I'm not always willing because my addict voices whisper to me that I'm better than this. But when I go to a meeting, I'm reminded of where I could be and that the Steps are working in my life. I need to give back in order to keep it.

I pray for guidance and the willingness to do my Higher Power's will today.

January 23

NEWCOMERS

Each of us in...(S.L.A.A.) knows the confusion and difficulty of walking into the first few meetings, feeling like a newcomer in new surroundings. Whether we took this courageous step out of pain and hopelessness, sought relief from longing and emptiness or were directed to attend, we move toward recovery by being here. – from the "Welcome" pamphlet

What is it like to enter a meeting for the first time? Some people are scared. Others are angry. There are also those who walk into a meeting simply to please someone else. There are even a happy few who are able to walk into a meeting proud and relieved to be there. It is important to remember those feelings. When someone new walks into a meeting, we can put ourselves in that spot again. What would be important to hear from the group as a newcomer? What will help keep them coming back? It has been said that the newcomer is the most important person in the room. It is our primary purpose to carry our message to the sex and love addict who still suffers. When that person walks in the door and we hear them tell their sad story, we see ourselves the way we were not so long ago. Nothing puts our recovery in perspective like hearing the fresh pains of addiction. We are reminded of how far we've come. Further, we have the responsibility and the privilege to share our experience, strength and hope. We do it for them because someone did it for us.

Old-timers are the backbone of the program and newcomers are its lifeblood. Today, I take responsibility to welcome the newcomer.

January 24

MAGICAL THINKING

My earliest memories [are] of...dreaming of this or that girl in school who would save my life...and the transforming magic of losing myself in the fantasy of loving. All at once the turmoil in life seemed to stop and the fantasy was enough to temporarily obliterate pain. – S.L.A.A. Basic Text, Page 197

I wanted so badly to believe that I was going to get what I wanted from the person I was obsessed with, that I turned them into the ever-elusive unicorn. I thought my brain was that powerful–that if I thought about it enough I could change reality. I once heard a speaker say, "We try to manage and control our thinking." I get lost in magical thinking, especially when I can't handle the reality of my life, or when I want something desperately. That's probably why video games are so popular. But no one gets back up after you kill them in real life. That's the danger of getting lost in the fantasy world. Sometimes I don't even know I'm doing it because when there's another person involved, it can seem like reality. My qualifier and I thought we were in love and going to live a dream life. But while we focused on the fantasy, we didn't notice the complete devastation of those around us.

Today, through prayer and meditation, I live in reality.

January 25

THIRTEENTH STEPPING

Each lonely addict, hungry for fellowship, and trapped in the compulsive need for some specific indulgence that only increases the yawning void within, is in a kind of pain which he or she feels only someone who has similarly experienced it in his or her form of addiction can truly understand. – S.L.A.A. Basic Text, Preface, Page vii-viii

We need to have a boundary we don't cross when it comes to making program friends. Twelve Step work and fellowship are some of the best parts of the program. I know from experience the desperate need to find a partner in crime. I found that someone in the rooms of S.L.A.A. Most people think of thirteenth stepping as some lurking predator who preys on any newcomer who walks through the door. But predatory behavior can be subtle. In my case, it was the late-night talks after the meeting (about God) and the fellowship "dates" (They would even order my food for me.). Before they showed up, I felt like a kid again in fellowship get-togethers and connected to the program. But as soon as they showed up my addiction was off and running. We are told to make outreach calls and go to meetings and work the Steps. But when that person is the only one we want to talk with, the situation has crossed over into addiction. It's good to make program friends who can help you through withdrawal but if that spark starts it's better to shut it down than to get stuck in the mud of thirteenth stepping.

I choose healthy program friends and set appropriate boundaries. I know that I am worthy of real love.

January 26

THE ELEVENTH SIGN OF RECOVERY

We learn to value sex as a by-product of sharing, commitment, trust and cooperation in a partnership. – S.L.A.A. Core Documents "S.L.A.A. Signs of Recovery"

Learn to value sex? Why would I have to learn that? I thought I did value sex above all else. But like the Basic Text says, when it's a "rapid consumption commodity on an open market" it has no value. When it's a means to an end, and done out of desperation, it has even less. When I first heard this Sign of Recovery, I thought it impossible that sex could ever be a by-product of anything. It takes center stage in our society. It sounded like it would become an afterthought and that horrified me. Sex was an easy way out of problems in a relationship. Why should I have to work so hard at sharing, commitment, trust and cooperation? I was never good at those things. Trust was not attainable after all that people had done to me. Cooperation means compromise and I was too fearful for that. I felt that if I compromised, I would lose myself. Compromise, to me, meant always doing what the other person wanted. But I can honestly say that after all my work in S.L.A.A. and reliance on my Higher Power, I have seen this Sign come true in my life. Instead of the boredom that I thought I would have felt, I have a life-affirming dignity that I wouldn't trade for anything.

I value sex as a by-product of a healthy relationship. Today I focus on openness and intimacy in my partnership.

January 27

POSITIVE THINKING

We were coming to know that our own attitudes and actions were the only aspects of our lives which we stood any real chance of influencing. – S.L.A.A. Basic Text, Page 98

We mirror our world, and our world mirrors us right back. If we laugh, the world can seem to laugh joyfully with us and when we're sad the whole world seems to cloud over. This is no mere metaphor. Scientists have discovered special brain cells called mirror neurons that respond equally in action or in observance of another's action. This means our very cells experience the world around us as if they are that world—one more reason why it's important to surround ourselves with healthy images to build our bodies, our consciousness and our future. When we feel that everything is going wrong, sometimes it can help to look at all the things that are going right. It might not always work and sometimes we might even need to feel bad for a little while before we feel good again. But more often than not, this is a technique that is healthy for us and a technique that works.

If I get lost in negative thinking, I pray and make outreach calls to S.L.A.A. fellows, remembering to be grateful for the little things that make my life better.

January 28

REPUTATION

We needed to find some bedrock from which to assay, without illusion, who and what we had been in the world, what we had held ourselves up to be to others and to ourselves. Furthermore we needed to...understand the payoffs we had derived from our addiction. – S.L.A.A. Basic Text, Page 79

People deal with reputation in different ways. Some people keep their addiction very hidden, so any sign of the addiction in their outer world would be devastating. Other people act out however they please, calling their addiction a lifestyle. I've done both. I kept up a false front in my life and it was important that no one knew what was going on with me. I tried to hide everything. If people were starting to question or find out about my secret life, I would just pretend it wasn't happening. There came a point where my acting out started happening so much that I just started to embrace it as a lifestyle. I started to be proud of how many people I slept with, and how sexually provocative I could be. At the same time, I was really focused on protecting my reputation. A lot of energy went into trying to control what people thought about me. I never once thought about controlling the behavior that was the cause of my bad reputation. It wasn't until I joined the program and started getting recovery that I realized what a futile endeavor it was to try to control my reputation. The only way that we can change how we are perceived is by living up to our own values, integrity and principles.

Today, I let go of fear and take actions that boost my self-esteem.

January 29

LONELINESS

We found that we were forming warmer relationships with friends, coworkers, and even casual acquaintances. Today we may live alone, but we have found rewarding friendships and companionship without sex, and we are not lonely. – S.L.A.A. Basic Text, Page 140

Many people in recovery are familiar with the acronym, H.A.L.T. This is a tool for assessing ourselves, a way of taking a spot-check inventory. The "L" in H.A.L.T. stands for lonely. Loneliness is a trigger. We don't need to be exposed to provocative images or messages from a past lover in order to be triggered. Feelings can trigger us too. Picture the addict, alone at home, with nothing exciting to occupy their time. Who wants to do the laundry or the dishes on a Saturday night? One of the most important things we can do for ourselves when we feel triggered by loneliness is to take an action that is contrary to our feelings. My sponsor says when I'm feeling lonely and no one is calling it's because I haven't been reaching out in meetings. We have a network of people available to reach out to when we are struggling. The thought of acting out may be far from our minds, however if loneliness is a trigger, we recognize it. Left unacknowledged, the feeling can grow into something bigger and lead to acting out down the road. If I'm feeling lonely, but I don't feel like calling anyone, then that is exactly what I need to do.

I use the tools of the program. If feeling lonely, I make outreach calls, go to a meeting or seek fellowship.

January 30

PHYSICAL ATTRACTION

We began to recognize that our disease, far from being just a way to stop the clock with pleasure and intensity, had molded our personalities in ways that would maximize our ability to get the addictive returns! Our physical appearance, our mannerisms, the way we went about our careers or other activities, many of the traits we thought of as our identifying trademarks, as who we were, had been designed to serve our sex and love addiction. – S.L.A.A. Basic Text, Page 73

Whenever I felt an attraction to someone, I would lie, cheat and steal to be with them. If they looked good and I hated their personality, I ignored that red flag. A lot of flaws can be overlooked when distracted by beauty. When I had a strong physical attraction, I thought it was a chemical reaction (our body chemistry matched so it must have been a match made in Heaven). I spent a lot of time and money searching for that spark. In sobriety, it's tough to find a balance between caring about my appearance to have healthy self-esteem and trying to attract someone inappropriate. Once my qualifier started lurking around my meetings and I started wearing more and more revealing clothing, rationalizing that it was "business attire." A fellow called me on it, saying that I was being predatory and trying to entice a spiritually sick, vulnerable person. I woke up, checked my motives and went back to normal "boring" business attire. I can dress up when it's appropriate and my motives are clean. Sexual charm is best left to those who can handle it.

I care about how I present myself today. I keep my thoughts about my appearance in perspective.

January 31

BETRAYAL

The anger and outrage filled me, and I yelled and screamed at him, hoping that it would lessen the intense pain of betrayal that I felt...if I could...believe that he was truly an uncaring and wicked person, I could save myself the immense suffering of losing someone I really loved. – S.L.A.A. Basic Text, Page 54

Sex and love addicts often choose partners who are the type to betray us or we betray others to try and get our needs met. When we rely on other people (instead of ourselves and God) to meet all of our needs, the betrayal is more intense. If we are doing the betraying, the consequences are more severe. We need to have a support group to rely on. But in the dredges of our disease, we can't help it when we break trust. We are powerless. We need to have multiple partners, lie about mistakes, keep secrets and trust untrustworthy people. Keeping our supply of sex and love is more important than any degree of honesty or dignity. S.L.A.A., through prayer and the Twelve Steps, shows us a way out. We learn to slowly shed our secrets in shares with our sponsor and fellows. We learn to be honest in our Fourth and Fifth Steps and eventually in our everyday lives. We walk with dignity and don't have to worry anymore that the house of cards will come crumbling down around us in a dramatic display of our betrayals.

I show those I love who I really am. I am open, honest and direct.

February 1

THE SECOND STEP

Came to believe that a Power greater than ourselves could restore us to sanity. – S.L.A.A. Core Documents, "The Twelve Steps of S.L.A.A."

It was by a lake in a park when I had my moment of crisis. I realized that business trips and acting out were going to be synonymous. I had read spiritual books on dealing with sin and living the overcoming life. I tried every strategy I could think of. I prayed, wept and spent an entire vacation retreat studying what I hoped would be the victorious key. I even threatened myself with consequences, and yet here I was again. This time I had moved even further into an area that I had believed was morally off limits. What was I doing back here again? In my shroud of shame, I hadn't realized that this place of powerlessness was a good thing, providing I didn't give up in despair. My only choice was to embrace the possibility that my cycle of degeneration could be broken through the initiative of a benevolent power, distinct and separate from myself. "I can't do it" really does mean "I can't do it." Yet, this isn't a place of despair but of hope. For when I come to the end of my hoarded resources, I find a Higher Power who is graciously willing to act.

I accept my powerlessness and see the door of hope that my Higher Power has provided.

February 2

TROPHY THINKING

Advertisements, films, TV, magazines constantly promote the idea of attractiveness, beauty and sexual charm as the objective of our otherwise dull lives. It seemed ironic that because I excelled so well in these highly touted virtues, my life became such a mess, and finally unraveled. – S.L.A.A. Basic Text, Page 216

S.L.A.A. helped me discover that a lot of my ideas about prestige and social status were wrong. In my addictive thinking, I saw myself as a trophy wife, I was attractive smiled a lot, but I was dying inside. Trophies are given in victory or conquest and mounted on a shelf. They have no other use than to look good for the victor. They have no thoughts or feelings. Their purpose is only to feed the ego and social status of the person who won them. I thought love was a game. So, if someone "won" me I must be a trophy. I liked the idea that I was attractive enough that someone would try to win me. But being preserved on a shelf and feeding someone else's ego all the time doesn't leave room for my hopes and dreams. I didn't pursue my interests because I had to conform to the game. I had my own trophy-thinking about my partner. I didn't like him as a person, but when he showed interest, I transformed from the nerdy little girl into the glamorous girlfriend of the most popular kid in town. I spent a lot of time and money making sure I stayed attractive to him. S.L.A.A. showed me that I have value outside of my appearance and sexual charm. I wouldn't trade the freedom that this idea brings for anything.

I treasure the trophy of emotional and sexual sobriety today, knowing I am worthy of love and respect.

February 3

THE COMMON DENOMINATOR

We find a common denominator in our obsessive/compulsive patterns, which transcends any personal differences of sexual orientation or gender identity. – S.L.A.A. Preamble

The disease doesn't discriminate. People in the rooms of S.L.A.A. are from all different levels of society and stages of life. We are people who would not normally mix. I have no reason to meet and talk to a Wall Street tycoon and yet sometimes I can find him sitting next to me at a meeting or fellowship. I laugh at myself when I'm shocked to find out what people do. It's as if I forget that rich or famous people can get struck down by sex and love addiction too. Newcomers may be uncomfortable with being around people who are different. But we can't afford to let personal differences get in the way of recovery. The Traditions help us with that. Tradition One states that "our common welfare should come first; personal recovery depends upon S.L.A.A. unity." We care about others. We practice love and tolerance and create a safe space for recovery. We don't fight about religious or political beliefs. We stay focused on our primary purpose—to carry the message of recovery from sex and love addiction to the addict who still suffers.

I focus on unity today and know that I am of service to my fellow addicts.

February 4

CHILDHOOD FEARS

Behind this staged setting [my adult life] was a driven, scared boy who didn't believe he had any intrinsic value, whose goodies might be taken away at any moment, and whose only workable tool to handle this papier-mâché world was a series of ongoing love affairs and intriguing escapades around the world. – S.L.A.A. Basic Text, Page 216

When I was young my father was called away to war. He went away for 21/2 years and my mother cried every night and thought he was going to die. I've dealt with abandonment my whole life by being afraid of it. I got abstinent in S.L.A.A., went on a dating plan and married my partner. Still, every time he went away for a business trip, I would feel immense abandonment. I'd be so depressed I couldn't take care of myself and I wouldn't be able to do my Step work. I realized it was a childhood fear that I was feeling and that I didn't have to feel abandoned. I had a program, I had support people and my sponsor to go to, and I had meetings to take me out of the childhood trauma. Most of all, I realized my Higher Power never abandons me. No one can abandon me today except myself. People do leave, but it's usually not about me.

I value myself. I make healthy and loving choices today.

February 5

ENVY AND JEALOUSY

I had been subjected to yet another of the now routine bouts of intense craving and desire, stimulated by still another temptation which was compounded by the agony of seeing someone else help himself to what would formerly have been "my" territory!* – *S.L.A.A. Basic Text, Page 33

Envy means I want something that someone else has. Jealousy means I'm afraid I'll lose something I have to someone else. Recognizing envy in oneself can be painful. Perhaps I see a friend or family member who has the success that I desire, and I envy them, maybe even resent them. I am unable to experience happiness for that person because I am too caught up in what I want. Further, I make their accomplishment into a reflection of my lack thereof. Rather than focusing on what others have, it is more productive for me to express gratitude for what I do have. If I desire greater accomplishment in my life, I must be willing to put in the work to attain it. Addiction has held me back and obscured my goals. It made me lose sight of what is truly important. Through the process of recovery, it is possible to realign my priorities and be the person I want to be. I can be happy for others while working to attain my goals and be grateful for the blessings I already have.

Higher Power, thank you for the gifts you have given me. I focus on and take pleasure in the good fortune of my friends and family.

February 6

REFLECTION

Many of us found that both daily and on a periodic basis we needed to set aside times for solitude and reflection. These times of self-overhaul provided an opportunity to touch base with ourselves and our progress, and keep perspective on our spiritual development. – S.L.A.A. Basic Text, Page 97

The dictionary definition of reflection contains the idea that we form thoughts and opinions through meditation. Before S.L.A.A., I would not have made the connection between meditation and reflection. I thought I should draw my own thoughts and conclusions from the quiet. They were my own ideas and opinions even if they came from thin air. In the days of my addiction, I didn't have much time for reflection. I was too busy trying to get ahead or find "the one" and forgetting to touch base with myself and my progress. Why sit in solitude with yourself if you're just going to beat up on yourself all the time? I didn't like the direction my life was going, never asked for God's help, and didn't like any of the ideas that my brain came up with anyway. With practice, I have been able to quiet those voices and be honest with myself about my progress in S.L.A.A. and in life. I sit quietly and ask for my Higher Power's direction. Anything that is revealed to me, I take to fellows to be sure it's not my own selfish ideas.

Today, I set aside time for reflection in my busy life.

February 7

SAFE SPACE

The only real "safety" any S.L.A.A. group (and S.L.A.A. as a whole) can ever have is a desire to get well which is held in common by a majority of group members, and the availability of that Grace, bestowed by a Power greater than us all, which alone makes recovery possible. – S.L.A.A. Basic Text, Page 133

Safety in the rooms is so important. When I came to my first meeting, I wasn't sure what others would think of my past behavior. I thought I might end up an outcast among the outcasts. But even in the tiny group that welcomed me for the first time, there was someone whose story was nearly identical to my own. Because that person felt safe sharing the details of their past, it felt safe for me to reveal my shame and tell all the secrets that I held for so many years in my addiction. We create a safe space by sharing openly and honestly from the heart. This opens up space for the newcomer. That was a key for me, knowing that other people shared the same feelings and pain and that it's all right to share those experiences. When a newcomer is present, I share the difficult, shame-ridden details of my acting out, because they could be just as scared as I was the first time. Maybe they're just waiting for someone else to say what is already on their heart, so they will know they're in a safe space and it's okay to be vulnerable.

I feel safe in meetings and with friends in S.L.A.A., people who understand and accept me.

February 8

IF IT'S HYSTERICAL, IT'S HISTORICAL

All of us, without exception, went through periods during which we were extremely vulnerable to mental and emotional shocks. Often these seemed to occur as a result of coincidental meetings or contact, direct or indirect, with old addictive situations. – S.L.A.A. Basic Text, Page 111

Quite often in my withdrawal, I would come away from a situation saying, "Why did I overreact like that?" I was crying for days, or screaming at someone with no cause, or so sad that I didn't want to do anything. On my first intimate sober date, I made spaghetti and the entire time I was cooking, a voice in my head said, "You're doing this wrong. He's going to hate it. He'll never date you again." I was a wreck by the time he came over for dinner. Later I realized that as a child whenever I tried to help my mother make dinner, I got berated for everything I did and eventually banned from the kitchen until my next attempt. This was my insanity of trying the same thing over and over again expecting different results. As an adult, I was playing those tapes in my mind from my childhood and torturing myself. When I realized this, I was able to let it go and be kind to myself. My date loved the spaghetti and asks me to make it even today. I don't have to listen and believe my mother's voice in my head anymore. If I start to get hysterical in a situation, I will pause and ask myself, "Is this historical?" If so, I will give it to my Higher Power.

I love myself exactly as I am. I choose to stay in the present.

February 9

BEST THINKING

If our sex and love addiction was such a fundamental part of our personality…then we had to ask whether all our prior ideas about who and what we were might be incorrect or ill-founded. We had to admit to the possibility that anything, if not everything we believed could be faulty. – S.L.A.A. Basic Text, Page 76

My best thinking got me into the rooms of S.L.A.A. My addiction was so much a part of my personality that I couldn't separate the unhealthy addict ideas from the healthy ones. I was working towards goals that had no basis in reality and thinking that crazy schemes would fix me. Often, my foundation for any goal was, "Maybe this will work." It usually ended up making things worse. I engaged in a "glamorous" career that sometimes satisfied my need for attention and love but gave me no real sense of personal worth or dignity. Even when I thought I was trying to help others, my ideas were twisted by the addiction. Step Two says that we "came to believe that a Power greater than ourselves could restore us to sanity." When I pray and meditate over an idea rather than running right out and trying it, I get a clearer picture of my motives and how it will affect my life. My sponsor taught me to think the idea through to its logical conclusion. I had to list pros and cons and possible outcomes. We aren't supposed to futurize, but in this case, it's helpful in spotting faulty thinking that is dressed up by the disease as best thinking.

I analyze my best thinking by praying, meditating and talking to fellows before acting on anything important.

February 10

THE SEVENTH CHARACTERISTIC

We use sex and emotional involvement to manipulate and control others. – S.L.A.A. Core Documents, "Characteristics of Sex and Love Addiction"

"Why do all our arguments end in sex?" was a question my boyfriends asked often. I usually got my way. I used emotional involvement to control my friends if I couldn't have sex with them. I had to control everyone in my world or I didn't feel safe. I wished the world was a stage and I could be the director. I believed the only way to control someone else was to manipulate and threaten. If someone was emotionally involved, the threat of abandonment was a powerful tool. If they were a sex addict, the threat of withholding sex would pull them over to my way of thinking, even if I wasn't prepared to carry through with the threat. When I joined S.L.A.A., I had to start letting go of all my tools of manipulation. The phrase 'Let the chips fall where they may" helped me so much. My sponsor would constantly remind me that what my partner was doing was none of my business. I had to stick to working on my sobriety and my side of the street. If someone let me down, I couldn't manipulate to change the outcome. I had to look at the reality of every situation and take care of myself honestly.

I let go and let God. I keep the focus on myself and my own recovery.

February 11

SOCIAL NORMS

To the observer, my life was the American Dream come true: beautiful wife, two handsome children, large home, pool and tennis court, cars, travel, etc. Behind this staged setting was a driven, scared boy. – S.L.A.A. Basic Text, Page 216

I live in a city where there is no longer the "normal" family with 2.5 kids and the white picket fence. That didn't prevent me from chasing some unknown and ever-elusive ideal. I just wanted to fit in. I thought sex and love was the way to do this. I played mind-reader. I thought I knew what God and society wanted. Before S.L.A.A. I thought the point of life was to be sexy and catch the rescuer who would make me "normal" and help me fit into society. The rooms of S.L.A.A. and Twelve Step work made me question all of that. I realized that my idea of what society wanted wasn't what Higher Power had in store for me at all. I have none of the assumed prizes: big house, career or children. My role in the world is to try to be humble and of service; I never would have thought of that or been willing to take on that role. I'm grateful to S.L.A.A. for opening my eyes to the truth. What other people think about me is their business and not mine.

I focus on humility today and how I can be of service to others.

February 12

ANXIETY

It wasn't too long...before the floating anxieties became anchored. I began experiencing full-blown panics, the kind that would make me grip the table to make sure I didn't float off into space...The mounting sexual activity and growing deceit had finally broken me. – S.L.A.A. Basic Text, Page 217

Usually when I feel anxiety, it's because I'm afraid of losing something I have or not getting something I think I need. Fear creates all kinds of havoc in my life. It's one of the worst emotions, making me want to act out and numb out. Dealing with fear using sex and love addict behaviors only creates more fear and anxiety. S.L.A.A. taught me tools gave me tools and taught me how to deal with fear. I share my fear with others and they give me their experience, strength and hope. Building self-esteem instead of tearing it down with acting out saved my life. I saw only hospitals and institutions or suicide in my future when I was acting out. When I saw that I could stop with the help of a Higher Power and Twelve Step action, I had a glimmer of hope. Over the years, that glimmer has turned into a beacon that steadies me whenever the storms of anxiety hit. It doesn't disappear completely from my life, but it's much more manageable.

I share my inventory work with my sponsor and Higher Power, knowing that it helps me manage my feelings and sobriety.

February 13

SHARING THE MESSAGE, NOT THE MESS

The summation principle, the Twelfth Step, is the affirmation of personal recovery through accepting the responsibility to take the commitment to this way of life into action by sharing it with others. And it is here that true love, which is of God, and makes it possible for one person to touch the soul of another, is found and expressed. – S.L.A.A. Basic Text, Page vii

For many years, I went to S.L.A.A. and couldn't get sober. I had one sponsee that my sponsor told me to let go of because I was just sharing the mess with her. Despite this, I was still asked to do the long share at meetings. Every share was garbled. I went through a year of crying everywhere I went. Today, with many years of sobriety and many service commitments and sponsees I give back where I can because of all those years of sharing the mess in every meeting. Through all the pain, the people in the rooms accepted and loved me anyway. That's what the message is today for me. I was really messed up for many years but S.L.A.A loved me anyway, and today I'm the kind of respectable person I always wanted to be. The old-timers who knew me back then attest to the power of the program when they compare the old me to the person in recovery that I am today. Seeing my transformation gave them hope. I've seen people with completely wrecked lives recover and become leaders in the world. It's a beautiful thing to watch people recover.

I let go of ego and carry the message of recovery.

February 14

AUGUSTINE FELLOWSHIP

Augustine of Hippo—as those who have read his autobiography, Confessions, ***know—was probably one of us...the dynamics of Augustine's story, the inner workings and struggles of the person himself, left us with little doubt that he would have understood, and felt welcome among us. - S.L.A.A. Basic Text, Page 130-1***

It was rumored that when he was young, Augustine had many affairs and believed that humans are naturally inclined to sin. His famous prayer is "Grant me chastity and continence, but not yet."* Some might worry that naming S.L.A.A. "The Augustine Fellowship" might be considered religious affiliation. The Basic Text explains the first group's reasons for adding "The Augustine Fellowship" to our name. Meeting places often have difficulty with any group that has the word "sex" in their title. Getting something in the mail from The Augustine Fellowship draws much less scrutiny from over-observant mail carriers and nosey neighbors than "sex and love addicts" does. Even our Basic Text no longer has the name on its cover. Even though most of us have been rebels our whole lives, we had to find a way, as a group, to work within society. We had to deal with skepticism and fear in an adult way. We have a responsibility to the fellowship. When people needed reassurances in the early days of S.L.A.A. they accommodated their needs by using The Augustine Fellowship as their name, and eventually started using both names. It takes time to earn trust and respect and that's what they did.

*Augustine of Hippo, Confessions, 8:7

Today, I have faith that my Higher Power has a plan. More is revealed as I stay on the road of recovery.

February 15

GETTING ARRESTED

One evening I met someone, went into one of the stalls with him, and within minutes was under arrest by vice police who were watching behind a wall. In that moment, I felt totally devastated. I thought my life was over. I was now a criminal. At nineteen, I was caught...and no one in my family knew that I was gay. Not the best way to come out to your parents.
– S.L.A.A. Basic Text, Page 172

Twenty-five years ago, I was arrested for public lewdness by an undercover cop. At that time, I had 10 years sober in A.A. but had done no serious Fourth Step work on my sexual inventory. I was seeking what I thought was a suitable substitute for love in all the wrong places. It took this first arrest to get my attention about sex and sobriety. Court-ordered to S.L.A.A., I attended meetings, obtained the S.L.A.A. text, and began work on the Steps with a sponsor. Shortly after my probation ended, I attended fewer and fewer meetings and stopped working the Steps. I relapsed. In 1996 I was charged with indecent exposure. I was again court-ordered to S.L.A.A. and on probation for two years. All this to say, I qualify for this program. Today, I do not act out on my bottom-line behavior. I attend meetings regularly, read Twelve Step literature, work the program and meet with my sponsor weekly. Sponsoring others helps me remain active in sobriety. Finally, and perhaps most importantly, I invite God into everything I do. Without God, I am lost to my addictive nature.

It is with a grateful heart that I choose to live my life sober.

February 16

SATISFACTION

The sex and love addict would come to substitute the thrill of sexual adventure or intensity of "love" for the more encompassing satisfactions, founded first and foremost on self-respect, and later realized in family, career and community. – S.L.A.A. Basic Text, Page viii

I used to live by the phrase, "I can't get no satisfaction." I thought it made me cool to be continually on the search for more—more attention, more and better sex, etc. When my sponsor told me to embrace the boredom, it sounded like assigning myself to hell. Life without the thrill of sexual adventure made me feel like I needed to jump out of airplanes in my early withdrawal. But I was told to sit with the feelings and act like I thought a "normal" person would. It was uncomfortable for a very long time. I had to grieve my former thrilling life in order to let go of the longing for "the one." But the self-respect I gained in return was definitely worth the effort. The freedom of holding my head up high and giving back to family and community is all the satisfaction I need.

Today, I enjoy dignity and self-respect.

February 17

DAILY MAINTENANCE

Time and daily consistency of action are the tools with which we fashion our release, under God's guidance, from the tyranny of the psychic realm. This may be the last domain of the addiction to relinquish its power, but it does happen
– S.L.A.A. Basic Text, Page 111

It's hard to be consistent with all the ups and downs of a sex and love addict's life. Society's view has been that the nature of love is fleeting. A whirlwind romance, intense passion, basically a rollercoaster ride was much preferred over the boring drudgery of day-to-day life. It takes time to change lifelong patterns. The thing that I and my sponsees get stuck on is time. We would complain about working the Steps so thoroughly. My sponsor told me, "You had 17 years of learned acting out patterns. What makes you think you'll change that overnight?" I thought my God should be powerful enough to wave his magic wand and change me quickly without any help from me. Sometimes working the Steps and going to a meeting every day can seem like sawing at metal with a nail file but eventually it does give us freedom from addiction. Every day I wake up, read recovery literature, say a recovery prayer, journal call my sponsor, go to work and then a meeting and that's what works for me. Some meditate. I think the point is to find something that works and do it daily. Our disease is doing push-ups, so, why shouldn't we?

I use the tools of the program daily to help me recover.

February 18

THE THIRD TRADITION

The only requirement for S.L.A.A. membership is the desire to stop living out a pattern of sex and love addiction. Any two or more persons gathered together for mutual aid in recovering from sex and love addiction may call themselves an S.L.A.A. group, provided that as a group they have no other affiliation. S.L.A.A. Core Documents, "The Twelve Traditions"

I naturally assumed that I was a pretty open-minded person. The truth is, I was like most. My circle of friends was generally made up of those who were in similar camps politically, religiously, economically and culturally. My addiction was a game changer. It put me in a room with people with very different perspectives on life. "We are people who normally would not mix," says the Big Book of Alcoholics Anonymous. One fear of beginning in meetings is the fear of becoming like one of "them," whatever "them" happens to be. What we find when we enter the rooms are people whose worldviews, support systems and belief structures served them well in so many ways but failed to help them stop living out a pattern of sex and love addiction. A desire to stop acting out and a common cure forged an insoluble bond. I sit across from people with whom I would never have chosen to acquaint. I have a sponsor who believes differently in so many ways. Yet, I find that as different as we are, we are not so different. We all want to get sober. We are here to help ourselves and help one another. That is more important than all the things that typically divide.

I choose a sober way of life and to truly connect with my fellows.

February 19

AUTONOMY

In an [open-energy-system] relationship...the failure of the relationship would not spell "death" to the individuals involved. The loss of the individual's own autonomy, and the forfeiture of personal dignity, would be seen as being far worse. – S.L.A.A. Basic Text, Page 145

In my addiction, I was striving for autonomy, yet, I was so dependent. If a relationship failed, I didn't know how to live with myself or who to be. I remember thinking that I was no one without a partner. All I could do was cry and eat junk food until I found the next love interest or completely threw away my values and beliefs in order to win back the relationship. That self-defeating pattern continued into my thirties, until I got sober in S.L.A.A. finally learned how to be a person of dignity in the world without a partner. I let go of my belief system that a person is nothing in the world without a relationship. I found interests that fed my soul (and self-esteem) that didn't require anyone else. I stopped taking everything personally and allowed myself and others to have their own thoughts and feelings. I can finally say today that I am more autonomous than I've ever been in my life. I'm so grateful for the opportunity to grow up in this program. I know that I am valuable regardless of whether I receive outside validation or not.

Today, I remind myself of my personal worth and maintain my dignity.

February 20

OXYTOCIN

An entrancing moment with her, ephemeral in real time, took on the qualities of eternity, and in such a moment all awareness of how my mind had been altered was lost; I was overwhelmed. – S.L.A.A. Basic Text, Page 16

The research on oxytocin is very new at this time. We know that it is a chain of just nine amino acids long, but it has big effects. It speeds child delivery and results in milk production in mothers. It is hypothesized that increased oxytocin may create the state we associate with being loved, sexually stimulated and socially bonded, while decreased oxytocin appears to lower our desire to socially interact or be emotionally expressive. There is even the possibility that oxytocin works outside the brain, speeding wound healing and reducing inflammation. During my withdrawal experience I was shocked to find myself shaking and crying, my grief overwhelming, my anxiety spiked and my body hurt. Even if science isn't sure, the possibility of a biological basis to addiction helped me believe that sex and love addiction was "real." I know that for me I needed the Twelve Steps, the slogans, the tools and the supportive social network of recovering companions to produce in me the spiritual awakening and personality change needed for recovery from sex and love addiction. Too much or too little oxytocin is not too much to handle for my Higher Power, the program, and me.

Today, I find balance through exercise and fellowship.

February 21

COMPULSIVE CONTACT

Obsession and compulsion, now our masters, meant that control over our sexual and emotional lives no longer resided with us, or within us. We had lost control, regardless of whether we admitted it to ourselves or not. – S.L.A.A. Basic Text, Page 69

My intellectual recognition of my need for contact with my qualifier, despite the consequences, was baffling to me. I was intelligent, educated and psychologically aware. Why would I repeatedly return to interact with a person when afterward I would feel demoralized, abandoned and worthless? It was only through working the Twelve Steps that I could understand the addictive nature of this compulsion and with my Higher Power's help, cease listening to the relentless lies my addiction whispers to me. "Call him, you'll feel better. See him, and it will all be good." My addiction is cunning, baffling, powerful and very convincing. On my own I am unable to resist its seductive voice. I can recover, one day at a time, with help from my Higher Power, honesty and regular contact with others in S.L.A.A. who have learned to reject the lies their addiction tells them.

Truthful and honest, I claim my recovery today.

February 22

NOT ENOUGH

The feelings of inferiority and insecurity, which we petitioned God to replace with confidence, were openly admitted, and as we accepted the support or the confessions of similar insecurity from others, we felt comforted. – S.L.A.A. Basic Text, Page 89

When I was told to "humbly" ask God to remove my shortcomings it became clear to me that my two most damaging defects of character were arrogance and shame. After a while I discovered that the defect of arrogance was only a cover-up for my shame. It was a false sense of pride and superiority that was behind my acting arrogantly. My low self-esteem and need to be accepted fed my belief that I knew best, that my way was the only way and that I was smarter than others. Acting out my phony self-importance was demonstrated by undesirable, shameful behavior which just led me back to the core belief that I am truly unlovable and if anyone gets to know me, they will surely find out what an awful person I am and will leave me. Underneath that false power of control was shame and intense self-loathing. Without realizing it I would disrespect myself by acting out in shameful, self-denigrating ways. It seemed that I always thought I was better than or less than others, never equal to my fellows. Now, when I find myself falling back into that kind of black-and-white thinking I can affectionately remind myself that I'm not better than/less than and I can then ask God to restore me to a state of humility.

Today, I heal my shame with the tools of the program, reminding myself that I am enough.

February 23

TRUST

We came to trust the guidance that was helping us navigate away from the old addictive patterns. If God was helping us manage our external lives, it was easier to become open to clearing out the inner debris to trust God's guidance for the inward journey
– S.L.A.A. Basic Text, Page 79

Coming from an abusive relationship, it was hard for me to trust other people. I couldn't even trust myself to leave an abusive situation. That translated into not trusting God to protect me. When we do the Twelve Steps, we are given the tools to see that we can trust God, others and ourselves. The Steps take us into and through the inward journey. In the Fourth Step we put down on paper the resentments of the past. Sometimes our anger was justified. But in every situation, we are hopefully able to see our part. This helps us to steer clear of situations and people in our sober life. It may be painful to look at how others have hurt us and how we have hurt ourselves, but it is necessary to build up a new foundation of trust where we choose the people in our lives more carefully and give less of our power away to our sex and love addict tendencies. With God and S.L.A.A.'s guidance, we navigate away from old patterns of co-dependency, love for abusive or unavailable people and any other character defects that made us love untrustworthy people.

I trust myself to stay sober, knowing my Higher Power and S.L.A.A. guide me.

February 24

LONGING

We asked to have our longing for a person or a particular sexual hunting ground removed, and found ourselves given a choice. When we voluntarily chose to avoid those places and those people, the longing eased. – S.L.A.A. Basic Text, Page 89

I used to revel in longing. I listened to all the tragic love songs repeatedly. I played every tragic scene with my qualifier over and over again in my head like a bad movie. It was a source of comfort. Even in relationships with other lovers I always secretly had this one person whom I was pining over. I would get so stuck in the mud of longing that I couldn't get clear of my addiction and I would inevitably run back to my qualifier. Longing is about living in the past or wishing the future could be different. My sponsor made me realize that I was assigning magical qualities to my qualifier instead of facing reality. The many long years spent wasted in longing made it seem so difficult to stop, but because of my recovery in other parts of my addiction, I do know that recovery is possible in this area, too. S.L.A.A. taught me to live in reality.

Today, I live in reality, taking responsibility for my life and doing the next right thing.

February 25

ENABLER

Many of us had the feeling of "needing to be needed" that left us clinging to the addict, certain that if we made ourselves necessary, or "indispensable" to the addict, we would be "safe." We...sacrificed our personal dignity and [hid] behind self-deception in order to make the relationship work. – S.L.A.A. Basic Text, Page 63

I always wondered if Kate from our Basic Text was a sex and love addict herself. A lot of partners of sex and love addicts end up in S.L.A.A. to confront their love addiction. Just like with my alcoholism I could point to my partner and say, "They are so much more of an addict than me, so I don't have to look at myself." I was so busy trying to rescue him that I didn't see my own sex and love addiction blooming. He was out there cheating on me with three people and getting women pregnant. Why deal with petty things like self-esteem when there are big dramas to confront? Being an enabler allows the addict to continue acting out with less fear of repercussions. If we can't stop being an enabler, maybe we need to look at our own sex and love addiction. Partners in long-term recovery can help each other because they speak the same language and understand.

I let my Higher Power and S.L.A.A. help heal my dis-ease.

February 26

THE SECOND SIGN OF RECOVERY

We are willing to be vulnerable because the capacity to trust has been restored to us by our faith in a Higher Power.
S.L.A.A. Core Documents, "S.L.A.A. Signs of Recovery"

Being vulnerable means allowing all of my defects and all of my fears to be seen by another human being. It means taking a chance on getting hurt by trusting someone else with the reality of who I am. Six months into my recovery, I started dating a close friend. It was the first time I allowed myself to be myself with a potential love interest. In my active addiction, the name of the game was "obscure, deflect and withhold." I was an expert at changing myself to conform to what they wanted. I didn't realize that being myself was even a choice. In my first relationship in recovery, I opened myself up to my partner. I let her know when I was upset, even when I feared she might leave me. Instead of abandoning, she listened to me. Instead of anger, I received compassion and understanding. She was an excellent partner with whom I was able to test the waters of honesty. I know that if someone is unwilling to listen to my concerns and feelings, we will not be able to have an honest and open relationship.

It is okay to be myself. I open myself up to the people I trust.

February 27

THE S.L.A.A. LIFE PRESERVER

Alcoholics Anonymous grew from the principle that one alcoholic could maintain recovery by reaching out to help another one...That "carrying the message" principle of the Twelfth Step of recovery insures that lonely sex and love addicts...will have the opportunity to find that special friendship and fellowship with others which is so vital—so life giving. – S.L.A.A. Basic Text, Page viii

The symbol of the life preserver is about someone throwing a lifeline. Members of S.L.A.A. save each other's lives. The life preserver doesn't work on its own. Someone has to choose to throw it into the water and the person in the water has to choose to grab it. That lifeline comes in the form of our Basic Text, fellowship, sponsorship and meetings. An outreach call could save someone's life. Our message of hope is in the S.L.A.A. Basic Text, but the addict has to read it and choose to hear the message and follow the plan of recovery. Sponsors, fellowship and meetings are all available to help. As long as the newcomer is willing to reach out for that help, they can recover instead of drowning in addiction. The life preserver logo is on all of S.L.A.A.'s literature, chips and medallions to remind us that we are not alone. Other members are there for support. We help ourselves by helping others. It feels good to see others recover and lead happy, more productive lives. If we can have some small part in making that happen, it strengthens us to continue this journey of recovery.

Today, I reach out to my fellows and help in whatever way I can.

February 28

TIME APART

In human relationships, two individuals could be nourished by each other and also exchange energy through experiences outside the relationship. Rather than being completely dependent on each other, individuals in open-energy-system relationships might have a degree of autonomy. – S.L.A.A. Basic Text, Page 144-5

I used to be so self-centered that once someone left the room, it was like they were dead to me. I would either feel alone in the world or fall into negative fantasy about life without them. They couldn't have a life going on without me. The threat of abandonment was too great. As soon as they walked out the door, I had to call or text or have plans to see them soon. They had to be constantly doing things for me so I knew they were at least thinking about me during our time apart. If all of these elements weren't in place, I was convinced we were doomed. This would require that I find a "backup" partner. I would occupy myself with them (wasting their time and mine) until my real partner came back. With the help of S.L.A.A., I saw how destructive that scenario is to my well-being. I learned how to spend time apart without fear of abandonment. We can support our partner in work and other activities that we don't necessarily share, and we can respect their connection with friends and family as well as their need to be alone.

Today, I respect solitude. My Higher Power is with me.

February 29

LEAP OF FAITH

Where would we find even the rudiments of a faith that could carry us through this dissolving and reconstruction of our whole personality? ... through contact with sober people at our regular S.L.A.A. meetings who had surmounted the need-for-faith barrier themselves. – S.L.A.A. Basic Text, Page 75

My first leap of faith was to enter the program. I didn't know what I was getting myself into. I had a feeling that I would find all kinds of crazy things behind the doors of meeting rooms. But I walked through those doors anyway. I just knew that my way didn't work. I had hope that I would find the answers in S.L.A.A. My second leap of faith was sticking around, getting a sponsor and doing the Steps. I had no proof that going through such pain would work for me. Seeing sober members who had recovered because of the program helped but couldn't allay all of my fears. Not having a Higher Power made it a struggle. It's difficult to jump off a cliff and trust that a net will appear underneath you when you don't think there's anyone there to put up the net. But I just kept believing it would work. Finally, I had a spiritual experience. Since then I have had some really big decisions to make that I agonized over and couldn't find answers. My faith that my Higher Power would be there to catch me if I fell gave me the ability to attempt my best effort. I have always had great success. That may not always happen, but I know I have support and love from fellows and my Higher Power.

I put faith in my Higher Power to do for me what I cannot do for myself.

March 1

ABSTINENCE

This process of increasing awareness led eventually to a final surrender of the whole addictive pattern, and thus we were launched into withdrawal and sexual and emotional sobriety. - S.L.A.A. Basic Text, Page 105

Prior to abstinence, pain and despair lingered. A sponsor's suggestion that I "cycle down" for 60 days seemed like a temporary surrender—marginal at best. To surrender to a 60-day abstinence period signals acceptance and a belief that sobriety and serenity is possible. To "cycle down" means no contact with qualifiers while avoiding unsafe places and unsafe people. It excludes spending significant time with anyone who disrespects my values and program. Over time, with patience and daily spiritual practices, feelings of loneliness and despair lessen. On sharing at meetings there are those occasions where I sense subtle reactions that spell disbelief and doubt in my fellows—especially younger men. Yet there are times when I hear shares that indicate that abstinence can be a reality for skeptics who eventually report up to 90 days of sobriety and abstinence. With five years of sobriety, I am no longer drawn to inappropriate people or places. Such a way of living and thinking is awesome. Abstinence heightens awareness and brings hope and acknowledgement of personal needs, priorities, programs and practices. Each day is a new opportunity to trust in a Higher Power, knowing that the surrender of my will does not spell defeat. Freedom from self-will running riot reveals unimaginable opportunities.

Every day that I surrender to my Higher Power is a victory.

March 2

SUFFERING

As addicts we had become accustomed to pain. More often than not, pain was a central characteristic of our romantic involvements and even many of our sexual pursuits. Some of us even equated pain with love, so that in the absence of love we would at least be comforted by the presence of pain. – S.L.A.A. Basic Text, Page 85

When we cease to perceive value in suffering, healing is instantaneous. When a fellow said that to me, I got angry with him. What possible value could I find in suffering? But I was using emotional pain to insulate me from hurt and fear. My twisted thinking was, ***If I can solicit anger and jealousy from my partner then he must love me***. I was in the habit of creating chaos in my relationships in order to keep my partner constantly engaged. But the reality was that I was pushing him away with my behavior. I created distrust and partners often left me. Left with my pain, I would listen to love songs, get drunk and cry. Sometimes I would get dramatic and lie on the floor and scream, plotting my suicide. Grieving the loss of the relationship in this way ensured that I would stay involved in it long after it was over. In sobriety, we go through pain so we may let go. We give our character defects to a Higher Power. Hopefully they are removed, a day at a time, and we are able to build trust and intimacy in our relationships.

I let go of my old emotional habits today and rely on my Higher Power to get me through hurt and fear.

March 3

ROMANTICISM

Some of us were caught up in the hypnotic intensity of sexual and romantic encounters or relationships, merging ourselves into our lovers or spouses. These experiences became overwhelmingly compelling, carrying us along with them, exuberantly at first, and then less and less willingly. – S.L.A.A. Basic Text, Page 69

For some of us, obsessive romanticism was a key aspect of our overall sex and love addiction. As a teen, my interactions with female peers became overwhelmingly focused on winning their approval of me as a sexual being. While other boys naturally developed "the hots" for this girl or that, romantic impulses in me were much more intense. Romance addiction became all-absorbing, profoundly affecting my sense of emotional well-being and capacity to function. To hide the truth from myself, I reasoned that I was only expressing true chivalry in this cynical modern age. All of this was preparing the way for full-blown sexual compulsivity as I moved through my teens. Recovery from sex and love addiction must include recovery from obsessive romanticism and relationship addiction. Once the compulsion of acting out itself has been lifted and recovery begins to expand in us, we notice that romantic idealization and fixation on imagined relationships begins to fade. How liberating it is to view others not as gods or goddesses, but simply as fellow human beings, deserving of respect, honesty and right conduct from us. I thank God, who, by way of the program and fellowship of S.L.A.A., has awakened me from the hypnotic trance of obsessive romanticism.

Today, I stay rooted in reality. If my mind starts wandering into romanticism, I pray and meditate.

March 4

SURRENDER

True surrender of our sex and love addiction meant not only being willing to take ourselves out of the painful situation at hand. It meant, most importantly, being ready to be free of our whole life strategy of obsession with and pursuit of love and sex. – S.L.A.A. Basic Text, Page 71

It helps to remember that ours is a spiritual disease requiring a spiritual solution. Somewhere along the way, there was emptiness, a longing that we tried to escape from or fill in a variety of mind-altering but ultimately addictive ways. In recovery we identify this need as a spiritual hunger. Nothing else seems to work. We get to "give up," say "uncle," surrender. We get to take inventory of our lives and realize that we have this disease of sex and love addiction. We see that our way of living doesn't work. This is a gift. Out of sheer desperation is born in us the willingness to get down on our proverbial knees to admit that we are powerless over acting out with the behaviors and emotions of our disease. When we do, something happens. We have made contact with a Power greater than ourselves, which we are free to define and redefine, that "can do for us what we cannot do for ourselves."

Higher Power, let me be willing to surrender my disease to your loving care, that I may be a beacon of light to those who still suffer.

March 5

THE THIRD STEP

Made a decision to turn our will and our lives over to the care of God as we understood God. – S.L.A.A. Core Documents, "The Twelve Steps of S.L.A.A."

The concept of turning my will and my life over to a Power greater than myself was one of the hardest, most confounding things I was asked to do in this program. I thought God should be a voice in my head, like a GPS telling me to go right or left. It was only when I was in enough pain that I realized I couldn't rescue myself and I became willing to pay attention to the more subtle signs of a Higher Power in my life. Little by little, I began identifying these elements all around me. A Power greater than myself is a room of 10 people. A Power greater than myself is someone who's got more recovery than I do. A Power greater than myself is the shifting tide and the flowers blooming. Being willing to listen was the beginning of my developing a relationship with my Higher Power. If I pay attention, it will reveal itself to me.

Today, I surrender my will to my Higher Power, opening myself to what is in store for me.

March 6

GIVE TO KEEP

I give all I can, in whatever way I can, so that when the time comes that I get the insane urge to throw myself away on an abusive sex or love partner, I will be saved. – S.L.A.A. Basic Text, Page 260

I never want to drive all the way across town after a long day at work to give the lead share at an S.L.A.A. meeting and participate in another hour of sharing. But I do it every time I am asked. I think of it as insurance against a slip. Carrying the message gives my life a purpose that it's never had before: to hopefully help the suffering sex and love addict. Service commitments, sponsoring and being present at meetings, all give back to the program and ensures that S.L.A.A. will be there for the suffering addict in the future. The program works because newcomers come in and there are sober people to help them by sharing their experience, strength and hope. Then the newcomer becomes sober and helps others. Watching the newcomer go through this transformation also helps the old-timer remember how it works. Give to keep is a solid foundation principle in S.L.A.A.

Sharing my experience, strength and hope helps me gain another day sober.

March 7

THE SECOND CHARACTERISTIC

Fearing abandonment and loneliness, we stay in and return to painful, destructive relationships, concealing our dependency needs from ourselves and others, growing more isolated and alienated from friends and loved ones, ourselves, and God.
- S.L.A.A. Core Documents, "Characteristics of Sex and Love Addiction"

I used to pride myself on being a "tough girl, just one of the guys." I didn't whine like other girlfriends when my boyfriend cheated on me—I got drunk and chased him with a bat, secretly hoping I wouldn't catch him. I stayed in abusive relationships for years, hoping something would change. But it never did. My friends all abandoned me because of the insanity of our volatile relationship. When I finally got sober in S.L.A.A., my new relationship and the intimacy of it scared me so much. I was convinced that the more he got to know the real me, the more likely he would abandon me. In the past I concealed my dependency needs by finding a "back burner" guy, smoking, drinking and eating too much (cigarettes never abandon you until you die of lung cancer). But in recovery, I had to give these up. Thank God, I found that a loving Higher Power was all I needed. The structure of S.L.A.A. made it impossible to isolate from friends and loved ones, myself and God. It doesn't seem possible to isolate from oneself, but speaking from experience, it can be done. When I got so lost in a fantasy world that I didn't know what I truly wanted or believed, I was isolated from myself. S.L.A.A. broke me out of my delusion. I hope I stay.

I stand with dignity today because I have S.L.A.A. and my Higher Power beside me.

March 8

FEELINGS AREN'T FACTS

Abstinence from acting out on bottom-line behaviors opens us to the vulnerability we have desperately sought to avoid. Some helpful suggestions [are to] ... Find a safe place/person where you can cry, rage, grieve. Avoid stuffing your feelings ...Remember that feelings aren't facts—you won't die from them. – from the "Withdrawal: Gateway to Freedom, Hope and Joy" pamphlet

Before I got into recovery, I was so controlled by my feelings I would get into a state of hysteria about a relationship when I felt my emotional needs weren't being met. I would get scared, fear abandonment and become angry. Fear overwhelmed me. I would have so many feelings, and some of them I wouldn't even be able to identify. When emotions ruled my life, I made up stories in my head to explain why I was upset. If I felt it, I assumed it was reality. What I've learned from recovery is that feelings aren't facts. I don't have to act on them the way I used to. It's okay to sit with my feelings and just recognize that I have them. I can take a moment, check in with my Higher Power, read a meditation or take an outreach call. I can slow down, identify my emotions and acknowledge that I don't have to act on them.

Higher Power, help me to recognize my emotions today and accept them as a temporary state of being.

March 9

SPONSORSHIP

We discovered that we could continue to affirm our recovery by working with other sex and love addicts. No experience in living was more meaningful for us than letting ourselves become channels through which healing and redeeming grace could flow. - S.L.A.A. Basic Text, Page 102

Getting a sponsor secured my investment in S.L.A.A. and helped me to become accountable to someone else. It gave me a lot of strength to share my shameful history with my sponsor. He could hear my story without thinking that I was a terrible person and still loved me. It helped me to feel better about myself. It has been essential to work with a sponsor because he could identify the patterns that I was blinded to. I wanted to change, but I couldn't see what I was doing and I couldn't change on my own. Today, I'm working with four sponsees and have found that each time they call or we get together, I'm reminded of the importance of the program. When they call me and they're upset because of recent frustrations or challenges, I'm reminded of how I do not want to go back to that life of confusion and suffering. When they have a positive "Aha" moment, it's inspirational to me and reminds me of the times that I've also grown as a person. When they have a need that's not being met by the program, it spurs me into action and has encouraged me to take on new service commitments. Having sponsees and having a sponsor has been critical in making progress and staying sober from sex and love addiction.

I sponsor others as I have been sponsored, giving back the gift of recovery that has been shared with me.

March 10

INTEGRITY

The discovery of personal dignity and integrity has become a new standard by which we apply to our ventures. We prize a more holistic understanding of ourselves and seek to affirm this in all areas of our lives. We find that nothing short of this is fulfilling to us. – S.L.A.A. Basic Text, Page 47

Honesty and moral principles were not the focus of my attention in my acting-out days. Forget about being fair. In the world of feeding my desperate desires, fairness flew out the window in favor of whatever would fulfill my needs. Honesty would just get in my way. Integrity requires internal consistency. When my addict is constantly doing battle with my healthy side, it's impossible to find stability without Higher Power and the Twelve Step program of S.L.A.A. Altering my beliefs was a way of life. If one of my values was getting in the way of what I wanted, I threw it under the bus. S.L.A.A. and the Twelve Steps taught me honesty at all costs. The cost of honesty only takes its toll once and gives dignity in return. But the cost of keeping a secret can only give misery for a lifetime. S.L.A.A. helped me uncover long-buried moral principles and stick to them. In the past, I never thought I could live up to them, so I thought, why even try? Being a sober person today is what I desire. Finding integrity daily helps me towards that goal.

I live in integrity today and stand by my recovery values.

March 11

RECONCILIATION

Through the deep destructiveness of active sex and love addiction, through the foreboding uncertainties of a difficult reconciliation, through a prolonged period of learning how to cope with a maze of conflicts and irresolutions, our partners and ourselves emerged onto a plane of true expansive living, in loving partnership with each other. – S.L.A.A. Basic Text, Page 153

Reconciliation can be a difficult subject for sex and love addicts in recovery. Sober addicts wonder if they are going back to their disease if they reconcile with a partner. There needs to be a lot of soul searching before this journey is embarked upon. Were the foundations of the relationship basically good and did they have room to grow? Was it just that our disease got in the way and messed everything up? Or was the relationship fatally flawed? Can we be truly present in the relationship, without addictive distractions? If we are on solid spiritual ground and have discussed this thoroughly with our sponsor and partner, reconciliation may be an option. We take it one day at a time. S.L.A.A. can help us stay out of fantasy and to rebuild good communication with our former partner if we use the Twelve Steps, prayer and meditation. I've heard it said that addicts expect a medal for running out of a burning building. We may feel entitled to accolades from a renewed partner simply because we are sober now. Our partner may still be suffering from past harm done by our addiction. We need to be prepared for some stress. But it may be well worth the effort.

I seek help from the program and my Higher Power when considering reconciliation. I stay out of fantasy.

March 12

SETTING BOTTOM LINES

The "freedom" to define our own addictive pattern could not be used in a self-serving way. Our addictions are a reality that persists regardless of any short-sighted, convenient definition – S.L.A.A. Basic Text, Page 72

I've had difficulty setting boundaries for myself and my life so I didn't know how to set bottom lines. I started with very clear definitions, such as "Don't have sex with married people." It was helpful to be specific and to work with my sponsor every step of the way. If I put "having a sexual thought" on my bottom line, I'd have to pick up a desire chip every couple of hours. But if I left off some items because I wasn't ready to let go of them, it wouldn't be long before I ended up back in the same pit of despair. As I grew in recovery, I became more aware of how my addiction controlled me on subtle levels. The definition of my sobriety grows with me If I make an excuse like, "It's not on my bottom line, so it's okay, what once was not a problem could become one. It's important that I am honest with myself and with my sponsor in evaluating how I define my sobriety, whether I've been sober for three days or three decades.

As I make progress in recovery, I check in with myself and my sponsor to stay mindful of my behavior.

March 13

WILLINGNESS

We were willing to be available not to the next lover or new sexual fantasy, but to whatever might happen next within ourselves. Paradoxically, this was not willingness that came from strength, but from the certainty of the dire consequences of continuing on in our addiction. – S.L.A.A. Basic Text, Page 73

When we walk through the door into a meeting, we are demonstrating our willingness to face this disease and get help. Each action we take towards recovery strengthens our willingness to stay on the healing path. It also lights up the path for others. The Steps prepare us to walk the road of recovery. When we see others who have walked the road before us, we hear their message and are able to open the door to become willing. Letting go of old ideas is difficult. We may not wake up with the idea that we can stay sober that day. But prayer and meditation, even if we don't believe in them, show that we have the desire to stop. The Founders Meeting of S.L.A.A. gives out a desire to stop chip. In my opinion, anyone who has the courage to stand up and take that chip shows willingness. Some of us don't give up the addictive behavior easily. I always said that God had to hit me over the head with a baseball bat before I was willing to notice I had a problem with sex and love addiction. Being ready and able to turn my will and my life over to a Higher Power that I didn't understand went against everything I ever believed. It took a lot of work and reflection, but God and the program helped me through it and carry me today.

Each day, I pray for the willingness to do my Higher Power's will.

March 14

QUALIFIER

Our justifications generally sounded very convincing to us..."It feels crazy not to be talking to this person that I care about." "I have as much right to be at a certain location or function as s/he does"..."I haven't seen this person for several days...that must mean I'm not addicted"...The dilemma was that we didn't realize that we were culling "intrigue" from these behaviors. – S.L.A.A Basic Text, Page 108

The first time I took a contrary action to avoid going somewhere where I thought I would run into my qualifier, it hurt. It hurt so badly I was in my car cringing and it was at that moment that I came to believe this was a real addiction. At that point I went into withdrawal. Even though we hadn't been in contact for over a year I often wondered what would happen if he were waiting at my front door. What if he called? What would I say? Before S.L.A.A. I might have called and stirred up some drama. Now I can call my sponsor and confess how much I miss my qualifier. I can let my sponsor know how lonely I feel. Sometimes we think we've been away from our qualifier for so long we can handle it again or that they've changed, but we don't need to go back to relationships that caused us pain.

I stay away from my qualifier today. I believe that my Higher Power has something better in store for me.

March 15

DIVERSITY

The experiences of addiction which bind us, in sharing, to one another in S.L.A.A. are far more compelling than the differences of gender and sexual choice which serve to divide more "normal" people. – S.L.A.A. Basic Text, Page 47

At the first S.L.A.A. meeting I ever attended, the other members included one straight woman, one straight man, and one gay man. I wondered about the possible conflicts of having both men and women in a meeting of sex addicts. I wondered about the conflicts of having gay men in a meeting with other gay men. But none of that was important enough to me to keep me from listening to what they had to say. Sex and love addiction is not isolated to any one type of person. We should feel safe to express ourselves in a meeting, but remember that others want to feel safe as well. For some of us, recovery from our addiction might involve getting beyond prejudices. This doesn't mean we need to agree with everything someone else does, but we can certainly make room for tolerance and compassion. The Twelfth Step states that we try to carry the message to sex and love addicts. We can do this by helping others feel accepted the first time they walk into a meeting. That acceptance may encourage them to keep coming back.

I welcome the diverse backgrounds and experiences of others in the program and recognize our common ties.

March 16

INTIMACY

Most wonderful of all, when we walked through each day with the sense of being hand in hand with God, as a spring of love seemed to flow from within, available to help us quench the thirst for love of ourselves and others. Thus, we came to find intimacy with ourselves, intimacy with God, and the intimacy with others. – S.L.A.A. Basic Text, Page 101

Intimacy means the willingness to be vulnerable, to be honest about who we are. If we learn to love ourselves, then we can become more willing to share with others. It takes a lot of trust to be intimate with another human being. Some of us have never experienced that level of intimacy. We have been too afraid to let someone see who we really are, warts and all. To attain this level of intimacy, we must let go of fear. This process takes time and patience. If the person we are partnered with truly loves us for who we are, there is nothing of ourselves that we cannot share. If we love ourselves, we no longer need someone else to provide us with validation. If we feel judged or rejected, then we may need to reevaluate that relationship. We can seek out love with someone who is a true and equal partner and who accepts us just as we accept ourselves.

I am honest today. I share myself openly with those that I trust.

March 17

GOLDEN RULE

We had to conclude that it was silly and futile to let ourselves be upset at what we saw as diseased actions by others, especially if we hoped that others would continue to be tolerant of our own frequent lapses into dishonesty or manipulative behavior.
– S.L.A.A. Basic Text, Page 97

"Do unto others as you would have done to you." Reciprocity was very important to me. If I did anything for anyone, I expected something in return. If they didn't respond in kind, that meant they didn't love me. If it was a stranger, that meant there was no justice in the world or that God didn't love me (if God even existed). I wasted so much energy trying to manipulate and control others into doing things my way. I felt entitled and judgmental. If everyone would just follow the Golden Rule, the world would be a beautiful place. But not everyone is capable of that. People aren't objects that I can move around on a chessboard. Maybe my idea of reciprocity doesn't work for them. If I sit around getting resentful about lack of participation in my blueprint for life, I'm only hurting myself. S.L.A.A.'s Steps and Traditions taught me to be of service without expecting anything in return. Through the process, I have seen that I will never get what I really need from human beings. I need a spiritual solution. The serenity that the program has given me is better than any token I can receive from the physical world.

Today, I am of service to others and let go of expectations.

March 18

THE TWELFTH TRADITION

***Anonymity is the spiritual foundation of all our traditions ever reminding us to place principles before personalities.* – S.L.A.A. Core Documents, "*The Twelve Traditions*"**

Perhaps the greatest roadblock to getting help for our addiction is the fear of being found out. How can we be sure, when we walk into a meeting, we won't see someone we know? We cannot be sure. But if we do run into the ghosts of our past, we can be confident that they are sitting in that meeting because they also want relief from the pain of addiction. Revealing the identity of an addict can do a great deal of damage to their personal, professional and social life. For this reason, we respect the anonymity of our fellows and ask that they do the same for us. We must also maintain our anonymity for the sake of the fellowship. If we preach the wonders of S.L.A.A. at a public level, then suffer from a slip or relapse, the program itself may suffer. A.A.'s ***Twelve Steps and Twelve Traditions*** states that anonymity is "humility at work." We seek recovery for our own sake, not for recognition. As we maintain the anonymity of ourselves and others, we ensure the integrity of S.L.A.A. so that it continues to exist for the addict who still suffers.

I maintain the anonymity of myself and my fellows, as they would do for me.

March 19

MULTIPLE ADDICTIONS

[People] could not seem to understand that an addictive appetite never gets "enough," and that insanity is insanity regardless of whether it is encountered in drinking or romance. - S.L.A.A. Basic Text, Page 34

I heard in A.A. that if you're not in more than one Twelve Step room, you're in denial. I always blamed my sex and love addiction on my alcoholism. But when I got sober in A.A. the behavior didn't stop. It only got worse. I knew I had another addiction to deal with. When I was sober in S.L.A.A. and standing in the aisles of the grocery store about to blow up my healthy relationship over a food obsession, I knew I needed a Twelve Step food program. I know quite a few fellows in S.L.A.A. who had a "no drinking alcohol on dates" rule on their dating plan, and came to find they needed A.A. I can see more clearly that it's not necessarily which way I avoid life (for example, through alcohol, sex, food, money, etc.) that I need to focus on. It's the Twelve Steps that I need to focus on. My spirituality will keep me sober in all areas. It's not necessarily about which program I joined this week, it only helps point me in the right direction each time. It helps to hear people share about the same problems that I am going through. I use the Twelve Steps to try to stay sober in all areas of my life today. If I find myself numbing out on any substance or behavior, I get help.

I use the Twelve Steps and get help daily.

March 20

NO CONTACT

It is important to understand what your part is in the pattern. It may be tempting to say, "I can't stop the affair because they keep calling me." But that is blaming others for your behavior. What are you doing to stay in these miserable places? – from the "Setting Bottom Lines" pamphlet

For six months before I got sober, I tried to stick to a no-contact rule with the married man that I was trying to stop having an affair with. He was also in S.L.A.A., which was a very small community at the time. I would inevitably run into him. I asked my sponsor what I should do. "No contact means no contact," she said. "Block his phone number, don't read his emails, if you see him in a meeting and he says 'Hi,' stare at your feet, mumble something incoherent and walk away. All of our addictions call out to us, but when you're dealing with another human being it's tangible. When I was quitting smoking, the cigarette company never called me at 2 a.m. asking me why I don't smoke their cigarettes anymore." I knew her words were true, but it was so difficult not to read an email with the subject line "I miss you." I would get a numbness throughout my body that was like taking a shot of whiskey. When I finally got the concept of "no matter what," I was able to get and stay sober.

I concentrate on conscious contact with my Higher Power, releasing the object of my obsession.

March 21

CHOICES

I now felt I had reached a point in withdrawal where I had been granted the Grace of choice in my sexual and romantic life. This new state of affairs was born of the long struggle between addictive temptation and personal autonomy. The balance was tipping in my favor at last, even if just barely! – S.L.A.A. Basic Text, Page 33

For the alcoholic, the choice to drink or not disappears the moment the first drop passes their lips. For the sex and love addict, the line is not so clear. Once we have made it through the withdrawal process, we regain the ability to choose. No longer do we blindly react to our first impulse. Options are available to us and each option has associated advantages and disadvantages. Additionally, it becomes clearer what the right choice is among our options. But it's important to define our bottom lines clearly with the help of a sponsor, and not fall into the trap of engaging in accessory behaviors because they're not on our bottom line. It's a slippery slope that leads us to break our sobriety. That is why it is important to stay current with our sponsors and our fellows in the program so that we remain aware of our danger zones. The freedom to choose is precious and it takes work to maintain it. By listening to that small yet strong voice within us, we usually know what decision is best for us.

Today, I think through my options and make thoughtful decisions.

March 22

MY FIRST LEAD

The first time I qualified was a cleansing experience for me. It helped me to understand that I was not alone. There were people who identified with my story and with my pain – S.L.A.A. Basic Text, Page 176

Sharing my story the first time, I could barely stumble through a few words about how crazy my addiction was. The voices in my head told me that everyone in the room was either bored or hated me. When I broke out in tears, I was mortified. But when I looked up and saw all the concerned faces nodding in agreement I knew that everything was going to be okay. I realized that others had gone through similar experiences or feelings. When laughter broke out, my first thought was, ***They're laughing at me.*** Then I realized they were laughing with me and I felt the calm of quiet support come over me. When my share was over, almost everyone thanked me (as if I wouldn't enjoy the opportunity to talk about myself). Some said they thought they were the only ones who felt that way and were glad they were not alone. Some said they didn't go through the same experiences but identified with the feelings. I was amazed that people listened to me for 20 minutes No one ever listened to me. I was taught that children are to be seen and not heard, and girlfriends need to keep their opinions to themselves or they get hit. I could never find my voice before I came to S.L.A.A. Meeting shares helped me discover what I really thought and felt about myself and my experiences.

I share my experience and remember that I have support.

March 23

WALKING THROUGH PAIN

When the pain comes now, I don't automatically resort to a sexual thought or solution. I have time to process the feelings and to realize they can't overwhelm me, by going to either my higher Power or a member of the S.L.A.A. Fellowship for help. – S.L.A.A. Basic Text, Page 205

Imagine a bed of hot coals. You stand to one side, your bare feet sweating in anticipation of the task at hand. Weigh the potential outcomes in your mind. You could walk across swiftly, not giving the coals time to burn the soles of your feet. Or you could make your way across the 1,000-degree heat, only to stop in the middle out of fear. If fear overcomes us while we walk through our pain, we could become overwhelmed. If we get stuck in the problems of our lives, addiction will be waiting there, ready to burn us. What drives us to take the next step? What tools can we use to remind ourselves that there is hope? The resources are there for us to use. A firewalker makes it across the pit by continuing onward, even when it hurts. This can't be done on sheer willpower alone. It takes time and confidence to brave the fiery paths of life. We each have our support team, cheering from the sidelines, telling us we can make it through. With courage, we can lift our feet up and make it to the other side. No matter what I am going through, I can stay sober today.

Using the S.L.A.A. tools, my Higher Power helps me maintain my sobriety.

March 24

THE SIXTH SIGN OF RECOVERY

We become willing to ask for help, allowing ourselves to be vulnerable and learning to trust and accept others. – S.L.A.A. Core Documents, "S.L.A.A. Signs of Recovery"

I was ashamed to ask my father for help when I was suffering financially. I would have rather incurred the overdraft fees than allow myself to be vulnerable with my father. The program taught me that it was okay to ask for help, so I swallowed my pride and approached my father for assistance. As is often the case, I found that my fears were unfounded. Asking for help in those instances has given me courage to ask for help in other situations. When I am tempted to act out, I can call on my sponsor or someone else in the program without fear of being judged. My fellows in the program are always willing to help me if I am brave enough to reach out and ask. I have even built relationships with some friends and loved ones in which I can tell them that I am triggered and need to remove myself from a situation. When I admit that I am struggling, my Higher Power acts through the people I care about and does for me what I cannot do for myself. We all need a little help now and then.

The assistance I need is around me and I ask for help.

March 25

DATING

This readiness for the possibility of a new partnership was evident in the apparently contradictory absence of feeling any particular urgency to enter a new relationship. – S.L.A.A. Basic Text, Page 153

Dating was always easy in addiction because I had a boyfriend after the first date. As the joke goes, I brought a moving van to the first date. But in sobriety, dating brought up all the fears I always tried to push down or numb out with addiction. Being truly sober means I don't try to push those fears away with any of my ancillary addictions. I don't eat or drink too much during or after the date. Even though flirting is healthy while dating, I watch my behavior so it doesn't become predatory. All my old fears come up. I fear I'm not enough or too damaged for normal relationships. I'm never satisfied, and I'm uncomfortable with boredom. It's hard to trust people, and dating requires trusting another human being, ourselves and God. The dating plan that my sponsor gave me helped a lot with that. I didn't have to overthink the process and it freed me up to enjoy it. Some of the dating plan seemed ridiculous to my date, but I chose to trust my sponsor. The person I was dating was willing to date according to the plan despite his misgivings. This showed me he was the right person with whom to build a foundation for a relationship.

I have and use a dating plan.

March 26

AWARENESS

Disregarding how much better off we really were now, we yearned for our former ignorance. And yet we found that the door to awareness, once opened, could not be closed. We had seen—we had even felt—occasional hints of what a healthy existence could be like. – S.L.A.A. Basic Text, Page 78

Awareness is difficult for people who have based their lives on finding ways to numb out. It can be painful. It can also be unobtainable when our disease masks it so well by telling us lies. I cultivated so many multiple personalities in my disease in order to fit in and get the attention I so desperately needed. Sometimes my lies were so convoluted I didn't even know I was lying. Steps Five through Seven force us out of the hiding places in our minds. We bring situations to light in the Fourth Step and think about them—bringing them to the awareness of ourselves and God. When we tell another human being in our Fifth Step, we learn even more. Putting our character defects on paper, we are given the gift of knowing ourselves and our patterns. We are able to walk around with our eyes wide open. When I got into a relationship, I had to work on my awareness even more. A healthy person is honest and has boundaries. It was painful to admit that I had engaged in a character defect. But I wanted the relationship to continue, so I admitted my mistake and worked on changing my behavior. My sponsor often said, "Constant vigilance is the price we pay for sobriety."

I examine my character defects today. I am grateful for the aware person I have become.

March 27

TOP LINES

I find it more useful to keep in mind what I call my top line rather than my bottom line. My top line is what I do want for myself, my program goals...These things are beginning to happen for me. – S.L.A.A. Basic Text, Page 270

The distracting influence of addiction leaves undiscovered corners of our life left unexplored. What dreams has our addiction kept us from realizing? What might we have done with the weekends spent trolling the internet for porn, the hours spent obsessing about our qualifier? What goals did we let fall by the wayside? Recovery gives us our lives back. We can pick up old hobbies, spend more time with our family or even return to school to pursue a new field of interest. It helps to have positive goals to strive for. Too much time spent dwelling on not acting out can be intensely frustrating. Rather than constantly striving not to do something, we can place our focus instead on what we can do to better ourselves. Recovery allows us to uncover the bright, talented and interesting human beings we were meant to be. What will we do with our new lease on life?

Today, I explore the neglected areas of my life, growing mentally, physically and spiritually.

March 28

SELF-ESTEEM

The addiction was affecting every area of my life. I especially devastated my emotional well-being and self-im age...I felt isolated and unworthy unless I felt I was wante and needed by a man. I was so absorbed in the pursuit of "lov that the rest of my life seemed meaningless and unfulfillin – S.L.A.A. Basic Text, Page 213

There is a voice inside of me that tells me I am not what I ar supposed to be and I will never be enough. This voice tells m that I fall short of everyone's expectations, that I'm not as goo as the people around me. Addicts try to shut this voice up b numbing themselves with their addiction. When we remove ou substance of choice, what do we put in its place? Do we replac the negative voice with one that is nurturing and positive? Th process begins with acts of self-love. It starts when we take the firs step of recovery. We deny the self-defeating statements and replac them with positive affirmations. We can start the moment we ente the program. When we truly love ourselves, we no longer need t escape from who we are. We enjoy our own company and desir to experience life as ourselves. This is one of the many benefits o healing and living in recovery.

I am a valuable human being. I love myself for who I am.

March 29

OUTREACH CALLS

Contact with those already recovering from sex and ove addiction was also a source of practical help in ustaining our day-to-day sobriety. Suggestions on how to void addictive situations were given, and the simple act of xplaining a current temptation or situation to someone else ho understood seemed to help us stay honest with ourselves.
S.L.A.A. Basic Text, Page 75

One of the most difficult actions for me to take in recovery s to make outreach calls. Isolation fueled my addiction. I have n anorexic side that wants to hide out and withdraw. The more I solate, the more I experience feelings of deprivation and loneliness. his makes me want to act out to reduce the pain. In recovery, I irectly counteract these impulses by making outreach calls and onnecting with people at meetings. My first outreach call was very ifficult. Someone gave me their phone number after a meeting n case I needed to talk. I thought it was a ridiculous suggestion. didn't want to do that. But that was my addiction talking, some art of me that feared recovery. I used contrary action and called he person and had one of the best phone calls I've ever had. They ontinue to be a great outreach partner in my recovery and have elped me to reach out to others. The telephone is a lifeline in ecovery that can help me have positive experiences.

I make outreach calls daily.

March 30

FAMILY OF ORIGIN

Humbly, we turned to God. "I am not responsible for th conditions which created me, but I am willing to try to b responsible for myself," we prayed. "Help me to be willing t make right what I have done to each and every person in m life." – S.L.A.A. Basic Text, Page 92

"I am not responsible for the conditions which created me, m parents are," was my mantra before sobriety. I harbored resentmen against my parents for most of my life. They weren't the caretaker they were supposed to be. Maybe if they had taken better car of me or if my sister hadn't been such a bully, I wouldn't have s many addictions. But I hear people in S.L.A.A. share all the tim that their home life was normal growing up and they still suffe from the addiction. Regardless of what happened in my famil of origin, I need to be willing today to be responsible for mysel I need to focus on my actions and make amends for what I hav done instead of blaming my upbringing. I need to rely on God t help me let go of resentment. Blame allows me to stay lazy an avoid working the Steps around my past. If I use the excuse tha my childhood was messed up, I don't have to change. Once I coul put those thoughts aside, I could take action to heal.

I am responsible for myself today and make amends for an harm I have done in the past.

March 31

REVENGE

If we had just been jilted by someone we felt was "indispensable," surrender meant that we accepted our loss, and refused to take revenge or recriminate. – S.L.A.A. Basic Text, Page 73

Revenge is such a part of society that it can even be commended and encouraged sometimes. If I plotted revenge on a lover, I continued to feel connected to them long after the relationship was over. I could continue to obsess about them. In my twisted way of thinking, it gave me a better excuse to stalk them. I felt entitled to this behavior because they were cruel to me and deserved it. This rationalization in order to hang on to character defects was never good for my emotional well-being. It just dug a deeper hole for my self-esteem to be buried in. My revenge plots never worked out as well as the scenario in my head anyway. Most of them just stayed as fantasies that took up too much of my time. Accepting loss was never my ego's strong suit. I had to be in control of everything in my life in order to feel safe. If I couldn't control someone with sex and love, I had to do it with anger. When I surrendered my sex and love addiction, this was a difficult character defect to let go of. The no-contact rule on my bottom lines helped. I prayed to stay out of negative fantasies and to deal with the pain of loss in a healthy way instead of being self-destructive. This has worked for me and my sobriety.

I seek healthy coping behaviors like prayer, meditation, forgiveness and fellowship when someone harms me.

April 1

HEALTHY BOUNDARIES

Early in S.L.A.A. we coined an expression, "In order to maintain sobriety, we have the right to be a jerk." – S.L.A.A. Basic Text, Page 116

Before S.L.A.A., I didn't have any boundaries. I spoke inappropriately at gatherings. I went with inappropriate people and did whatever they told me. I didn't really care about my well-being or my life. I met people in S.L.A.A. who knew how to hold healthy boundaries. I invited a fellow somewhere and I remember knowing that I was crossing a boundary with her. She simply said a polite, "No." I was shocked. She didn't care about my feelings or try to mitigate it. Nor did she try to explain herself so I could try to manipulate her further. She realized what I was doing and brushed it off. I thought she was a jerk but that was only because I didn't get my little addict's way. I learned so much from that. I started to get my own healthy boundaries and realized that it's better to keep myself safe than to be liked by everyone. I don't have to worry about what other people are thinking of me. I can leave that up to Higher Power. I can say "no" to something that is not good for me. The people who take the time to get to know the real me know that I'm not a jerk. I know that I'm a good person. I'm even better now that I have healthy boundaries.

I let go of codependency enough to maintain healthy boundaries.

April 2

THE FOURTH STEP

Made a searching and fearless moral inventory of ourselves.
– S.L.A.A. Core Documents, "The Twelve Steps of S.L.A.A."

I followed the traditional Fourth Step format from Alcoholics Anonymous, and I listed every person I had a resentment against. I wrote what they had done to make me resent them, and how it affected me. I was searching and I was fearless. But somehow, I managed to skip over the section that addressed my part in those events. When I took my Fifth Step, my sponsor pointed this out to me. It was an eye-opening experience. I'd been so focused on what others had done to me, it never occurred to me that I might have any blame in those situations. My Fourth Step was the groundwork for the enlightenment found in my Fifth Step, and I took this into my Sixth and Seventh Steps when examining my character defects. With the knowledge of my own faults, I was able to forgive the faults of others and carry out my Eighth and Ninth Steps. None of this would have happened without the thorough work I did on my Fourth Step. Some people say that the Fourth Step separates the men from the boys. I'd rather say that it separates those who grow from those who go.

Higher Power, help me to be honest with myself about my assets and liabilities.

April 3

H.A.L.T.—HUNGRY, ANGRY, LONELY, TIRED

Though abstaining from addictive, bottom-line behavior(s) is painful, the pain does not last forever. One of the tools in the withdrawal survival kit is "Don't get too 'Hungry-Angry-Lonely-Tired' (H.A.L.T.)." Most of all, don't despair! Remember—You are not alone! – from the "Withdrawal: Gateway to Freedom, Hope and Joy" pamphlet

Three meals a day, constant resentment inventories on every little detail, a meeting every day and eight hours of sleep no matter what. My sponsor was like a drill sergeant when I was in withdrawal. She knew the dangers of any one of these when we're trying to stay sober. When I'm too deprived of food, I get lightheaded and my guard is down. Old feelings come in and it becomes about cravings for other past acting-out behavior. When I'm too angry, I don't feel the conscious contact with God because I'm focused on revenge. Lonely is dangerous because I start to feel like nothing can fix me but "him." When I'm tired, I get confused and my decisions aren't rational. When any of H.A.L.T. is in play, I'm thinking of ways to get release. Past numbing-out behaviors may look like a way to get what I need. Once I get mired in that mud, it's all the more difficult to pull myself out. That's why I need to yell for help. I need to tell an outreach partner or share at a meeting that I'm experiencing H.A.L.T. These actions can help lift me out of the mud.

I practice self-care today and remember to stay out of H.A.L.T.

April 4

SOBRIETY DATE

The people who recover from sex and love addiction are those who define their bottom-line addictive behavior. They start now and add to it later if necessary. This is the sobriety definition. They don't act out—just for today, this hour, this moment, no matter what. – from the "Questions Beginners Ask" pamphlet

In the first four years of S.L.A.A., my sobriety date changed so many times that I thought, What's the point? I used to go to meetings and say, "Sobriety time doesn't matter." But when I had my spiritual experience and set my bottom lines, my sponsor had me write that date in my S.L.A.A. Basic Text in permanent ink. When I reached 114 days (a point that I could never stay sober past before) she made me a t-shirt with a countdown to 114 days with the S.L.A.A. life preserver on the back. This made me feel loved and forced me to recognize the importance of keeping that date and taking sobriety chips in recognition of that. When I share, I pass around my sobriety medallion so newcomers can recognize the importance of sobriety. On my twelfth sober anniversary, my partner bought me a medallion that was pink with bling. It makes me so grateful that I have a partner who understands and celebrates me. Acknowledgement and celebration of my sobriety date solidifies its importance. It helps me to not act out one day at a time.

I celebrate my sobriety date and know that if I keep it, I will have peace and serenity in my life.

April 5

OBSESSION

We who are plagued with romantic obsession have found hope and recovery in S.L.A.A. The program shifts the focus from the idealized romantic relationship that our disease craves to a working relationship with a Power greater than ourselves. – from the "Romantic Obsession" pamphlet

Obsession has created so much anxiety in my life. It isolated me and forced me into a fantasy life that eroded my sense of self and well-being. I thought so much about him and how he could fix everything. If only he could be the person I wanted him to be and not the reality that he was. This left no time for me to do my life. But the obsession had such a hold that was stronger than even heroin, that I didn't care about life without him. The ironic thing was that I didn't really know him. I was assigning him magical qualities that he didn't have. I never wanted to be the kind of person that was so fixated on one person that everything else in their life suffered. I wanted to be a well-liked, well-rounded person. All that was gone the minute he walked into my life and my mind. I used to wish that I could just cut out that part of my brain that contained thoughts of him so I could continue with some sort of life. S.L.A.A., God and the Steps performed that surgery for me and I will be well as long as I continue on this path and don't invite the obsessive thoughts back in.

I let my Higher Power and the Steps relieve my obsession today.

April 6

SEXUAL ANOREXIA

Sex was more fulfilling than we had ever previously experienced, even as it was no longer the source of tyranny which had constricted so many of us. – S.L.A.A. Basic Text, Page 158

When I joined a food program and stopped binging on gourmet foods, I looked at the food plan as torture. I thought I would never enjoy food again. But I discovered that it tasted better because I was no longer grabbing for all I could get and ignoring the experience of it like I used to. It was the same with my relationships. I was in a committed relationship, so my sexual anorexia didn't have excuses to back me into a corner and make me obsess so much that I ran away. Sometimes it's a struggle to feel joyful about sex but I have a support group and close S.L.A.A. friends to reach out to. A subject that used to be taboo is now a source for healing. Through sharing about my anorexia, I realized that I've always been anorexic, even in my acting out. Going through the actions without really being present or being with someone who I would never see again, or didn't even know their name, was my anorexia. For me, the only way out of anorexia is intimacy and commitment.

I stay present and experience the joy in my relationships.

April 7

POWERLESSNESS

We began to recognize that we were powerless, not merely to change some specific sex partner, lover, or situation. We were powerless over an addictive pattern, of which any current, specific circumstance was just the most recent example – S.L.A.A. Basic Text, Page 71

We are the owners of our patterns. These patterns are ways of thinking and behaving that are embedded and unconscious and therefore acted out without recognition of another choice By honestly writing out our history and experiences with power lessness and unmanageability, as most do in formally working a First Step, we will inevitably uncover our non-working patterns and the progression of our disease. When we listen to others share their stories of unmanageability, we can usually identify the same thoughts and feelings, if not the behavior. Sometimes we hear people that reveal our own powerlessness to us where we thought there was none. We thought we could handle it, but it overwhelmed us. Admitting and accepting this part of our sex and love addiction as it is now documented in our First-Step writing and therefore undeniable, is crucial in beginning to take personal responsibility and in changing. We can no longer point the finger as we have done in the past.

Today, I commit to focusing on myself with the help of the program, my Higher Power and my sponsor.

April 8

THE TENTH CHARACTERISTIC

We stay enslaved to emotional dependency, romantic intrigue, or compulsive sexual activities. – S.L.A.A. Core Documents, "Characteristics of Sex and Love Addiction"

Most people come to know that they are enslaved to their addiction at some point in their lives. Nicotine addicts need to smoke even when it's inconvenient or killing them. Alcohol and drug addicts end up in the hospital or jail and go straight back to buying the substance when they get out. But enslaved to sex and love? You're supposed to be emotionally dependent on the one you love, right? Most of society believes that romantic intrigue and sexual activities are the point of life. But I wasn't happy unless I was constantly making romantic gestures or fantasizing. If I wasn't having sex, in some form or another, six times a day, I was miserable and full of fear or plotting to get more. When these activities become self-destructive and consume us, we hopefully realize that we are enslaved to sex and love addiction and find S.L.A.A. The program helps ease the need to be sickeningly dependent on one person by teaching us how to be independent and self-loving through Higher Power and the Steps. We are able to stop spending all of our money and time on romantic intrigue. Sex becomes a by-product of sharing, commitment and trust instead of a voracious desire.

Today, I focus on the work that needs to be done and feed my soul instead of my disease.

April 9

FELLOWSHIP

A fellowship of others who can truly say, "Yes, I understand—I felt that way too" is a vital part of what makes recovery possible in each avenue of addiction. - S.L.A.A. Basic Text, Page viii

Left to my own devices, I can make the simplest of situations chaotic and unmanageable. I can misconstrue and misinterpret the people and situations around me. I can become so frustrated that the lure of my sex and love addiction—with its empty promises—seems the only way to assuage my fear, anger and resentments. Just for today, I can choose to try another way. I can reach out for support—through prayer and meditation, by telephoning a fellowship member and by attending an S.L.A.A. meeting. I see others in S.L.A.A. doing this. If I trust Higher Power, I know that he/she/it will give me the strength and courage to be humble and to ask for help. The Steps, Traditions and Concepts were all set up to make a durable, workable fellowship of people who are uniquely situated to help each other. They may be from all different cultures and backgrounds, but they have all felt the pain of sex and love addiction. The first day that I went out to breakfast after a meeting with a group of fellows was when I truly realized how blessed we are to have found S.L.A.A. I knew I never had to be alone again.

Instead of trying to do everything on my own today, I reach out for support.

April 10

HOPE

The difference between this despair and loneliness and those same feelings I had during my active addiction is that today I have hope alongside those feelings. Today I have hope that I can have a life as full and free as I've always wanted.* - *S.L.A.A. Basic Text, Page 189

Life was devastating when I walked into the rooms. My patterns seemed inescapable. They showed themselves definitely in love relationships but also with friends, coworkers, neighbors, anyone I met. I did not want to get close to people because I feared the conflict I grew up with, which seemed to be my inescapable destiny. Coming to the room and listening to old-timers who spoke from their experience, strength and especially hope was so grounding for me, and inspiring, and really was the one thing that kept me coming back. It was more than the words they were saying, it was how they said it—the tone of their voice, the way they could just be present in their bodies and face the room. Their words echoed within me and were the promise of a better life. It's amazing that I have been able to find recovery from my addictive patterns. Now I'm one of those people who can sit in my body and face the room and let the Higher Power of the program work through me and reach out to other people.

Today, I find hope in the rooms of S.L.A.A. and share it with others.

April 11

ROMANTIC LOVE

Whatever novelty we held for our partners in the beginning it had to wear thin, and then wear off. For those who were getting more involved with us, our ability to take a suddenly sick cat to the vet's, or pick up a bag of groceries on the way home, or come through with some real childcare help, was worth a lot more than a professional reputation, or romantic dinners by candlelight in extravagant restaurants, or magnanimous gifts or gestures.
– S.L.A.A. Basic Text, Page 155

Romantic love is addictive. It's the stuff of Hollywood movies and escape fiction. We long to be with the person we desire, without considering his or her own wishes. The fantasy of long walks on moonlit beaches is alluring. Addicts want that above all else while the realities of life suffer. Goals fall by the wayside as we chase the high of romantic love. Often, the objects of our affection can't live up to our romantic ideal and we become resentful and vindictive. If sex addiction hides underneath the romance, it will eventually come out and our incessant demands for more will only lead to disillusion. People who don't want to live in reality become exhausted and the romance dies. Dramatic romantic gestures are seen for what they are: manipulation. After the honeymoon period, most sex and love addicts run. They don't have time for the boring errands of life. I always dreamed of having that romantic love but settled for what I got. I would obsessively watch movies and read books to get high on romance. S.L.A.A. taught me how to live in reality. Today I have a healthy relationship that gives me serenity and fulfillment. I wouldn't trade that for some crazy idea of fleeting romance.

I let go of my fantasies of romantic love and live in reality today.

April 12

RELATIONSHIP CONFLICT

We have learned by painful experience that life with a sex and love addict cannot and will not be without growing pains and often severe conflict. This is true even, and perhaps especially, in recovery. If we try to keep the surface of the relationship smooth, we begin to compromise our own feelings... Our own success in partnership rests first, as does the addict's recovery on maintaining a sense of personal dignity. – S.L.A.A. Basic Text, Page 64

It's difficult for my addict brain to look at the big picture when I'm having conflict in my relationship. All I can see is the fear. I'm afraid he's not right for me, I've made a mistake, he'll abandon me because of this particular character defect that we're arguing over, etc. When I talk to my sponsor and fellows, I realize that I'm blowing everything out of proportion. Sometimes conflict can involve deal-breakers. But if I and my Higher Power have chosen well, and if I stick to the principles and tools of the program, relationship conflict can be worked through. Finding a way to work it out and getting through to the other side makes the relationship stronger. In each situation, I remind myself, "Do I want to be right? Or do I want to be happy?" If I hold onto my need to be right instead of looking where I can be of service to my partner, the conflict will last forever. I heard a woman who had been married 40 years say the secret to a happy relationship is to never go to bed angry. If I can take my ego out of the argument, I never go to bed angry.

I use the principles and rely on my Higher Power and S.L.A.A. fellows for relationship help.

April 13

FAKE IT 'TIL YOU MAKE IT

Nothing less than going through the death of all that I had been in the world up to that time—of experiencing the dissolution of my former self—seemed required...I could have no guarantees for the specific results. I would have to let it take me where it would. – S.L.A.A. Basic Text, Page 23

Through withdrawal, while I was becoming the person I was supposed to be, I felt like an imposter. I had never had true self-dignity before. My reactions to stress had always been to act out in some way. My sponsor told me to act as if I was already the sober dignified person I wanted to be. She said that the more I took positive actions, regardless of whether I felt capable of them or not, the more normal those actions would become. Taking sober action felt strange, as if someone else was doing it. But the more I practiced, the better I was able to make that my first reaction. When I was wrong, Higher Power showed me another way or revealed something I needed to learn. In college, I remember saying that people with big vocabularies were "actors" and "snobs" and I went around cursing all the time in order to "stay real." The reality of the situation is that I looked ignorant and those "actors" went on to do great things. I don't have to put myself down to be true to who I am. I can "act as if" and still be real.

I allow myself to fake it 'til I make it, trusting in my Higher Power.

April 14

VIGILANCE

It would have been a serious error to attribute all of our troubles to the addiction alone, for our character defects affected all other areas of our lives as well. This was not the time to relax, for we needed to continue our vigilance against the constant sexual and romantic temptations and the illusion of "the perfect romance." – S.L.A.A. Basic Text, Page 85

Sex and love addiction is sneaky. It can creep into every area of our lives and tell us a work friendship should turn into an affair because that person is perfect for us, or it's okay to take a little comfort in going to an adult bookstore. It tells us that cable television programs aren't harmful. For some people it might not be, but when we start rationalizing behaviors that make us dance around our bottom lines, we're in dangerous territory. My sponsor said it was as if acting out was a big dark hole that we keep falling into, until one day we walk really far away from it in order to avoid falling in. If I start doing a behavior that doesn't feel right, I check with sober partners. If they think it sounds sketchy, I avoid it. Sometimes just the act of telling on myself stops the behavior. If I'm ignoring how I'm feeling, I can get caught in the trap of addiction. Journaling, praying, meditating, outreach and all the tools of the program keep me in touch with myself and my sobriety. Sometimes it seems like too much work, but it's worth it.

I use all the tools of the program to stay vigilant today.

April 15

SELF-CARE

I was beyond the point of feeling that solitude was only deprivation, and was faring well. I had done many things which I had always depended on others to do for me. I had learned to take real pleasure in my ability to take care of myself. – S.L.A.A Basic Text, Page 37

In this quote from the Basic Text, Rich had been living alone and going to S.L.A.A. He says, "I had learned how to cook a good meal for myself, to do my laundry, to maintain my apartment." Sex and love addicts usually try to manipulate others into doing mundane (or big) tasks for them. When we depend on others they don't do it right or they end up resenting us or they take control. In my case, it was my parents who did everything for me because I could never get the unavailable men to do anything for me (talk about repeated blows to the ego). I felt like a little kid in my thirties. My sponsor told me to take a 30-day no contact and to stop taking money from them. The time alone made me realize how much work it is to take care of myself. But I got to pursue my own interests and felt real pride and dignity for the first time. I wasn't looking to anyone else for approval, only myself. That feeling is so freeing, getting off the hamster wheel of trying to manipulate others to do what I could do for myself.

Higher Power, help me to focus on loving myself, so that I may be healthy enough to love others.

April 16

CHARACTER ASSETS

We had begun to develop spiritual qualities which we had never had, or had allowed to go unused during our active addiction. – S.L.A.A. Basic Text, Page 89

I've always had character assets, but they were so hidden under acting out that I didn't notice them or have the chance to build on them. I often tried to claim my partner's character assets as my own. Sometimes I would bury my good qualities out of fear of losing the attention of someone I thought I needed. If I got the sense that a prospective partner would be intimidated by intelligence, I played dumb. If my boyfriend thought I worked too much, I became irresponsible and called in sick when I wasn't. With the help of Higher Power in sobriety, I let go of the fear of losing someone in favor of letting my character assets grow. Once I could identify and clear out many of my defects, I got to work on cultivating the opposite of those defects. It was sometimes a long painful process, but Higher Power and the program helped me through. Today, I am the kind of person I used to look up to and wish I could be.

I list my character assets and add to them daily.

April 17

STARTING A MEETING

A regularly scheduled S.L.A.A. meeting, even if only two are present, can lead to a deepening sense of personal commitment in furthering the recognition of sex and love addiction...A meeting can also serve as a focal point for sharing experience, strength and hope concerning recovery from sex and love addiction.* – *S.L.A.A. Basic Text, Page 121

In my early recovery, I was in a small college town. At that time, there were only two meetings. I had to drive two hours, and sometimes, when I got there, I found out that the meeting no longer existed. That's how desperate I was for recovery. I soon realized I needed recovery right where I lived, so a friend and I decided to start a candlelight meditation meeting. I don't know if it still exists, but it was an amazing meeting that gradually grew. When I left that town, they were up to about five meetings. That's how the fellowship grows. It just takes one person reaching out to another sex and love addict and it grows from there. I think I take it for granted that I can go to a meeting now every day. I was more desperate back then, and it showed me that I would do anything for my recovery. It makes me grateful that I do have a lot of meetings now and can put more energy into other forms of service.

If I see the need, I will start a meeting today.

April 18

REAL LOVE

We travelled the road towards greater communication, understanding and cooperation; that is, towards partnership. – S.L.A.A. Basic Text, Page 43

Real love requires attention and acceptance. It does not imprison the beloved. It is not fantasy or projection of our own needs but respect for the other person's. In real love, both parties are willing to relinquish control of each other and let go of the outcome of their efforts. In real love, we understand, too, that other people have their own relationship with a power greater than themselves and must make their own choices. We want for our lovers whatever they understand as best for them, even if we think they are mistaken. After all, each of us can only learn from his or her own mistakes. We can only hope that whoever we love will seek the guidance of a Higher Power in pursuit of their own good. The Twelve Steps help us clear away the wreckage of the past and build a stronger foundation for relationships with others. Our primary relationships must first be with ourselves and a Higher Power. Then we can enjoy cooperation in a partnership.

I use the tools of the program to clean up my side of the street and grow towards real love.

April 19

THE EIGHTH TRADITION

S.L.A.A. should remain forever nonprofessional, but our service centers may employ special workers. – S.L.A.A. Core Documents, "The Twelve Traditions"

Money and spirituality don't mix. One sex and love addict talking to another, freely giving what was given to them is the only way the Twelfth Step works. If the motive is money, the speaker or sponsor is compromised. Sex and love addicts stop listening and refuse to believe a paid Twelfth-Stepper. Special workers get paid to help S.L.A.A. function but they never get paid to be speakers or sponsors. This Tradition has helped me in my personal life because I used to see people in terms of their accomplishments and careers. I was often in a state of "compare and despair." The Eighth Tradition tells me that there's actual value in identifying ourselves as who we are inside rather than what we do. A sober S.L.A.A. member who has a tiny apartment in the city is better situated to help another in Twelve Step work than a non-sober member who lives in a mansion on the hill.

I keep my Twelfth-Step work nonprofessional and focus on deepening my spiritual connection with my Higher Power.

April 20

SECRETS

We even took pride in our ability to keep a secret, to keep our stories straight, to keep our feelings hidden, to go it alone...If we were able to manage the maze of intrigue without discovery... then we apparently never had to deal with the consequences of our actions. – S.L.A.A. Basic Text, Pages 81-2

There is a saying, "We are as sick as our secrets." What we are able to say out loud to another human being and to our Higher Power is what we are able to admit to ourselves. With rigorous honesty, we can name and claim the thoughts and deeds that get us into trouble, cause us pain and compromise our dignity. When we share deeply from the heart, the love comes through no matter how painful or embarrassing the content of what we have said. This creates openness. When we see the unconditional love fellowship members have for each other no matter how shameful or painful their patterns of acting out, we begin to open ourselves to this love. The love in our hearts connects with the love in the room and thus begins the healing. Our judgments and doubt dissolve long enough for us to hear the strength and the hope.

Higher Power, let the fear in my heart be replaced by honesty, openness and willingness. Let me take an action today to strengthen my recovery.

April 21

PORNOGRAPHY

In my early teens, I spent hours in fantasy and masturbation, the only means I had to express my feelings. That pattern of withdrawal from human contact and solitary concentration on sexual release...became a growing part of my active addiction. – S.L.A.A. Basic Text, Page 164

For many of us sex addicts, using pornography was such a large part of our disease that it ended up totally consuming us. We locked ourselves up in our rooms with the glow of a computer or a glossy magazine. We entered a different world to escape the one in which we felt we could not function. Pornography has the power to twist our personal ethics to fit into a mold that will produce the greatest addictive outcome. Healing from the frequent use of this substance is a long process. Sometimes the images can pop back up when we are at our most vulnerable. Entering recovery means realigning ourselves with the person we are without pornography. We no longer need to live that detached painful existence where we objectify and use images for our own selfish ends. We no longer torture our brains with those mind-numbing images, losing ourselves and our humanity in the process. Our identity will reveal itself as we continue the slow process of healing. We can live happy, fulfilling lives without our substance of choice. We can reform our identity to become the person we were always meant to be. I have dignity without pornography in my life.

I love and respect myself. I look forward to getting to know the real me.

April 22

UPS AND DOWNS

Addictions, however, are like internal hurricanes. Periodic lulls may occur, but a tidal onslaught may recur at any time. - S.L.A.A. Basic Text, Page 9

They say that life has its ups and downs. In dealing with addiction, it always felt much more dramatic than that. The downs felt like a deep dark pit that I would never get out of and the ups sometimes felt manic. I would trade anything in the world to always stay in the highs and do anything to avoid the lows. Being depressed felt too personal, like God or the world was out to get me. With S.L.A.A., Higher Power and the Twelve Steps, I'm learning to stick around and deal with the bad times. I also experience the good times with a more realistic perspective. I can experience joy with my feet on the ground now. I have found with this stability that the roller-coaster ride has stopped. My sponsor compared it to a pendulum that swings wide in addiction. You just need to wait over time for it to come to center. But with sobriety, we don't have to wait so long to get to center. Dealing with problems helps me to avoid despair. Having sober fun helps me avoid the crash when the party's over.

Today, I stay centered through meetings, prayer, meditation and outreach.

April 23

GENDER STEREOTYPES

Many persons with difficult sex and love addiction histories seek to blame "others" for them. These others can be labelled under such stereotypes as... "emasculating feminists," "male chauvinists,"... ad nauseam. – S.L.A.A. Basic Text, Page 132

This section of the Basic Text goes on to say that, "The truth seems to be that until we 'own' our sex and love addiction as a personal condition about which we assume the responsibility to do something within ourselves, hostility directed outward towards some designated would-be 'persecutor' is a waste of time." Yes, my mom tried to tell me I had to cook and clean and take care of a man or I wouldn't amount to anything in this world. I wanted to be able to "drink men under the table" instead of wearing dresses and looking pretty like my sister. Rebelling against stereotypes caused me a lot of pain. I felt like a failure and an outsider because I couldn't conform. When I came to S.L.A.A., that all changed. They accepted me for who I was, flaws and all. They told me I didn't have to conform to society's rules. That was between God and me. I only needed a desire to stop acting out. I could put all outside judgment aside and just concentrate on getting sober.

I concentrate on the Twelve Steps and my sobriety today and I let go of worry and judgment.

April 24

RED FLAGS

If our frustration level was up due to difficult circumstances in our work or our relationships with other people, these situations needed to be flagged. Flagging them meant disclosure of them and our frustration about them to our partner. – S.L.A.A. Basic Text, Page 157

Frustrations need to be communicated so we don't act out over them. Maybe something can be done to change the situation. If red flags appear in a dating situation, it might be best to discuss them with a sponsor before speaking with our partner. Early on in my dating plan, my date admitted to lying about a past relationship. I took it as a red flag against the relationship. I told my sponsor about it and that I wanted to stop dating him. Her response shocked me. "If you came to me every week and said, 'He lied to me again,' I would tell you to run. But you lied to him also about a past relationship. Is it possible you could give him the benefit of the doubt this time?" My partner and I communicated about it, he apologized and ever since he has proven himself to be an honest, caring man. People are human and they will make mistakes. Something is only a red flag if it erodes the foundation of the relationship or if we will certainly act out over it. With Higher Power and the program, we can strive for a solution.

Today, I practice open and honest communication.

April 25

RESENTMENT PRAYER

Whenever we were troubled by things other people said or did...we needed to make a quick assessment of our own spiritual condition...We found that one easy way to do this was to ask ourselves, "If I were doing to someone else what I think is being done to me, would it be a symptom of my own illness?" – S.L.A.A. Basic Text, Page 96

Resentment is a burden on my emotions, my thinking, and my soul. It is one of the biggest obstacles to freeing myself from obsession and anxiety, fear and regret. When I first got in the program I was paralyzed with resentments and was told to pray. I was given a resentment prayer which instructed me to shower this person with love, but I could not see beyond my rage and indignation. So, my sponsor gave me his emergency resentment prayer: just say, "PRAYER." It helped me so much. I liked recognizing that the person was spiritually sick and I could identify with that myself. It helped me become right-sized when facing the person every day. I liked taking contrary action in praying for them and wishing the best for them. What I especially liked was asking my Higher Power for help with giving up the resentment. This is a tool I use throughout my recovery, which is basically the recognition that I am powerless even over my own ability to turn stuff over.

I pray to be relieved of obsession and anger when I feel resentment.

April 26

STRENGTH

I felt myself getting stronger in both insight and steadiness of behavior as I continued to share my experiences, both before and after recovery, with others, even if they were not receptive. - S.L.A.A. Basic Text, Page 39

Strength before sobriety meant fighting everything and everyone to prove I was strong. Inside, though, I was insecure and scared. That's a lonely place to be. I've heard people say, "There's strength in numbers." I never felt that to be true until I came to S.L.A.A. and saw people helping each other through their struggles. The fellowship held them up when they felt too weak to go on. We share our experience, strength and hope. With the help of the Twelve Steps and the S.L.A.A. Program of recovery, I gained insight into myself that helped me get through many of life's difficulties. Instead of sticking my head in the sand, I engaged in self-care, went to the doctor and found out I needed surgery. Instead of running into addictive behaviors, I prayed and asked for help. I got through it all feeling like I was standing tall with my Higher Power instead of groveling in despair. I have steadiness in my behavior now that draws people to me instead of the erratic behavior that used to push them away. Sobriety yields more and more strength every day.

I rely on my Higher Power and the S.L.A.A. Fellowship when I feel as if I am lacking strength.

April 27

THE NINTH SIGN OF RECOVERY

We begin to substitute honesty for self-destructive ways of expressing emotions and feelings. – S.L.A.A. Core Documents "S.L.A.A. Signs of Recovery"

When my relationship with my partner was new, I used to start arguments with him so he wouldn't hang up the phone right away. I was afraid of losing him and my disease told me this would keep him around at least a little while longer. I didn't see how self-destructive this was in that it was harming the relationship. If the relationship went away because of my ignorance I was always able to beat myself up gloriously for that. My partner called me on it. He told me to stop finding things to argue about just so he wouldn't get off the phone. Thank God that because of S.L.A.A. I found a partner who was good at being honest about his emotions. I instantly realized what I was doing and the fear of abandonment I was feeling. I did a fear inventory and realized I was self-sabotaging. I prayed for the character defect to be removed. It's not that I never feel the feelings, it's that I have S.L.A.A. tools to deal with them appropriately.

Today, I look for constructive ways of expressing emotions and am honest about how I'm feeling.

April 28

HEALTHY BREAK-UP

Encountering and facing any and all pain along the way through this process of withdrawal, I could become capable of making some decisions about how to live my life. This would now be based on the discovery of who and what I really was, which might emerge during my time alone, in full awareness of my addictive past. – S.L.A.A. Basic Text, Page 23

Six months into my relationship, my boyfriend and I broke up. It felt like I was experiencing a death—the death of hope for a sober relationship. I read a book about grief in recovery, and I learned that you don't replace the loss. My biggest fear about losing a relationship was that I would act out again in S.L.A.A. I had to trust God, and when I experienced that loss, I found that I could turn to the program, I could go to more meetings, I could go up to the desert and visit my family and just be closer to God and rely on my Higher Power for everything. I could get through the grieving process. I had to feel the grief instead of numbing it out or not allowing myself to cry, or whatever avoidance habits I had in the past. I got through it. I felt stronger and closer to God because of it. I feel like I could get through any grief with the tools and support of the program.

I use grief as an opportunity for learning and growing. I remember that pain is the touchstone of spiritual growth.

April 29

CONSCIOUS CONTACT

From someone or something to bail us out of scrapes or to pray to only amidst crisis, we had progressed beyond an overseeing caretaker or parent-like God to the sense of being in conscious partnership with this Power. – S.L.A.A. Basic Text, Page 99

Working toward a relationship with God instead of only using him in emergencies has never been attractive to me. For some reason (addiction maybe) it has seemed tedious to pray and meditate every day. Asking for God's direction has been like something magical that only other people can do. I always felt that God wouldn't listen to "poor little old me" or I wouldn't hear him. Sometimes the noise in my head was so loud that I couldn't hear anything, so forget about meditating. When my sponsor told me to set a timer and meditate for five minutes a day, I refused. I didn't have enough time in my day. "I'm too busy" is a logical excuse but not a good one for my recovery. There's a block to building partnership with a Higher Power because I don't always trust him. I've always thought of God as an authority who punishes me. It's difficult to change childhood beliefs and be on equal footing and open communication with someone (or something) you can't see and are afraid of. I forced myself to go to meditation meetings and pray whether I believed it or not. Gradually, I learned to trust and believe in a loving Higher Power that I have a partnership with today.

Today, I set aside time to pray and meditate and to keep the lines of communication open with my Higher Power.

April 30

POWER STRUGGLE

What security we had derived, knowing we could foster insecurity in others, making them all the more needy and dependent on us, thus insuring our own sense of well-being. We enjoyed the power our sex appeal gave us in enforcing our dominance over others by hinting that they could be replaced.
S.L.A.A. Basic Text, Page 74

I remember so much crying and dramatic situations in my relationships before sobriety. Everything I did was about gaining the power in the relationship. I strategically flirted, ignored, abandoned or created dramatic situations. I needed a reaction from the other person that would let me know I had power over them. Even if I was deathly afraid of losing them, I would hint that they could be replaced. It didn't matter that they lost trust in me over this behavior, as long as I felt a twisted sense of security in fostering their insecurity. This is where the power struggle backfired on me. As long as I relied on these strategies, I was destroying the relationship. What a mess I was in if they called my bluff. Sober members in S.L.A.A. showed me that openness and honesty works much better at building trust and intimacy. It's okay to compromise sometimes in a relationship, it's not a life or death situation. Whenever I feel the desire to have power over another, I can do a fear inventory and check my motives. The feeling is usually lessened when I turn it over to my Higher Power and trust that everything is as it should be.

I surrender my need for control while promoting harmony and healing in relationships.

May 1

THE FIFTH STEP

Admitted to God, to ourselves, and to another human being the exact nature of our wrongs. – S.L.A.A. Core Documents, "The Twelve Steps of S.L.A.A."

Why is it so important to unburden oneself, to let the unflattering truths of who we are be exposed to another individual? Some of us can remember a time when we shared deeply personal information with people we barely knew out of an incessant need to release the pressure valve of guilt or pain. Others felt the need early on in recovery to inform all the people we loved that we had this thing called sex and love addiction, and that was why we'd behaved so poorly. But the Steps are in an order for a reason. We must admit our problem, give our will over to a Higher Power and take our inventory before we are truly ready to share ourselves completely with someone else. Through the humbling relief of taking a Fifth Step with a sponsor (or another trusted individual), we learn how to be vulnerable. We learn how to be honest with another human being. This is practice for every encounter we will have in the future. To present ourselves honestly is a foreign experience, but with the Fifth Step, we move closer to rigorous personal honesty in every aspect of our lives.

I admit my shortcomings to the people I trust.

May 2

HUMOR

We had come to know ourselves more as we really were... We had begun to develop spiritual qualities which we had never had, or had allowed to go unused during our active addiction. Working hand in hand with our new partner, God, it was time to begin making our peace with other human beings. – S.L.A.A. Basic Text, Page 89

The disease of sex and love addiction can be humorless. When we learn to laugh at ourselves, we gain humility. Laughing with others can be a way of creating healthy intimacy. Early in sobriety, I went to an S.L.A.A. party with a sign around my neck that said, "Confront me if I don't ask for help." My sponsee and I laughed about that all night. Before the program, if anyone laughed at me it was like experiencing a death. I couldn't prevent myself from plunging into anger and fear. In order to get and stay sober, I had to learn to laugh at myself. If I took every little mistake I made (and there were many of them) personally, I would have run from S.L.A.A. a long time ago. Laughter with my fellows eased the pain of withdrawal. I knew they understood my suffering and were laughing with me instead of at me. That moment of relief motivated me to reach out to fellows and become part of the group. This gave me the support I needed to stay on the road to recovery.

I find laughter today to combat despair and negativity.

May 3

LET GO AND LET GOD

Affirming our Spirituality—relying upon a Power greater than ourselves...Becoming open to accepting the unexpected turns in our life. Practicing acceptance when situations don't go our way. More easily sensing we are being guided by our Higher Power. Trusting that our Higher Power is using our personal struggles for a greater good. – from the "Measuring Progress" pamphlet

In active addiction, we hold on to people or situations that aren't good for us because we don't know what will happen if we let go. Often, Higher Power has something better in store for us. It's difficult to trust that God will be there for us. It turns out Higher Power had a much better plan for my life than I ever had for myself. It just took the opening of the door to let him in. It's difficult to trust something we don't understand or have never believed in. Doing all the Steps in order helps us come to a place where we can start to believe. First, we surrender to the addiction, then we come to believe. We turn our lives over and clear out the wreckage of our past. If we truly let go, we are able to do this painful task willingly. God takes over for us when we are too weak to continue, if we let him.

Today, I accept life's struggles and trust that my Higher Power will be there for me.

May 4

PASSION

Even if we seemed to possess some positive traits, such as authentic concern for others, we could see that these had been perverted by our addiction, leaving us full of conflict and working at cross-purposes. The line between compassion and passion had never been clear to us. – S.L.A.A. Basic Text, Page 73

The dictionary defines passion as a strong feeling of enthusiasm or excitement for something or someone. The feelings can be sexual, romantic, angry, etc. It says that strong feelings can cause you to act in a dangerous way. Sex and love addicts know that all too well. In my addiction, I tried to rationalize my behavior as "I'm just a passionate person." But that passion got me in dangerous, dramatic situations all the time. Most situations ended in anger and someone getting hurt. The sexual feelings seemed easier to handle because I could numb out. But the romantic feelings (love addiction in my case) made me lose my mind. As addicts, we never knew how to control feelings. Once felt, they overwhelmed us. Fellowship, Steps and reliance on a Higher Power are a map out of the maze of dangerous passions. We emerge into enthusiasm and excitement for service work and our family and fellows. Passion can be a good thing if managed with the tools of the program of S.L.A.A. It takes practice and commitment, but it can be done.

Today, I rely on my Higher Power to guide my feelings.

May 5

LIVING THESE PRINCIPLES

The principles are simple enough: admission of the true source of the problem (addiction to the activity itself); reliance upon God or some other source of power beyond one's own resources for guidance in recovery; willingness to inventory one's own character defects and share this inventory with another; a readiness to come to grips with basic character flaws and make restitution to others; and commitment to these principles as a continuing way of life. The summation principle, the Twelfth Step, is the affirmation of personal recovery through accepting the responsibility to take the commitment to this way of life into action by sharing it with others. And it is here that true love, which is of God, and makes it possible for one person to touch the soul of another, is found and expressed. – S.L.A.A. Basic Text, Preface, Page vii

This is a tall order to present in the Preface of the Basic Text. It could scare newcomers away, but instead it becomes a goal to strive for. Living the principles gives us dignity of self and what we have been seeking our whole lives: true love. Newcomers see people in meetings who really are following the Twelve Step way of life: being honest, accepting responsibility and sharing love. This goal of living the principles takes a lot of work to achieve but is well worth it.

I do my best to live the principles of the program today.

May 6

GIFT OF FORGIVENESS

We could not make our forgiveness of others conditional on their having redeemed themselves, or righted their wrongs. We had to forgive them because, like us, they were sick and afflicted, and presumably had not set out in life to be so. - S.L.A.A. Basic Text, Page 90

Forgiveness never seemed like a gift to me before my involvement in Twelve Step programs. It seemed like a weakness that others would take advantage of. I thought withholding forgiveness gave me some sort of power. But it only sapped my energy and harmed my emotional well-being. When I'm lost in resentment, I'm more vulnerable to acting out. It's a waste of time. Since I started working the Eighth and Ninth Steps, I see that forgiveness is a gift to both the giver and the receiver. When I let go of resentment and anger, I get freedom from obsession. That obsession no longer has the power to stress me out and force me into self-destructive behavior. When I went back through my past in writing my Fourth Step and gave up many of my resentments in Steps Five through Seven, I felt the burden of all of those harmful feelings being lifted. Making amends helped me see that others weren't entirely to blame, I had a part in almost everything that happened to me. When others forgave me, I realized I wasn't a horrible person, only human.

I give and receive the gift of forgiveness as often as possible.

May 7

DATE 'EM 'TIL YOU HATE 'EM

We anorectics begin to realize that we have been living our lives for a long time without love. We observe the absence of closeness in certain areas of our lives and we observe that we are engaged in a policy of dread of others, and a strategy to keep them at bay. – from the "Anorexia: Social, Sexual, Emotional" pamphlet

Most of my life I've stumbled upon relationships. Someone else always let me know of their interest in me. It was rare that I ever expressed an interest in someone else. I was always too afraid to step out there and admit my feelings for someone. Even in recovery, my attempts at dating began through the anonymous safety of a smartphone screen, rarely making any real connections. But once, I asked out a woman I met at a social gathering. At first, she seemed just my type, but it didn't take long before I realized we had very little in common. She was more concerned with grooming me into her ideal partner than with getting to know the real me. My sponsor didn't say "date her 'til you hate her," but he might as well have. He said I needed the dating experience. But eventually, it was too much for me. I finally told her how I felt. She told me that she had certain expectations of people she dated. I told her that I wasn't interested in meeting her expectations. It's not worth it to stay with someone who doesn't like or love you for who you are, but it might be worth it to spend enough time with them to figure that out.

I work through my fear of connection and check my motives before leaving a dating situation.

May 8

HELPING OTHERS

The effectiveness of our efforts to help others would be directly related to the level of our own "spiritual awakening."
- S.L.A.A. Basic Text, Page 102

Before recovery, I never gave a thought to helping others. My goal was to get ahead at any cost. Ambition and pride blocked me from giving to anyone. Fear that there wasn't enough money, power and prestige to go around or to satisfy my addict desires forced me to sabotage people. When I came to S.L.A.A., I saw people doing things differently. People raised their hands when asked if anyone could sponsor. Sponsors reached out to me and met me even when it was inconvenient for them. Volunteers kept the meeting going each week. Even watching a fellow put away chairs after the meeting helped teach me about concern for others. I saw a serenity in these helpers that I had never felt in my own life. But I worked the Steps a few times and followed the direction of my sponsor and got service commitments (albeit begrudgingly). I started to feel more peace and freedom from the obsessions that had plagued me my whole life. Even though in the beginning I was only helping others in the hopes that I would rid myself of the disease of sex and love addiction, forced service eventually became sincere concern and care.

I look for ways to be of service to others today.

May 9

THE FOURTH CHARACTERISTIC

We confuse love with neediness, physical and sexual attraction, pity and/or the need to rescue or be rescued – S.L.A.A. Core Documents, "Characteristics of Sex and Love Addiction"

What is love? Of course I confused it with a bunch of other things before sobriety. Sex and love addiction twists many things including definitions. But not only sex and love addicts confuse love with other emotions. It's a story passed down through the generations: rescue someone and then marry them. We are taught to value physical and sexual attraction in society. We are taught that we need a partner in life to be whole. My neediness was about feeding my ego, needing attention. Physical and sexual attraction was about finding a way to numb out. Pity and the need to rescue made me feel better than the other person. Emotions that are about ego and fear cannot be love. With the help of S.L.A.A., I was able to put my needs aside and care about other people. I felt true love from my Higher Power and as a result was able to express that with another human being. Love is no longer about finding a way to break free from my painful isolation. It's about feeling genuine affection based on honesty and reality. I never want to go back to the confusing fantasy.

I love openly and honestly today, releasing any expectations

May 10

RESPONSIBILITY

While it was not wholly appropriate to blame either our early experiences or ourselves for our behavior as sex and love addicts, we had to accept some personal responsibility for it. We needed not to hide our true motives behind cosmetic rationalization or blame. – S.L.A.A. Basic Text, Page 83

I always believed I could use the excuse of what happened to me to stay a teenager for life. I never wanted to grow up and take on the hard work of adult responsibilities. My numbing-out behaviors helped me stay incapable of living up to obligations. Rationalizing my situation with "It's because so-and-so did this to me" worked for me. The Fourth Step started me on the road to being willing to be responsible for myself. Fellows and my sponsor taught me the art of self-care. When I let go of immaturity it is often the more painful and difficult way of doing things but in the long run is much better for me. When I look at my side of the street and make amends, I am clearing out what keeps me stuck in the cycle where I need to be rescued. I am able to stand on my own two feet and maybe even be of service to others.

I ask my Higher Power to help me accept responsibility for my feelings and behavior.

May 11

AMENDS

But even if we could not see how we could find the courage to carry out these amends, the willingness to try to do so was vital to our progress. If fear and pride kept us from addressing this important step in our spiritual journey, we might go through life still trying to avoid the host of those with whom we had been involved in mutually destructive relationships.
– S.L.A.A. Basic Text, Page 91

Why even bother saying you're sorry if you're just going to do it again? Before S.L.A.A., I couldn't avoid doing it again, whatever destructive thing that was. But in order to make the person I was obsessed with stay, I had to apologize. I had to try to convince them I was truly sorry and would never do it again. I should have won an Academy Award for those scenes. In sobriety, I found that making amends is essential. I had to confront my bad behavior and take the actions to change it. If I didn't clear out the wreckage of my past, I'd spend a lifetime running. Pride gave me rationalizations about why I didn't need to make amends to someone who had also hurt me. Fear told me not to admit anything or I would lose everything. I opened the door to willingness by praying over each amends. That helped me realize that I would stay stuck in my disease and act out again if I didn't take action and proceed with Step Nine. Most of my amends were taken well and people could see that I had really changed. I had finally found serenity.

I apologize for wrongdoing today and amend my behavior.

May 12

"THE ONE"

The power of my long denied emotional yearnings for love completely overwhelmed me. My "lover," I thought, was my 'one and only," the one light in my life—made in heaven for me. - S.L.A.A. Basic Text, Page 4

I found "the one," my soul mate, the perfect person for me...so why should I care about another's spouse? That's how my disease spoke to me. Anything goes when you've found "the one." You go down in flames for them like Romeo and Juliet. I told myself, "It's okay that you're acting obsessive because you can't live without him." He was the air that I breathed. He was going to fix me. But that desperate neediness and inability to leave breeds contempt. All kinds of dramatic situations come from it. When no one else in the world can fix me, I need to get everything that I can from "the one." I remember a romantic moment when we were standing on a cliff after our tenth time getting back together and I thought, 'He's going to push me off of this ledge and kill me." That's how frustrated we were with the affair. The only one for me now is myself and God and people who come into my life for a season, a reason, or a lifetime. Because of my work in S.L.A.A., I will leave if it's not healthy. There is more than one person in the world.

I practice self-care today by letting go of finding "the one".

May 13

SLIPPING

However honest we became through any last-ditch efforts at "control," our sobriety did not really begin until the last reservation had been let go, and we gave up the right, for one day (or one hour) at a time, to have "one more" liaison with our addiction. – S.L.A.A. Basic Text, Page 107

There's a story in the Big Book of A.A. about an alcoholic walking into a bar (to get lunch) and thinking if he just had a little whiskey in milk it would be okay. Before he knew what happened he was pounding on the bar, drunk. That was me with my sex and love addiction. I thought, ***I can read this email even though I said no contact. I can manage. I know we said that if we saw each other's cars we would leave, but it'll be okay. I need to be here.*** Before I knew it, I had broken all my bottom lines and was left bewildered and afraid, wondering what would happen to me as a result of the high-risk situations I had just indulged in. Every time I slipped, my sponsor reminded me of self-care—play soothing music, eat something nutritious that I really liked, take a bubble bath and we would get back to work the next morning. I kept slipping until the pain of acting out kicked my ass enough that I was willing to try a different way, to give it to a Higher Power. Thirteen years ago, I opened the door to a spiritual experience and haven't slipped since.

I let my Higher Power, my sponsor and S.L.A.A. fellows love me through the ups and downs of my recovery.

May 14

LIFE ON LIFE'S TERMS

Real life is not without tensions, unhappiness, and conflict, if we are honest with ourselves and others. If we are to grow in sobriety, we must be willing to look for dishonesty and self-centeredness in all of our activities, lest we find ourselves seeking to escape from life once again. – S.L.A.A. Basic Text, Page 142

Life draws hard terms sometimes. I must work long stressful hours or take care of a sick child or watch a loved one die. I could never find hope or meaning in the midst of any of these things. I would run straight to the oblivion of addiction. "Someone yelled at me" was always a good excuse to act out. S.L.A.A. opened my eyes to the dishonesty of my rationalizations and showed me how truly self-centered I had been my entire life. Practicing prayer, meditation and the Steps brings us into reality and helps us deal with life on life's terms. I constantly ask myself, "What does Higher Power want me to do?" The answer is always about helping others instead of numbing out or grabbing for my selfish needs. When I'm met with particularly difficult times, I go to more meetings (90 meetings in 90 days is good for the soul). I ask a fellow what they need or how they feel. If problems keep me away from service work, I get back to it as soon as I can. I always try to put the program and God first.

I live life on life's terms today and remember to lean on my Higher Power and fellows when things get difficult.

May 15

UNRESOLVED ANGER

I could no longer deny that I did have a huge amount of unresolved anger, very subtly hidden, and unless I got it out I would eventually be destroyed by it. – S.L.A.A. Basic Text, Page 262

Unresolved anger can manifest itself in more than one way. Sometimes, it is the result of not having control over a situation as a child. Other times, it is the result of not dealing with anger at the proper time in the proper manner. Either way, it amounts to an inability to properly express this difficult emotion. When we have never known the right way to deal with anger, we often express it inappropriately with verbal abuse, internalized resentment or even acting out. As we get sober and allow ourselves to feel our emotions, we may continue to make mistakes in how we handle them. To properly handle anger, we need to take baby steps. We may need to let the anger out through physical activity, or write about our feelings first. As we mature in recovery, we can move closer to a state in which we feel the anger and express it appropriately while we are still in the moment. When we do so, we can let go of anger quickly, and the destructive influence of unresolved anger need no longer wreak havoc in our lives.

Higher Power, help me acknowledge my feelings and express them in a healthy way.

May 16

GENEROSITY

Some part of me felt quite unlovable just for being myself, and so I tried to earn [love] by being generous, forgiving, understanding, and seemingly selfless. – S.L.A.A. Basic Text, Page 49

I was generous to a fault. I was willing to give away everything I had in order to ensure my lover wouldn't leave. Generosity in this sense is self-destructive. S.L.A.A. taught me to look for the motives behind my desire to give. I was shocked to learn that giving in that way was selfish. My ego was trying to play the big shot. I was giving, expecting love or adoration in return. Giving does create higher levels of self-esteem but I need to be sure it isn't the only thing I do to feel better about myself. Sometimes, I need to take a fearless inventory of my motivation for giving. I need to find healthy ways to reach out and share my abundance, time and wealth with fellows. When I help someone in recovery, it often has the effect of helping me more than it helps them. Generosity in service work saves my life and ensures the growth of the S.L.A.A. Program.

I check my motives and am generous in service to S.L.A.A. and others.

May 17

CAREER

We found that personal or professional situations in which we could not affirm these spiritual values were expendable.. Careers that had been exploited mainly for material security at the expense of self-fulfillment no longer appealed to us. We either changed our way of going about them, or let them go
– S.L.A.A. Basic Text, Page 102

Many addicts are underearners. Like our love relationships, we stay stuck in jobs that don't fulfill us because we don't think we can get anything better. My sex and love addiction gave my self-esteem such a beating that I thought I needed to take whatever I could get. Before recovery, I remember having a panic attack when a job recruiter tried to get me to go on an interview for my dream job Instead, I took the first offer and have been working in a career for 21 years that I never would have chosen. Before sobriety, it only served as a place to make money in between liaisons with my qualifier. I stole countless hours from my employer, talking on the phone, emailing, fantasizing and sneaking out of work early. In my S.L.A.A. sobriety I tried to make amends to my workplace by getting more involved and helping wherever I could. I changed my way of going about my career and now I'm a trainer and supervisor. I still think of going back to school like I've seen other sober program members do, but right now, I have a degree of self-esteem around my career that is very important to me.

Today, I focus on being an asset to those around me.

May 18

SPIRITUAL AWAKENING

This spiritual awakening was itself the product of having hit bottom and surrendered, having acquired a faith, having accomplished a practical examination of our past and our character, having developed a deepening relationship with God, having accepted responsibility for the impact our sex and love addiction had on others, becoming aware of problem areas in our lives and resolving to deal with these constructively, making amends, and reaching into a spiritual domain through regular prayer and meditation to place ourselves in closer communion with the source of guidance and grace.
– S.L.A.A. Basic Text, Page 102

Sometimes people equate a spiritual awakening with a lightning-bolt spiritual experience. As soon as they humble themselves enough to work the Steps, they expect a Higher Power to take all of their problems away. For some people, this may be their experience. For me, it took four years of working Steps, becoming willing to believe and learning to trust a Higher Power. I needed to spend another 14 years continuing to grow. But that moment in the mind of this addict when I realized that God does exist, was magical. It changed me from a suicidal, insane person into a sober, responsible and peaceful person. My spiritual awakening cleaned out that darkness and I want to do whatever I can to keep it out.

Today, I am grateful to be of service to others because of my spiritual awakening.

May 19

THE ELEVENTH TRADITION

Our public relations policy is based on attraction rather than promotion; we need always maintain personal anonymity at the level of press, radio, TV, film, and other public media. We need guard with special care the anonymity of all fellow S.L.A.A. members. – S.L.A.A. Core Documents, "The Twelve Traditions"

Our fellowship seems to be following the path of A.A. with the public media. In the last few years there have been quite a few movies made about sex and love addiction. There are bloggers and reporters who believe in S.L.A.A. and its message. They guard the anonymity of individual S.L.A.A. members. Individuals who carry the message remain anonymous to the general public. Personal ambition has no place in the fellowship. Our policy on growing the fellowship is attraction rather than promotion. Hopefully the world will eventually see the good that S.L.A.A. does. Families see their loved ones changing for the better. Communities see people become productive members of society. We need to be content with slow growth. I wanted to shout from the rooftops the good that the S.L.A.A. Program did in my life. But I reserve that for newcomers in meetings and during sponsorship, not on a public level. Over the years, I have seen the wisdom of this Tradition and try to practice it daily.

Today, I practice attraction rather than promotion and guard others' anonymity.

May 20

SELF-WILL

It took me six or seven months in A.A. to learn about asking for help in the Third Step sense of "turn my life and my will over to the care of a higher Power." When I learned to do this, the higher Power handled whatever I turned over much better than I ever had. – S.L.A.A. Basic Text, Page 247

In preparation for my First Step, my sponsor cautioned not to get too detailed in writing out my personal history. ***He just doesn't understand,*** I thought to myself. This is how I do things. I wrote my story my way, all 80 pages of it. While recalling a particularly euphoric instance of acting out, I felt the impulse to return to my addictive behavior. It was the first time in recovery that I had any desire to act out again. I got up from my computer and went downstairs to spend some time with my roommate so I could distract myself from the triggering situation. I understood then why my sponsor had cautioned me. He had knowledge that I did not yet have. I didn't have all the answers and I couldn't keep trying to do things my way. I needed to open myself to the wisdom and experiences of others. This initial lesson prepared me for the greater act of surrendering my will and giving myself over to the will of my Higher Power.

I listen to healthy program partners and to my Higher Power to find my way in recovery.

May 21

OPENNESS

We knew how to be open with others in S.L.A.A. about virtually everything we were thinking, feeling, and experiencing. Through this openness we had come to know something about personal honesty, and we had also learned something about being emotionally consistent. – S.L.A.A. Basic Text, Page 146

Being open with others can be a struggle sometimes. It wasn't safe in my childhood to be open with my family. Honesty usually involved sabotage or punishment. With a rageaholic father, you never know what kind of reaction you will get. It was transformative to walk into my first meeting of S.L.A.A. and see people share openly and honestly without fear of repercussions. I saw the community love and support them instead of shaming them. When I started sharing, people thanked me for my honesty and said it helped them to know it was okay to be open. Getting current in meetings and outreach calls opens the door to let God in. We learn how to be emotionally consistent. We rely on others and this helps chase the fear away. Fear used to keep me isolated and stubbornly refusing to let anything into my life. This closed system fed my addictive behavior and kept me stuck in acting out. The openness that I found in S.L.A.A. and with my Higher Power allowed me to live a joyful existence for the first time in my life.

Today, I do my best to be open and honest.

May 22

CROSSTALK

[A] group of people seemed threatened and downright hostile when I shared my experiences, and I was brick-batted quite a bit...Sharing these things, regardless of whether I was met with sympathy, envy, or vilification, helped me immensely. – S.L.A.A. Basic Text, Page 34

When a group of addicts get together, there can often be crosstalk. Many meetings define crosstalk differently and have suggestions about how to avoid it. Some say, "We avoid specific references to shares but we may thank the speaker." I have often heard people ignore that and talk directly to the speaker during their shares. It's good to identify with the feelings being shared but advice-giving or unwanted comments can alter the safety of sharing. We need to hold a safe space for newcomers to practice openness and honesty. In Chapter 2 of the Basic Text, our founder, Rich, became frustrated with hearing a newcomer's constant acting-out stories. He confronted him about it and the newcomer ran from the meetings. I have seen many people, who once shared their delusional thinking, transform into level-headed sober people. They usually were allowed the time to come to realizations themselves through prayer, meditation and hearing other people's shares, not by being brick-batted by crosstalk. Sharing can be healing for everyone. Our responsibility is to hold a safe space for it and refrain from crosstalk even if we think our advice could save someone.

I keep the focus on myself and refrain from crosstalk.

May 23

PRAYER

Our growing relationship with God was like a stabilizing keel beneath us. No matter how stormy the winds above the surface of life's waters, or how much sail we sometimes hoisted into the gale in the form of commitments beyond the scope of our limited strength and energy, we found that the keel beneath us, meditation and prayer, guaranteed that we would not capsize. We would retain our buoyancy on the ocean of life. We could survive whatever life might throw at us. – S.L.A.A. Basic Text, Page 100

Life has been throwing a lot of difficulties my way lately. Sometimes my prayer to Higher Power is just, "Help. Help. Help." When I believe that something else in the universe is listening, I get the strength to go on. I have hope that things will change. I try to say, "Your will, not mine, be done" at the end of every prayer. Even if I prefer my will over God's will in a situation, saying this phrase anyway keeps me humble. I'm forced to realize that I'm not God and my job is to seek Higher Power's will. Asking in prayer for answers and waiting and listening for them in meditation is the best way to do this. I have trained my brain to thank God in prayer instead of only going to Higher Power in crisis. Prayer is life affirming, not just a survival tool. Since I started practicing it, it hasn't let me down. I repeat what my sponsor told me: "God doesn't drop people on their heads." Since my spiritual experience, I've found that to be true.

I pray for guidance today and believe that my Higher Power is listening.

May 24

STEPS

The Twelve Steps, as originally set forth in Alcoholics Anonymous, do provide a comprehensive and thorough approach to the problem of dealing with addiction, including sex and love addiction. – S.L.A.A. Basic Text, Page 67

The Steps gave me a way out of the deep dark hole that I had dug for myself in addiction. I did what my sponsor said and did all the Steps in order. I didn't rush ahead or skip a Step. They are brilliant in the way they are set up. The founders of A.A. must have had divine inspiration, in my opinion. I need to recognize the addiction before I can begin to believe that something can take it away. I need to have hope before I can surrender to a Higher Power and clear away the wreckage of the past. We must do daily maintenance, and then it comes full circle with giving back to the program. Each Step prepares us for the next one. We are reminded throughout to do each Step to the best of our ability. Everyone works the Steps differently. But they are set forth so clearly that even in their simplest form, addicts gain recovery in all kinds of addictions, including sex and love addiction.

I focus on the Step I am working today and give the other Steps to my Higher Power.

May 25

THE FIFTH SIGN OF RECOVERY

We learn to accept and love ourselves, to take responsibility for our own lives, and to take care of our own needs before involving ourselves with others. – S.L.A.A. Core Documents, "S.L.A.A. Signs of Recovery"

Sometimes people believe the purpose of S.L.A.A. is to find and keep a healthy relationship with another human being. For some, the relationship may be a happy by-product of their work in S.L.A.A. For most, the real task is learning to accept and love themselves. This sign of recovery reminds us that we are not alone in our quest for self-acceptance. When I hear people share the same feelings of insecurity, I realize that we are in this struggle together. I can make outreach calls to them or go to fellowship and learn how they are overcoming those fears. Usually, the answer is the Steps and meetings and prayer. When I let go of character defects, I become the person I want to be. When I follow my Higher Power's plan for my life, it's easier to take responsibility because I'm not doing it alone. Taking care of my own needs ends the rescue fantasy that used to put me in pain and obsession. Whether living alone or in partnership, this sign of recovery is necessary in order to have a happy, sober life.

I practice self-care and responsibility today.

May 26

OBJECTIVITY

Most of us found that writing down our inventory was very helpful. Looking at what we had done in black and white was a valuable aid to honesty and objectivity. – S.L.A.A. Basic Text, Page 79

My life lacked objectivity. When it came to me and my needs, I could never be open-minded or without bias. I was so insecure. My love addiction made me so needy that I couldn't take a step back and calmly observe myself. This is a necessary tool in recovery. I need to be able to say, "I did this and I need to make amends," without hiding out in the blame game. My strategy before the program was always to make excuses in order to keep whatever behavior I felt was serving me. But in reality it was doing more harm than good. Seeing it in black and white in my inventory made it seem like it could have been someone else doing it. I asked myself, "If I had seen someone else doing this, would I have thought it was right?" A synonym for objectivity is dispassion. I always thought a life without passion wouldn't be worth living. But once I started asking for my character defect of being a drama queen to be removed, I realized how selfish that had made me. I needed to stop trying to get everything for myself and start helping others. When the world doesn't center around me, I can be objective.

Today, I will write a Tenth-Step inventory seeking to be honest and objective.

May 27

THE NEXT RIGHT THING

I found I had to have definite destinations in mind or I was set up for trouble. It was always hard for me to ask for help from other people, but I found it absolutely necessary to let go of my false pride and pick up the phone when I felt things slipping away...I must put energy into my recovery and do whatever is necessary to stay sober. – S.L.A.A. Basic Text, Page 205

How do I know what's right? Pros-and-cons lists help, but to find answers, I pray and meditate. In my disease, I couldn't see the next right thing because I couldn't listen to Higher Power or fellows. I didn't have the humility to think that anyone else's opinion mattered. Often doing the right thing involved pain or inconvenience on my part. I hid from that at all costs. Doing the Steps of S.L.A.A. changed all of that for me. I started believing in a Higher Power. Once I started listening for God's will, I found it much less painful to take the actions that would lead to a much more happy and serene life. Doing the Steps in order with a sponsor revealed the next right action. I don't have to tackle the whole problem at once. I can take one step at a time and just do what's in front of me. Once I came to believe, I was able to turn my will and my life over to a Higher Power and clear out the wreckage of my past. I made amends and continued to work on spiritual progress. I may not always be on the right track but taking these actions helps me to see and do the next right thing.

I pray and meditate, listening to my Higher Power's will.

May 28

ACCEPTANCE

Although we had come a long way in our recovery, we were, however, still unable, by our unaided will, to shape our lives in a consistently positive manner. The reality of this estimation of ourselves was a truth we could now accept, if not gratefully, at least without struggle. This acceptance of truth, and willingness to allow a Power outside ourselves to continue to do what we could not do for ourselves, WAS humility. – S.L.A.A. Basic Text, Page 87

A story in the A.A. Big Book helped me so much with the concept of acceptance, I printed part of it on a sheet of paper and posted it in my apartment as a reminder. "And acceptance is the answer to all my problems today. When I am disturbed, it is because I find some person, place, thing or situation—some fact of my life—unacceptable to me, and I can find no serenity until I accept that person, place, thing, or situation as being exactly the way it is supposed to be at this moment. Nothing, absolutely nothing, happens in God's world by mistake. Until I could accept my alcoholism, I could not stay sober; unless I accept life completely on life's terms, I cannot be happy. I need to concentrate not so much on what needs to be changed in the world as on what needs to be changed in me and in my attitudes."* Refusing to accept something means I am trying to control things and that usually brings obsession and anxiety when things don't go my way. In every situation I ask myself, "Would you rather be right or happy?" I choose happy and doing things Higher Power's way instead of my own.

*Page 417 A.A. Big Book

I accept my disease and where I am in life today.

May 29

DESIRE

I would engage her in recitations of: "I love you"; "I need you"..."I can't live without you." An atmosphere of mutual hypnosis prevailed. Each of us seemed a candle into which the other's moth would fly. The world and time were insignificant in the face of our mesmerizing merger. – S.L.A.A. Basic Text, Page 11

Desire can be like kryptonite for a sex and love addict. Defenses are down and we're drawn into the tractor beam. But with the Steps it doesn't have to be that way. Steps Four and Five can show us where we are being delusional. Steps Six and Seven can help us take the ego out of desire so that even though we feel it, we don't have to act on it. When we have an attitude of being of service to others, it's harder to let the addict run wild when we know it will hurt someone we love. With the help of S.L.A.A. tools and fellows, we begin to learn the difference between desire and deserve. Ego tells us we deserve everything we desire, regardless of the consequences. But the true sense of service (when we find out what others need instead of trying to control) reveals that sometimes what we desire isn't the best thing to pursue. With the help of Higher Power and the program, we are able to decide rather than hypnotically chase a delusion.

I check in with my Higher Power and S.L.A.A. fellows before I act today.

May 30

COMPULSIVITY

Especially for us as sex and love addicts, the need for love had seemed insatiable...it was as though we were trying to quench a terrible thirst by drinking salt water. The more we drank, the more dehydrated we got, until our very lives were threatened...We found that this thirst...was a spiritual thirst, and the water was the God of our understanding. – S.L.A.A. Basic Text, Page 101

Before S.L.A.A., my pursuit of sex and love was irrational or contrary to my will. I pursued unavailable people. I never turned down the opportunity for love or sex even if I disliked a person's character or beliefs. It was a strong, irresistible impulse to have sex or a relationship. I needed to show the world that I wasn't broken and that meant having a healthy relationship. But the compulsive need for sex got in the way. I trashed my career and destroyed people's lives over that impulse. I tried everything to control my compulsivity: therapy, other addictions, moving, getting a bodyguard, acupuncture and even hospitalization. When I finally walked into the rooms of S.L.A.A, I thought my impulses would be immediately removed like they were for my other addictions. But for years I worked the Steps and went to meetings and still acted out whenever that impulse hit (which was quite often). It wasn't until I had a spiritual experience that I was able to stop. I didn't have to wander in the desert alone with my thirst anymore. S.L.A.A. brought me home.

I pray, meditate and make an outreach call if an impulse to act out occurs.

May 31

PEOPLE-PLEASING

Over time, without realizing it, I sacrificed my own individuality in my efforts to maintain this sense of emotional security derived from dependence on others. I thought that in order to be loved I must do whatever others would like me to do. – S.L.A.A. Basic Text, Page 196

People-pleasing was my character defect of choice in my acting-out days. If I was with a group of honor roll students, I bragged about my grades and spoke with a large vocabulary. If I was with my druggy friends, I drank people under the table. I never developed my own likes and needs because in order to feel safe everyone had to like me. If disliking anything I did meant they were going to leave, I had to change everything about myself to make them stay. That way of life doesn't leave a lot of room for getting to know myself. Even with the tools of S.L.A.A., it was difficult to find my voice in the first few years of sobriety. I was afraid to say, "No." I had to bring five different personalities into one that I could live with and like. I had to write many fear inventories about abandonment and emotional pain. What really helped me was when my sponsor said, "Look at who you're trying to impress. They're all crazy too." As long as I realize that I can meet my own needs, I don't have to compromise and feel bad about myself.

I practice self-love and acceptance while finding healthy ways to get my needs met.

June 1

INSANITY

We reaffirmed our undying intensity, both sexual and emotional—another brick of "quick-fix" on the wall of growing insanity. – S.L.A.A. Basic Text, Page 13

I heard once that true insanity is not doing the same thing over and over expecting different results, but doing the same thing knowing you'll get the same results and doing it anyway. In this quote, Rich kept going back to his affair even though he wanted a better relationship with his wife and the affair was destroying him emotionally. That's the way it was with all of my compulsive behaviors. I needed to feel the high of that quick fix even if it would destroy my life. I used to believe that the undying intensity was the point of life. It's the goal for everyone, right? But the reality is that the level of intensity I needed to feel okay burns out and takes me along with it. Each episode in my acting out is a brick in that wall of insanity which is my disease. That's why they say in meetings that God needs to demolish the house in order to build a better foundation. I need to fire my bricklayer (me) and let Higher Power build a better wall. Those bricks will be filled with self-esteem instead of insanity.

I search for and follow my Higher Power's guidance to help keep me sane.

June 2

EMOTIONAL SOBRIETY

Sexual and emotional sobriety are self-defined in our fellowship...What I really needed was to just take it easy and experience my feelings as they really were, face them square on and deal with them on a day-to-day basis, avoiding behavior that I'd come to identify as troublesome. – S.L.A.A. Basic Text Page 265

Being emotionally sober means we are no longer acting out in our fears. We aren't emotionally intoxicated nor buffeted by the storms of our emotions. In the past, we were swept away by our emotions, trapped in that vicious cycle of automatic behaviors and feelings that reinforced how badly we felt about ourselves. It's difficult to experience feelings as they really are in that warlike state. In sobriety, we identify and face the behaviors and negative thoughts that leave us emotionally wrung out. We surrender our past pain and trauma as well as the lies we tell ourselves. We let others affirm and love us. We are worthwhile people. We no longer need to escape into addiction because of overwhelming, unpleasant feelings. As we emerge from our emotional haze, we are more present and more willing to act from our heart. Now, when we begin to feel unhealthy emotions, we ask our Higher Power and others for help. We begin to feel a profound connection to God and to life. We have stopped struggling and are flowing with life. As we become emotionally sober, we are more open, honest, respectful, grateful and loving. We embrace our emotions, as they make us feel alive and connected to life.

I am emotionally present and learning to act from my heart. My emotions flow with the current of life.

June 3

ROLE MODELS

I will pass up the litany of my deprived childhood; I had screwed-up parents who offered neither role models nor affection so necessary to healthy growth. My desperate need for love/approval and my denial of this need, led to thirty years of frenetic behavior in a number of areas. – S.L.A.A. Basic Text, Page 216

All the adults in my childhood were flirty party people who made inappropriate sexual comments. I had too much information on who was cheating on who from my mother (even if it was only from the soap operas—I thought they were real). All the TV shows and movies were about sexy people getting what they wanted. The cute, good girl never got ahead. Guys had to be tough to survive. I wanted to grow up to be successful. But when I tried to fit that mold, it never quite fit. I was a nerd at heart acting like a femme fatale. When I threw away that idea of what a successful person is supposed to look like, I got to know the real me. S.L.A.A. gave me sober role models, like my sponsor, who I really wanted to emulate. That gave me peace and serenity that I had never known before. I threw away the old empty role models and found a way of life that works.

I look to sober members of S.L.A.A. as my role models today.

June 4

AROUSING SUSPICION

For those of you who are still suffering the pains of suspicion or the agony of discovery, we reach out in love and compassion. We are still only a few, a testimony to the power of this addiction to destroy relationships with those who do not share the illness.* – *S.L.A.A. Basic Text, Page 65

Every addiction carries a recognizable set of behaviors and traits that can clue others in to when we are slipping. We may not even be aware of it ourselves. Withdrawing from activities that we normally find enjoyable, being open and honest with our emotions, spending inordinate amounts of time on the computer or our cell phones: these can all be warning signs that the addiction is taking hold of us. As addicts, we have all been the source of suspicion at times. The questions of a loved one can bring back the fear we experienced when fully immersed in the grasp of our addictions. It also brings back fear for our partners, who have been there for the hard times and have had to tread the difficult path of rebuilding trust. It takes humility and honesty with ourselves to listen to what our loved ones have to say with an open mind. A spouse or a parent may be able to see things that we are incapable of seeing. When caught up in the hold of addiction, our perceptions become distorted. What was once the troubling paranoia of getting caught, can now be the way out of the addictive spiral.

Higher Power, help me be open, honest and direct with my loved ones. Help me see that they can be an honest reflection of myself.

June 5

THE SIXTH STEP

Were entirely ready to have God remove all these defects of character. – S.L.A.A. Core Documents, "The Twelve Steps of S.L.A.A."

How do we become entirely ready? Why does this Step use that word? Removing all defects of character? Aren't we supposed to work towards progress not perfection? It seems like this Step would create a lot of fear for addicts. But if we have thoroughly worked Steps One through Five, this Step isn't quite so fearful. God, our sponsor and fellows support us. Entirely ready doesn't mean all our defects disappear on the spot—it means we have enough humility to be ready to ask in the Seventh Step. We have seen our disease in Step One and know that we don't want to be that way anymore. We have seen clearly what the defects are in Steps Four and Five. Steps Two and Three prepared us by giving us hope that there is a Higher Power listening to our prayers who can help heal our defects. God doesn't remove them without a lot of help from us, though. Are we ready to keep asking? We may get fearful of doing the work of honestly looking at ourselves, of praying and of being humble, but others who have done it before us assure us that it's the best and only way to recover. Serenity is the goal and we can get there if we try and ask Higher Power and fellows for help.

Higher Power, I pray for the willingness to let go of my character defects.

June 6

CELIBACY AND ABSTINENCE

My bottom line also includes celibacy with no masturbation for a period during which I surrender to the S.L.A.A. program and the Twelve Steps and learn to apply them to my life. The energy transformation that is occurring is incredible. – S.L.A.A. Basic Text, Page 260

In my first few months of withdrawal in S.L.A.A., I went to an S.L.A.A. workshop at a nun's retirement home. I dreamt of escaping the world, taking a vow of celibacy and joining them. I realized that was just my anorexia wanting to escape from the difficulty of finding and navigating intimacy. Then I used this as a way to rationalize my desire to continue having sex even in withdrawal. But my sponsor suggested I try abstinence at least until I finished my Fifth Step. In order to gain clarity on my disease, I found I needed to be celibate for a period of time. The program wasn't just about doing the Steps and going to meetings. I needed to take back the energy I was squandering on sexual pursuits and focus it on Higher Power and creative endeavors. I needed to find out who I was without all the numbing-out behaviors. Because I was able to stay celibate during my withdrawal, I realized that sex isn't the most important thing in life and it's no longer my only goal. I have a newfound self-respect and love of life. Celibacy and abstinence can be a rich and powerful experience of developing intimacy with myself and my Higher Power.

I practice healthy sexuality including abstinence when necessary.

June 7

COMPROMISE

We were left face to face with each other, trying to respect the other's needs and thereby come up with a compromise that would make us both feel like winners instead of losers...If we try to keep the surface of the relationship smooth, we begin to compromise our own feelings. – S.L.A.A. Basic Text, Page 61

Compromise can be healthy or unhealthy. It's difficult for a sex and love addict to find the balance and decide what is a healthy compromise and what to avoid. We can't compromise our values and stay sober. When we give up our values to make a person stay or to avoid conflict we give away our dignity. Even small amounts of dignity depleted over time leave me a shell of a human being who can't even recognize my own feelings anymore. But if I determine that it's needed and compromise is pursued, I have to first determine if it's trustworthy. Will it help the relationship without giving away too much of myself? There is no relationship if my sense of self-worth is so depleted that all I can do is say "yes" to everything, even if it will harm me. My feelings matter as much as the other person's. Negotiations can seem to take forever and look like a waste of time. But with practice and learning to recognize healthy compromise, this skill has great value in the world and can make my life easier. There can be many pitfalls to compromise, but when done soberly, there are many rewards.

I pause and weigh the pros and cons of making any compromise today.

June 8

COMPARISON

At the height of our obsessing we may...compare ourselves with those who appear to "have it all". – from the "Romantic Obsession" pamphlet

My sponsor used to say that I shouldn't compare my insides to someone else's outsides. Every one of us has more going on internally than anyone could imagine by looking at us. We fantasize that every person is exactly who we assume they are by observing their physical appearance and social behavior. On more than one occasion, I was told by a coworker that I always seem so calm, that I don't let anything bother me. I responded once, laughingly, "It's all a façade." If the image I project to the world does not match my insides, then maybe the same is true of everyone else I meet. The vulnerable honesty displayed in Twelve Step meetings gives me a chance to look past appearances and listen to the experience of someone else. It allows me to sympathize with another's situation. If I can do this, I can develop compassion for all human beings, and forgive the flaws in myself and others.

I look for the things that I have in common with people today.

June 9

SEDUCTION

We felt safe in knowing that physically, emotionally, and mentally we could continue to attract new people to us, or further bind those already in our web...Through sex, charm, emotional appeal, or persuasive intellect, we had used other people as "drugs," to avoid facing our own personal inadequacy. – S.L.A.A. Basic Text, Page 74

Many people in our society think that having the power of seduction is something to be admired. It's used in advertising and actors use it to become instant celebrities. Some ability to seduce may be helpful for some. But for sex and love addicts, it can be the currency that feeds our addiction. Using any means necessary in order to have a constant supply of sexual companionship usually means we need to make empty promises. Seducing the same person again and again gets more difficult over time when they realize we're not capable of commitment or intimacy. Many addicts love that type of a challenge, but most go for the quick fix and find another to convince. Seduction is short-term validation. Once the goal of sex is reached, the true person comes out because no one can keep up a façade their entire lifetime. The truth always comes out. S.L.A.A. helped me stop playing games and present the real me in relationships. People were free to choose whether to accept me or reject me on who I was. I didn't have to run around wasting money, time and energy on crazy-making schemes anymore. The freedom to be me and find true love is worth more to me than anything else.

I treat others with respect today, staying true to myself and my sobriety.

June 10

RESENTMENT

Many of us...had learned to survive by cultivating hatred, anger, and resentment as motivating forces, seeking to insulate ourselves from hurt and fear. Now we discovered that we had crippled ourselves by using this monotonous strategy of distrust and isolation in all relationships, whether they were inherently hostile or not. – S.L.A.A. Basic Text, Page 86

When we feel pain, many of us look outside ourselves for the source. Who or what is to blame? Playing the role of the victim is much more attractive than accepting our own mistakes. Resentment provides the justification for any number of unhealthy acts. "I reported Mr. Long to my supervisor. That's why he's trying to get me into trouble now." Never mind that Mr. Long has a legitimate complaint against me for using company property without permission. "Robert has been spreading rumors about me. That's why my boss fired me." That may leave out the part where I was wasting company time on the computer and reporting late for work. When we examine our resentments, it becomes clear that we are not always free of blame. If we're still brooding over the perceived harm done to us, we'll be unlikely to see our own part in the situation. There is a saying that resentment is like swallowing poison and expecting someone else to die. All of that hatred builds up inside us, making us suspicious, spiteful and generally unpleasant to be around. If we can see our own faults, we can begin to let go of resentment and accept faults in others.

Higher Power, give me the willingness and compassion to help those who have offended me.

June 11

THE FIRST CHARACTERISTIC

Having few healthy boundaries, we become sexually involved with and/or emotionally attached to people without knowing them. – S.L.A.A. Core Documents, "Characteristics of Sex and Love Addiction"

Many of us don't know what healthy boundaries are before we come into S.L.A.A. I read many self-help books that tried to explain what they were but my love addiction always got in the way. Magical thinking, co-dependency and the need for acceptance were all more important than those rude old boundaries. How could something so seemingly harsh be healthy? Rationalizing away any need for rules made it easier for my addict to become sexually involved with people quickly and without knowing them. Sex addiction seemed easier to handle than love addiction, because it was like getting drunk and having a hangover the next morning. After every one-night stand, I would promise myself never to do that again. But inevitably, I would meet some fantasy and be off and running. Becoming emotionally attached to people without knowing them almost killed me. I stayed with abusive partners long after I discovered that they weren't the knight in shining armor that I had imagined them to be. S.L.A.A. gave me tools to stop the magical thinking and to start building healthy boundaries instead of anorexic ones. I had a dating plan to ensure that I would slowly, and hopefully patiently, get to know someone. I had outreach calls, sharing and sponsor-sponsee interaction to tell me if I was wandering into delusion.

I lean on my Higher Power and fellows to maintain healthy boundaries and sobriety today.

June 12

LIVING IN THE PRESENT

Be here now. This theme is at the core of any recipe for happy living. It involves, however fleetingly, the experience of a total trust, a total faith, that basically everything is just as it should be at this moment, including my desire for it to be different in the next moment. – S.L.A.A. Basic Text, Page 265

One of the tenets of recovery is living in the present, sometimes one minute at a time. We deal with our addiction-riddled pasts through working the Twelve Steps. The future often remains a constantly fluctuating and unpredictable concept. It is something over which we have no control. Events much larger than even our anxiety-ridden predictions can and do occur. In S.L.A.A., I am told that if I live the principles of the S.L.A.A. Program in the here and now, my future will be significantly better than my addiction-riddled past. Not only that, when difficulties do arise in my future, I will be much better equipped to handle them from a psychological and a spiritual perspective. As I encountered the constant fear in which I lived during my withdrawal period in S.L.A.A., I was told that I was "living in the wreckage of the future." This struck me to my core. From that moment on, I became willing to surrender my future to my Higher Power, knowing that my only task is to work my S.L.A.A. Program in the here and now. My future will emerge out of my commitment to recovery today. I can let go.

I release all thoughts of the future to my Higher Power. I work my S.L.A.A. Program to the best of my ability today, trusting that the future will take care of itself.

June 13

COMPLACENCY

Most S.L.A.A.'s who have been through [a slip] ...say they forgot that they were sex and love addicts and became overconfident. Or they became too preoccupied with business or social affairs to remember the importance of abstaining from acting out...they withdrew from taking advantage of the help available to them. – from the "Questions Beginners Ask" pamphlet

Wouldn't it be nice if we could just work the Steps once and be done with them? How long could we stay sober if we only did the bare minimum? Early on in recovery, I heard two things that stuck with me. The first was, "Be vigilant." The other was, "Everything you put before your recovery, you will lose." Sometimes I forget how cunning my addiction can be. Maintaining vigilance can be tiresome. Other interests and responsibilities can seem more important, because I think I've got my addiction under control. But when I start thinking that I'm the one in control, that's when I've lost perspective. It's only with the help of my Higher Power that I stay sober. If I stop doing my part, addiction's going to come back and hit me with a vengeance. I can't be 100% vigilant all the time. Sometimes it will take all my strength just to get to a meeting and call my sponsor. What's important is that I never lose sight of the danger of my addiction, and never talk myself into believing that, "I've got this." My recovery must come first if I want to stay sober.

Higher Power, help me to remain vigilant in my recovery and give me strength when I am tempted to slip into complacency.

June 14

STILL SINGLE

In the process of being alone and going through withdrawal, I had discovered, for the first time in my life, a sense of my own dignity. It was mine, divinely given to me as I was. I no longer needed to hold another person responsible for giving it, or failing to give it, to me. – S.L.A.A. Basic Text, Page 38

One of my sponsees has struggled for years with the fact that she is still single. She always believed that "success" in S.L.A.A. hinged on finding a healthy relationship. I can't count how many times I told her that it was about our relationship with ourselves and Higher Power. It didn't necessarily have to be about finding a partner. There's a whole section in the Basic Text devoted to living alone if one so chooses. She never chose that. It even sent her running from S.L.A.A. into a turbulent relationship. After she lost her career, home and a lot of money, she came back to meetings and went through the Steps again. Today her career is flourishing and I see a light in her eyes that I never saw before. She doesn't care about looking for a partner anymore. She's leaving it in God's hands. She's going through the painful work of changing herself for herself. Watching her process has proven to me that this program really works and that anyone can find dignity of self no matter what their situation.

I patiently accept my relationship status today, focusing on my goals and seeking my Higher Power's will.

June 15

RIGOROUS HONESTY

As I came to explore a new world of relationships in which I had some sense of dignity and the capacity for caring and commitment, I learned that old addictive patterns could slip back into my life in subtle ways. I learned the...absolute necessity of rigorous current honesty. – S.L.A.A. Basic Text, Page 167

In my addiction, I lied for survival. If telling the truth meant I was going to get hit by my abusive partner, then why would I be honest? In toxic relationships, honesty can be deadly. But I carried this entitlement into every other area. I lied when it was convenient or just because I could (ego). Lies are riddled with character defects. Telling untruths is really sloth and insecurity in disguise. I'm afraid I won't get what I need or keep what I have so I need to be dishonest. I find I can't lie and have my character defects removed at the same time. I can't have a sense of dignity when I'm afraid of getting caught in a lie. In relationships, there is no capacity for caring and commitment because my dishonesty hides my true self. If I'm dishonest with my sponsor and fellows, they can't help me. I walk around an imitation of myself and that's a breeding ground for a slip. When I lied in sobriety, my sponsor made me contact the person to reveal my lie—that painfully embarrassing task made me less likely to lie the next time.

I ask my Higher Power for the strength today to honestly face painful situations.

June 16

FREEDOM

God's grace would give us freedom from the burden of our old self. – S.L.A.A. Basic Text, Page 87

Sobriety never sounded like freedom in my acting-out days. It sounded like bondage to a God I didn't understand. When my sponsor told me to throw away my old God and get one that I could understand, I was able to let God in. But I didn't want to become a slave to Twelve Step programs. That was my excuse for not surrendering. A fellow pointed out that I was definitely a slave to my addictions. I had to have my phone with me at all times, I couldn't stop myself from going places and doing things that made me miserable, etc. The freedom from fear that I get by praying or going to a meeting is worth everything to me today. My old self was a rock around my neck, causing me to drown. It was as if I were walking around in a dark cave of fear and resentment my whole life and I found sobriety and stepped into the sunlight. It's not that I never go back to the cave, but God helps me out of it every time.

I answer the call of my true self today and thrive in my recovery.

June 17

EXPECTATIONS

In truth, the option to "tailor ourselves" to meet the expectations of another was untenable. We could not now, nor could we ever, sustain a relationship in which we had to destroy an essential part of ourselves in order to render ourselves more desirable to the eyes of another. – S.L.A.A. Basic Text, Page 154

When I "fall in love," all too often I expect my beloved to meet all my expectations, respond favorably to my demands and behave as I imagine a lover should. I cast my lover in my own addictive movie, then feel disappointed when they don't follow the script that's in my head. A friend in another Twelve Step program once said, "Expectations are premeditated resentments." If I project onto someone else what I think they should be or if I'm changing myself only to meet others' expectations, I am setting myself up to be let down. People have their own history, needs, feelings and agenda. They behave in ways I can't predict and may not like. To love someone is to accept uncertainty, because I can't control another person's reactions or behavior in response to my desires. Tailoring myself to meet the expectations of others means being untrue to who I am. The real me is hiding underneath that façade, and will always show itself in the end. By having realistic expectations, I not only experience less disappointment, but my expectations are often exceeded.

I release the need to change myself to meet someone else's expectations, acknowledging that same freedom in others.

June 18

THE FOURTH TRADITION

Each group should be autonomous except in matters affecting other groups or S.L.A.A. as a whole. – S.L.A.A. Core Documents, "The Twelve Traditions"

I've been such a rebel my whole life that when I first heard this Tradition, I laughed. A **bunch of ego-driven addicts allowed to do whatever they want**, I thought. **There will be chaos!** But I went to different S.L.A.A. meetings every day in the first few years of recovery and didn't see too many problems. Every meeting voted to follow a pretty standard format that they got from the F.W.S. office or other meetings. They may have had non-conference-approved literature that they wanted to read but someone usually brought it up at a business meeting. If it was too far away from the Twelve Steps, it was voted out. This Tradition tells me to be mindful that I affect others. I can't just make unilateral decisions in my meetings that would affect another meeting, any other service body or even people in the meeting itself. I've learned the quality of considering other people's needs when making my decisions. I don't come from a place of love addiction, trying to entrap people, or trying to defend myself in case they get mad. It's not codependent consideration. It's recognizing that people are autonomous and they have their needs that are separate from my own. I can do what I want as long as it doesn't affect other groups or S.L.A.A. as a whole.

I am mindful of how my behavior affects others and I place principles before personalities.

June 19

IMPLICIT MEMORY

I saw, for the first time, how automatically and unconsciously I was continuously creating a whole gallery of possibilities for loaded sexual and emotional events...Although I now knew that the payoffs from such intrigues were poisonous to me, I still found myself initiating them as second nature.* – *S.L.A.A. Basic Text, Page 28

I am powerless over my addiction, so of course I was acting off of implicit memory. I spent so many years acting out that sexual activities became like tying my shoes; I did it without thinking about it. In early recovery, I would start to drive down a street near my qualifier's house and suddenly wake up and ask myself, "What am I doing?" I didn't mean to put myself in danger. It was as if my car had a mind of its own. My foot hit the gas when it should have hit the brakes. Even at fellowship in S.L.A.A. where I was trying to gain sobriety, I would catch myself throwing out sexual hooks in conversation. I didn't want to continue to do things the way I did when acting out. The work to change myself was difficult. I had to get a whole new set of coping strategies. I had to act as if I were a person of dignity until I learned to respect myself and stop unconsciously going down the path of addiction. Meditation and prayer helped retrain my brain. Bringing my unconscious habits out in the open in my Fourth and Fifth Steps also helped. Fellows sometimes called me on my behavior and though painful and often humiliating, this was useful in helping me change and become conscious.

Today, I am a person of dignity. I make healthy choices.

June 20

THY WILL, NOT MINE, BE DONE

We saw that [the steps] were structured on the principle of Step 3. Our cup of diseased behavior would be emptied out, and we would cleanse it as best we could, making it ready for God's Grace to refill it, in accordance with God's plan, not our own. – S.L.A.A. Basic Text, Page 77

When I entered the rooms of Twelve Step programs, I was an atheist. Sometimes I thought if God did exist, he was playing tricks on me. If that's what God was like, why would I do God's will over my own? I spent years of slipping in S.L.A.A. on that excuse. The simple fact was that I wanted my way. I didn't want God to take over if he was going to give me hard work to do. But sobriety is hard work. When I finally did turn my will over, God worked miracles. Instead of the relationship that I thought was essential to my survival (the one that was, in fact, killing me) I was given a healthy relationship with someone who helps me grow. I never would have received this gift if I hadn't had those years of emptying out my cup of diseased behavior using the S.L.A.A. tools. The cleansing happened when I did Steps Four-Ten. I was ready for God to refill my cup when I finished all my Steps and set a sober dating plan with my sponsor and followed it. Today, I accept my life with gratitude and serenity.

Today, I let go of control so my Higher Power's plan can unfold.

June 21

MANIPULATION

Whether we were victims or victimizers...we had used the disturbed relationships about us for our own purposes, for obtaining the addictive payoff. Regardless of what others had done or failed to do, our own part in these relationships was riddled with dishonesty and manipulation of others, with willfulness and pride. – S.L.A.A. Basic Text, Page 90

It would be nice if we could say that we never manipulated anyone in our addiction. But if we are truly honest, we know that our actions were not so innocent. Perhaps we didn't lie, but we also didn't tell the full truth. Maybe we were aware that our partner was dependent on us, and we took advantage of the situation. To take an honest look at our character defects can be very difficult. We don't want to face the fact that we have manipulated our loved ones to get what we want. Recovery requires rigorous honesty, and we may not always like the truths we discover about ourselves. As we get sober, it is important to acknowledge when we have manipulated others, and when appropriate, make amends. It is better to recognize that we have this defect than to tell ourselves that we are incapable of such behavior. Once we recognize this, we can own it and let it go.

I am rigorously honest, willing to admit my faults and make amends.

June 22

FEELINGS

The difference between my feelings and what seemed to be acceptable was so great that I learned to deny my feelings, and look for excuses so that I would not have to label myself a "bad person."...I became so accustomed to denying my feelings and blaming my behavior on others that I truly did not know what anger or fear felt like, and I felt helpless to change my life. – S.L.A.A. Basic Text, Page 164

Today, I try to be responsible for my own feelings. I grew up in a family where children were to be seen but not heard. I gravitated toward people who were emotionally shut down or violently dramatic. There was no middle ground. Feelings were too painful. Even joy was overwhelming. They needed to be numbed with addiction. A fellow described the process of denying feelings as if he were driving around in a station wagon his whole life and just throwing junk in the back until there was barely any room for him. When he came to the program and started working the Steps it was as if he slammed on the brakes and everything came flying towards the windshield. All of my feelings needed to come out in sobriety and be dealt with. No more burying things. I dealt with past hurts and fears in Steps Four-Nine and continued to confront emotions with a daily Tenth Step. Sponsors and fellows helped me understand and work through confusing feelings. I am much more balanced today than ever before.

Today, I accept and honor my feelings seeking help from my Higher Power to achieve emotional sobriety.

June 23

TIME

If we were ever to be as cups running over with redeemed, non-addictive lives, then some Power greater than ourselves... would have to do the refilling. Such a Power (He, She, It, or They) would do that in Its own time, according to Its scheme of things, not our own. – S.L.A.A. Basic Text, Page 76

I've seen how my Higher Power's schedule doesn't necessarily correspond with my schedule. God knows exactly what I need and how to help me resolve difficulties. I've got about a three-day turnaround with Higher Power right now. I ask for help, and three days later I get the answer. Actually, that's about how long it takes me, right now, to clear up my stuff so I can see or hear Higher Power's answer. I get an answer right away, but I can't see it right away. How cool to know my Higher Power's faster than a computer and only wants the best for me. It may not always look that way to me according to my plan, but in the long run, I usually see it is. I just need to let go and let God and trust. Something that's painful in the short run may help uncover, discover and discard. It's all in God's plan to remold me in recovery.

Today, I let go and let God.

June 24

CHALLENGE

We were still plagued by sometimes prolonged bouts of obsessive thinking or emotional yearning for intrigue and romance for sexual oblivion. These could be set off by accidental encounters with our former addictive lovers, which seemed almost fiendishly psychic in the uncanny way they happened just when we were most vulnerable. – S.L.A.A. Basic Text, Page 78

Challenges come in many forms. Life is a challenge. It can seem particularly difficult for people who are used to numbing out instead of stepping up to meet life's challenges. Job loss, death, illness and even an encounter with the object of our obsession (whether that is a person or not) can send us reeling. In early sobriety, I never felt strong enough to live up to what was required of me. So, I went back to the familiar and broke my bottom lines. I used to say that if I broke a fingernail I would slip. But once I took the drama out of every situation (a character defect that made every challenge bigger than it really was) I was better equipped to handle whatever came my way. Fellows in the program helped me see the reality and supported me until I had the strength to meet the challenge. Reliance on a Higher Power gave me that strength. As long as I don't plunge into negative thinking and insecurity, I can look for ways to change my circumstances.

Higher Power, grant me the ability to accept those challenges that you set before me. Help me to meet this day with enthusiasm and certainty.

June 25

THE TENTH SIGN OF RECOVERY

We become honest in expressing who we are, developing true intimacy in our relationships with ourselves and others.
S.L.A.A. Core Documents, "S.L.A.A. Signs of Recovery"

Becoming honest in expressing who we are is difficult for most sex and love addicts (and all humans). Sex addicts need to lie in order to be able to seduce better. Forget about even finding out who they are—everything in their lives is structured around the hunt for their fix. I was a fake image of myself according to what I thought my prey needed in order to do my sexual bidding. I thought sex was the point of life so why bother finding other interests unless they would make you more interesting to other people? This applied to my life as a love addict as well. I was so concerned with making the object of my affection stay that I lost myself. When I lied to myself and others there was no room for true intimacy to grow. It was a numbers game—all about the quick fix and onto the next prospect. True intimacy requires time, honesty and compromise. I needed the time to get to know myself and work on my character defects in order to have a good relationship with myself, before I could attempt a partnership with anyone else.

I am honest with myself and others today.

June 26

TOUGH LOVE

Each of us, regardless of individual circumstances, was now willing to go to any lengths, a day at a time, to stay unhooked. This decision was unilateral. It did not depend on the cooperation or lack of cooperation of our spouses, lovers, or sex objects. We were willing to be available not to the next lover or new sexual fantasy, but to whatever might happen next within ourselves. – S.L.A.A. Basic Text, Page 73

For sex and love addicts, tough love is not desirable. It is a barrier to getting our needs met. Whether we are setting boundaries or someone else is showing us tough love, the emotions in those situations bring up a lot of fear. It takes courage to say, "No," when otherwise we would let our partner stay weak, dependent and active in their addiction. In my opinion, it's easier to go cold turkey from addictive substances like drugs and alcohol. Showing tough love doesn't hurt its feelings. The drug doesn't complain when you are throwing it away. Most relationships can only survive if there is compromise. Sometimes we can't do that if we want to stay sober. When our partner expresses displeasure, we may fear the loss of the relationship. We need to stay strong and let go of codependency. Higher Power can help if we ask. God and fellows can help us set and keep boundaries regardless of our fears or ego around tough love. Nobody wants to look like a jerk, but sometimes it's necessary for recovery.

Setting boundaries keeps me sober and sane today.

June 27

ACCOMPLISHING GOALS

A lot of what we thought we were, and thought we couldn't live without, was being boiled away. As this became clearer to us, our attitudes changed profoundly. We felt a deep desire to experience God's will in all areas of our lives for its own sake, rather than for some limited, self-defined objective. We were becoming vessels more suited to God's purpose. – S.L.A.A. Basic Text, Page 87

Before sobriety, goals were an inconvenience that got in the way of my sex and love addiction or they were overwhelming, insurmountable obstacles. All of my elaborate dreams of fame and fortune were to serve my sex and love addiction. Self-centered in the extreme, I didn't know how to set realistic goals, let alone accomplish them. Getting sobriety and working the Steps in S.L.A.A. reshaped my personality. Goals began to take form around my perception of Higher Power's will instead of my own. When I felt that God was asking too much of me and a goal was out of reach, I wasn't afraid to ask for help. I shared my difficulties as well as my triumphs. When I shared my difficulties, fellow S.L.A.A. members related and sometimes offered support. When I shared my triumphs, they applauded the effort and it showed newcomers the power of the program. Realizing that I am human and can't do everything all at once or immediately helped immensely. I take things one day at a time and let them unfold as Higher Power intends.

I set realistic goals and work towards them today.

June 28

ACTING "AS IF"

The fact that we needed faith in some Power, since we could not trust ourselves to be consistent in either behavior or motive, left some of us feeling even more shaken. Where would we find even the rudiments of a faith that could carry us through this dissolving and reconstruction of our whole personality?* – *S.L.A.A. Basic Text, Page 75

It used to concern me that agnostics and atheists might have a hard time in a Twelve Step program. The phrase "act as if" seemed like a denial of a person's right to their own beliefs. But when the time came that I needed recovery for myself, I had to suspend my disbelief. Though I was still skeptical about putting my trust in something I didn't understand, I came to believe that a Twelve Step program could restore me to sanity. When I worked the second and third steps, I put "act as if" into action. I started praying, even though I didn't know who or what I was praying to. By practicing the methods of a spiritual faith, my belief in a Higher Power grew with time. I found myself relying on my Higher Power more and more. I put faith before understanding, trusting that if I followed through with the actions, it would make sense as I went along. There is still much work to be done in my spiritual journey, but I know now that if I simply "act as if," my Higher Power will do great work in my life.

By practicing the Twelve Steps, my belief in my Higher Power grows.

June 29

SERVICE

We had sought full partnership with God, and knowledge of God's purpose for us. By seeking to live with honesty and integrity, and to be of service to others, we had discovered that the source of love, which was of God, had begun to flow from within us. We had lived our way into step 12. – S.L.A.A. Basic Text, Page 101

I've always believed myself to be an unreliable person. I learned from a young age that my parents would nurture and support me more if I failed to do anything for myself. Taking on service commitments within S.L.A.A. has taught me that I can contribute positively to a very important cause. Working a service commitment such as secretary, treasurer, literature, intergroup and starting a new meeting, has all taught me that I can do things for myself. Fears about failure and being unreliable have been removed from me as I've seen that I can show up regularly on time on a weekly basis for my service commitment. Recently, I was voted in for a second term of secretary which is a one-year commitment. People attending the meeting have reinforced that I can do what I'm supposed to do, and do it well or well enough. Perhaps most importantly, I can no longer deny that I am capable of being a responsible, competent person. That has shifted my outlook on life. This knowledge about myself is simple and humbling and so important because now I see the door is open for me to take on more and bigger responsibilities that I want to take in order to improve my life.

I find opportunities to be of service today.

June 30

TEMPORARY SOLUTION

The temporary addictive escape from a painfully perceived reality would be sought more and more, until the seeking itself felt like some primitive drive for survival in pursuit of which everything, including self-worth, would be sacrificed. – S.L.A.A. Basic Text, Page viii

We seek out temporary solutions for our pain, because any solution that will provide a lasting effect requires time and hard work. These are not things that the typical addict is willing to give. We want what we want, when we want it, and right now would be preferable. Acting out provides us with a momentary escape, a quick fix, but when we come down from that high, we're still the same person in the same situation we were in when we started. We choose these methods because they are easy and immediate, but they are also empty and fleeting. Whatever joy our acting out may produce, it is quickly replaced by shame and self-loathing. Recovery requires a rewiring of our way of thinking. We must learn to love the longer path to results. When we can appreciate that real growth comes through struggle and rigorous honesty, then we will no longer see the temporary solution as the better option.

My Higher Power helps me to recognize the lasting solutions in my life.

July 1

HEALTHY RELATIONSHIPS

True partnership is not built on fantasy or heroic expectation, nor on the availability of sex, on tap and on demand. – S.L.A.A. Basic Text, Page 42

When I first joined S.L.A.A., I saw marriage as the ultimate goal. It wouldn't be a healthy relationship unless you were married. The guy that I had gone through the dating plan with and was in a relationship with for a number of years told me that he wasn't the marrying kind and never wanted to get married. I thought, how can you have a healthy relationship without marriage? I went to my sponsor with it and she said that you have to decide what your goal is. Do you want marriage at all costs or do you want a healthy relationship? Do you have a healthy relationship? I realized that my goal was to be healthy in a relationship and that was what I had; I had a loving partnership. I let go of the idea that I had to get married. A couple of years later he asked me to marry him. My belief today is that both people grow in a healthy relationship and give each other the space to be themselves and to express their needs and feelings.

One day at a time, I learn to be in a healthy relationship by being open and honest with my partner.

July 2

THE SEVENTH STEP

Humbly asked God to remove our shortcomings. – S.L.A.A Core Documents, "The Twelve Steps of S.L.A.A."

My ego doesn't want to admit that I have shortcomings. That's part of what kept my disease alive and active for so many years Through working the Steps and the S.L.A.A. Program I experienced the gift of sobriety. In sobriety, I learned to love myself enough to admit that I have shortcomings. I don't have to judge or shame myself for them. I can accept them and surrender them to Higher Power to remove. Feeling that God has the power to remove my character defects allows me to look at them realistically instead of getting belligerent if someone points them out. Before I had faith in a Higher Power and the Twelve Step process, I would get angry whenever someone pointed out a mistake. Now I need to stop and ask myself if what they are saying has merit. If it does, instead of beating myself up, I ask God to remove the defect of character and do whatever I can to help. I just need to show up every day for sobriety and surrender my shortcomings to my Higher Power

I love myself enough to let my Higher Power remove my shortcomings.

July 3

SELF-DEFINED SOBRIETY

Those of us who tried to deceive ourselves in the way we defined our sex and love addiction either found ourselves slipping back into the old behavior, or getting into real trouble with our new steps forward." We learned the hard way that there was no such thing as half-surrender. – S.L.A.A. Basic Text, Page 72

Defining bottom lines was difficult for me. Half-surrender led me straight back to the dishonesty that had ruined my first marriage. My bottom lines such as "no contact with a qualifier" and "no sex outside of a committed relationship" were clear and cast a wide umbrella over a range of behaviors that I knew led me to act out. But this didn't address accessory behaviors such as looking at photos, letters or emails, or listening to songs that reminded me of qualifiers. Sobriety definitions are self-correcting if we are working a program. If I give myself too much freedom and independent choice, I find myself engaged once again in the behaviors that got me into the rooms in the first place. If I draw the lines too harshly, the program becomes an unsustainable system of "no," a breeding ground for joyless hanging on. My commitment is to get to the truth about myself. I seek to define my sobriety as accurately as I possibly can and live faithfully to it. As more is revealed, with the help of my sponsor, I adjust. Over time, as the plan approximates the truth more and more, I receive safety from a fall and experience the blossoming of my true self.

I experience freedom and joy maintaining my self-defined bottom lines.

July 4

CARRYING THE MESSAGE

[The] "carrying the message" principle of the Twelfth Step of recovery insures that lonely sex and love addicts, desperate for recovery...will have the opportunity to find that special friendship and fellowship with others which is so vital—so life-giving – S.L.A.A. Basic Text, Page viii

I always thought carrying the message meant doing the lead share in a meeting. But it's based on the beginnings of A.A. when the founders went to the hospital or friends of friends and talked one on one to the alcoholic. I'm carrying the message when I sit quietly in my home group each week and do my treasurer commitment. When I live my recovery, and stay sober, people can see that the program works. Sharing experience, strength and hope comes in many forms: Talking with sponsees, showing the people close to us how we have changed, being quiet when another member is sharing, being kind, having the strength to get through hard times, etc. There are many ways to help the newcomer. I can't count how many times life threw me a curveball and I met with a sponsee or went to a meeting anyway and was so grateful for the strength I pulled from those interactions. Contact with another S.L.A.A. member and the reminders of our addiction that carrying the message brings, have taken me out of my depression countless times.

Today, I live in my recovery and carry the S.L.A.A. message

July 5

SERENITY PRAYER

The Serenity Prayer took on great significance as we asked over and over again for the serenity to accept those people and events which we could not change, and for the courage to change what we could—with Grace and luck, ourselves. – S.L.A.A. Basic Text, Page 91

Before recovery, there is chaos. We may face pressure from family, friends, employers or significant others. We may fear we can never pay off our debt. Problems pile up and they seem impossible to overcome. Many of us come to S.L.A.A. when we have hit the absolute rock bottom. Every other method has failed. We have been unable to bring order to the chaos through our own efforts alone. The familiar and comforting words of the Serenity Prayer give us the peace we need to accept our disease and begin to heal one day at a time. The Serenity Prayer helps us to sort out which things we can control and which things we cannot. It is a request for greater discernment. We say the prayer and we work the Steps. We work with a sponsor and we do service work within our groups. One day, someone asks us to be their sponsor. We agree, listen to their problems and wonder how anyone could possibly be helped by anything we have to say. Then we hear some words escape our mouths without having any idea where they came from. That is the moment we know that our Higher Power has granted us wisdom.

I say the Serenity Prayer often because it empowers me to change the things I can.

July 6

SOCIAL ANOREXIA

Some of us feel overwhelmed in social settings. Others of us get high by socializing with a great many people in order to keep ourselves from intimacy with any one person. – from the "Anorexia: Sexual, Social, Emotional" pamphlet

Before S.L.A.A. I thought my ability to be outgoing was an asset. I was unaware that it was also a distinct facet of my disease. The concept of getting "high" or getting a "hit" off of socializing shocked me. At first I thought it was absurd. I eventually learned that the "high" I got from socializing came from the attention of others that I longed for to fill the emptiness I felt inside. Intimacy with any one person was way too scary. I even had three sponsors so I didn't have to tell everything to one person. I could compartmentalize. With the principles of the program I was able to let sobriety, the Steps and my Higher Power heal and fill this emptiness so that I was able to experience true intimacy with others. But even then, I would go to S.L.A.A. parties and the intimacy would wear me out. I would get a headache very early in the night and have to go home. Today, I check my level of self-care. Am I truly tired or does my anorexia want me to isolate? It's much easier to be around people when I let go of my character defects of fear and perfectionism and let Higher Power take care of my social anorexia.

Higher Power help me to experience true love and intimacy today.

July 7

SAYING "NO"

I now have increasing strength to say "no" to situations that I know are inappropriate and will lead to behavior I know from experience to be ultimately self-defeating, and to say "yes" to various other invitations from the circumstances of my life that I feel will be self-sustaining and self-freeing. – S.L.A.A. Basic Text, Page 266

Saying "no" was never cool in the days of my addiction. I had to be able to do everything in order to impress people. I needed so desperately for people to like me and I didn't believe in Higher Power, so I couldn't give the results of saying "no" to God. Never knowing or caring about what was good for me didn't help much either. Add to that the fear that if I said "no" I would get physically hurt or lose something valuable, and it was almost impossible. I went through life without boundaries. Then S.L.A.A. taught me that I needed to have no contact with certain people in my life who were harmful. I needed to stop saying "yes" to inappropriate behavior from myself and others. I needed to say "yes" to self-esteem-building actions. In the beginning, I needed help from my fellows to tell the difference between the two. But eventually I learned to recognize what actions were self-sustaining and self-freeing as opposed to being motivated by fear or a need for attention and love. I'm a different person, living in a different world today because of these S.L.A.A. life lessons.

I say "no" when appropriate today and leave the results to my Higher Power.

July 8

MEMORIES

In this phase of recovery we found that much of the emotional energy which had been spent on our addiction was now surfacing as feelings and memories that were charged with meaning. More and more of our past pattern of sex and love addiction was being revealed or becoming clearer to us.
– S.L.A.A. Basic Text, Page 78

I was sharing a nice night with my partner recently and a classic song came on the radio. It reminded me of my past relationship. I wanted to run into the next room and watch TV to hide. But I remembered how difficult that relationship was and what an addict I was in it and I saw how beautiful my relationship is now. Memories can either send me into longing for the past and a "do-over" or make me realize my character defects and mistakes. Before sobriety, I chose longing even if it was a fantasy. I was addicted to that type of emotional pain. Now that I have practiced self-care and can recognize self-destructive behavior, I can either pull myself out of longing with reality or ask sober fellows or Higher Power to help. When memories pop up from out of nowhere, it can be difficult to see reality. That's why I need to practice staying in reality every day. The Fourth and Fifth Steps gave me the tools to do that and the Tenth and Eleventh Steps keep me practicing it.

I keep my addictive memories in check by living in reality.

July 9

DISTRACTIONS

The original quest for distraction from life's tensions and responsibilities, for relief from past guilt and present frustration, now led us into oblivion. – S.L.A.A. Basic Text, Page 69

Distraction is my drug of choice. My favorite thing to do at a party was to get so drunk that I could barely lift my head and I could just watch the people around me like they were in a live movie. I can't just sit and watch TV without a video game in my hand. It numbs me out from the realization that I should be doing something else like cleaning the house or paying bills. In my active sex and love addiction, past guilt and present frustration were so dramatic that I felt entitled to the relief of sexual oblivion. It was much better than the alternative. But that oblivion was sand through my fingers. The emotional hangover left me depressed and craving more like a drug addict coming down from a high. Eventually it made me suicidal. I needed the tools of S.L.A.A. to help me find my purpose in life. Today, I feel useful working with sponsees and being of service to my meetings. I still want to bathe in distractions every day, but I catch myself and take contrary action. Doing service work that I love lifts me up.

I find serenity when I am of service to others.

July 10

CONTROL

To continue to live out our addictive patterns, or to be controlled by them, brought us in touch with the terror of irrevocably losing sanity…We now began to confront the second aspect of powerlessness: the paradox that surrender to the impossibility of control is the beginning of recovery. – S.L.A.A. Basic Text, Page 70

I knew I had difficulty abstaining from sexual acting out long before I knew the phrase "acting out." At the age of ten, I recognized how my pursuit of a sexual high consumed my time and made me oblivious to all other concerns. I began my first of many self-imposed moratoriums on acting out, all of which ended with me finally telling myself, "It's okay to do it again. I deserve this." Other times, I created rules for acting out that I felt would limit the behavior so that I wouldn't end up engaging in illegal activity. I restricted myself to specific types of pornography, but I kept modifying my rules until I returned to my original behavior, dangerously close to taking the step that could have labeled me a sex offender for life. These methods of self-control never work because I have no control over my addiction to begin with. The paradox of surrendering to attain victory makes sense for me, because when I try to control my acting-out behavior, I inevitably lose control again. When I surrender, I am no longer under the impression that I can act out without falling under the addiction's power.

I admit my powerlessness and turn myself over to the will and care of my Higher Power.

July 11

ASSUMPTION

Questioning one's attitudes and behavior concerning sexuality and emotional dependency is tantamount to questioning the very ground on which we have been standing—our whole identity as human beings. Our package of assumptions about the world and our own roles in it have had to be upended in the process. – S.L.A.A. Basic Text, Page 44

The Basic Text goes on to say "nothing short of this has been necessary to make us available to new life." Assumption can't exist unless I'm playing mind-reader. I heard someone say in a meeting, "When I assume, I make an ass out of u and me." I think I know what's right. That's playing God. Only Higher Power knows what's right. If I run around trying to change everyone and everything, I'm wasting precious time that could be spent finding out God's will and my purpose in life. My package of assumptions about the world was always negative. Everyone was either out to get me or didn't care about me. I believed this to be true without any real proof. Yes, my boyfriends treated me badly and my parents neglected me, but that didn't prove that my whole life was doomed. S.L.A.A. taught me to take one day at a time. My sponsor taught me to take people at their word unless they proved otherwise. I had to refrain from stalking and playing detective, thinking I knew what was really going on in any given situation. I couldn't assume facts not in evidence. God would reveal to me what I needed to see. Everything else was just unnecessary worry and misguided control.

My Higher Power knows what is best for me and I need only ask.

July 12

THE ELEVENTH CHARACTERISTIC

To avoid feeling vulnerable, we may retreat from all intimate involvement, mistaking sexual and emotional anorexia for recovery. – S.L.A.A. Core Documents, "Characteristics of Sex and Love Addiction"

In the beginning of sobriety, it may be necessary to retreat from all intimate involvement in order to go into withdrawal and get some clarity. Hopefully we have involvement with sober fellows during this time. But there has to be a point in recovery where we can emerge from isolation and trust that our Twelve Step work will give us strength to meet life's challenges. Many newly sober addicts dread dating because it triggers their disease. Fighting anorexia is difficult. The disease may want to rationalize and say turning down dates or social functions is recovery. "I can't go there because..." may seem rational, but it could mask a true motive which is to avoid the fear of acting out. Perfectionism pops up to say we don't need to continue down the road to a relationship because whoever we are dating is not right for us. It may be difficult to tell which voice is truth and which is disease. We need to rely on Higher Power and the S.L.A.A. group for guidance in learning the truth and staying out of anorexia.

Today, I turn to my Higher Power, Twelve-Step work and my fellows for strength.

July 13

TEMPTATION

"Success" in handling temptation was measured only by the outcome. The fact that I did not succumb, rather than the gracefulness (or lack of the same) with which I resisted temptation, was the payoff. Furthermore, the energy available to respond to a temptation...could be used inwardly to increase awareness.
S.L.A.A. Basic Text, Page 32

I live in a very "body-focused" city where the weather allows for beachwear all year round. We also have a large S.L.A.A. community. My sponsor told me there is no gracefulness to resisting temptation. I had to walk out of movie theatres if the movie was too triggering, stare at the ground and mumble like a crazy person and run away if confronted with a qualifier and fumble out of every situation that could harm my sobriety. Whatever I needed to do to maintain my sobriety was good, even if it made me look like a fool or an outsider. I would learn humility from the situation and have more awareness for the next temptation. Worrying about what other people think is at the core of sex and love addiction. But people in S.L.A.A. understood when I shared in meetings about temptations and my resulting awkward responses. Sometimes the laughter healed me and sometimes it helped me avoid a situation or be more graceful in handling it in the future. But I knew when they laughed, they identified. I was part of a loving community of people just like me.

My sobriety comes before people, places and things.

July 14

GENUINE

We had made something trivial of "love," with our long lists of those whose names we didn't even know, cheating them and ourselves of anything authentic or genuine. We...had lea everyone in our lives to expect from us what we could not or would not deliver. We had been masters of false advertising
– S.L.A.A. Basic Text, Page 91

Most of my life I was either so far in denial or so insecure that I needed to lie to the people I was with. I would call them "partners but that was a lie. I didn't even know their names so how could they be a partner? I told myself I was going to nightclubs looking for something genuine and getting upset every time the one-night stands didn't deliver a healthy relationship. If anything, ever did last long term, I was still cheating them and myself of anything authentic because I felt I had to lie about myself in order to make them stick around. They would expect me to be the person they saw in the beginning of the relationship—the one who never angered had no needs, gave extravagant gifts and was always kind and courteous. Meanwhile, I was ignoring everything and piling up resentments. My only outlet was to cheat and find new hope for a better relationship. I couldn't continue to live my life that way Worsening depression after every failed relationship was making me suicidal. The Twelve Steps and S.L.A.A. showed me a better way of life. I became the real me. I was able to have boundaries and be consistent. I opened up and became intimate. Instead of empty promises, I made real commitments and kept them.

I enjoy being the real me.

July 15

SECRETIVE LOVE

Our lives were divided into carefully segregated compartments, underscored by secrecy and confidentiality. Indeed, we even took pride in our ability to keep a secret...If we were able to manage the maze of intrigue without discovery...then we apparently never had to deal with the consequences of our actions. – S.L.A.A. Basic Text, Page 81

Secretive love was very enticing to me. Because I couldn't tell anyone else about my relationship, it created an "us against the world" bond. Saying, "If they found out they would be against us so we have to stick together" was very exciting, but created a closed relationship. The risk of being found out made my heart race and made planning each meeting very important. I felt like a spy, so intelligent that I was able to "manage the maze of intrigue without discovery." But I could only talk to him about our relationship. Friends didn't understand (or I thought they would judge me). Secretive love is not adult, because we don't confront other people's disapproval or hurt feelings. I had to keep my true feelings hidden from even myself because if I confronted them, I would have to leave the relationship. I wasn't happy going against my beliefs and I couldn't even talk to the one I loved about it. I finally told my secret and S.L.A.A. tools helped extricate me from the situation. Today, I am in an open, honest relationship where I can be my true self and not worry that the world will come crashing down around me.

I accept the consequences of my actions. I face them with strength and self-confidence.

July 16

INTROVERT

My solitude had become precious to me...I had gotten a grea[t] deal of insight into myself as an individual, not just as part o[f] a relationship. Most importantly, I had developed a vision o[f] personal wholeness towards which I felt able to grow. – S.L.A.A. Basic Text, Page 38

Sex and love addiction flourishes in isolation. For an introver[t] addicted to sex and love, spending time alone can seem like risky behavior. But it is possible to cherish solitude without falling prey to our addiction. The prevailing myth regarding introverts is that we are antisocial and don't have a lot of friends. In reality many introverts enjoy time spent out in a group and are capable of developing relationships with a wide array of people. Being an introvert just means that we need more time alone to refresh ourselves and be reminded of who we are. Solitude might feel scary at first, but as we wade through the troubling waters of temptation we find that we need not fear being alone. Freedom from fear is a blessing. It means we can still recharge our batteries without fear of acting out. We might need to make some outreach calls. We might need to relearn how to fill our time. But eventually, we will come to incorporate solitude as a beneficial and necessary part of our recovery. As we relearn what it means to spend time alone fear will drop away, and we will find comfort in our own company.

I am comfortable in solitude and enjoy spending time with myself.

July 17

ONE DAY AT A TIME

One day at a time. The past is gone, the future isn't here yet.* - *S.L.A.A. Basic Text, Page 265

It's very difficult to forget about the past or avoid dwelling on the future. We're told from a young age to plan out our lives. I would constantly worry about the future and obsessively think about the past, wishing I could change outcomes. My Eleventh Step in S.L.A.A. helped change this. Meditation and prayer allow me to see that I have a Higher Power in my life whom I can trust and have faith that my life is just as it should be in this moment. In meetings, I'm reminded not to tackle my entire recovery all at once. If I take it one day at a time, I can do each Step to the best of my ability and not feel overwhelmed about the rest of the work that I need to do to get to Step Twelve. If I'm truly taking it one day at a time, then it's okay to start over and believe that even slips are learning experiences.

I live in the moment today, knowing that my Higher Power shows me the way.

July 18

THE NINTH TRADITION

S.L.A.A. as such ought never to be organized; but we may create service boards or committees directly responsible to those they serve. – S.L.A.A. Core Documents, "The Twelve Traditions

Fellowship-wide services, Conference committees, intergroup and the ABM were all foreign words to me when I joined S.L.A.A. Even though I didn't care what they meant, these boards and committees were diligently working to make sure S.L.A.A. was there for me and for future newcomers. They weren't just going about their business doing with our money as they saw fit. They were having conference calls and meetings that anyone could attend. They also took votes to the fellowship at the Annual Business Meeting and through intergroup reps and the F.W.S. newsletter. Being "directly responsible to those they serve" helps to keep people honest and humble. If someone brings up the idea that someone has overstepped the bounds of their service commitment, there can be a discussion and vote. If that person is replaced, they can move on to other service work without retribution. This Tradition makes everyone involved more humble and aware. Asking what another person wants and really listening is a spiritual experience. But with all of this, how can we say we are never organized? We go with the group conscience over set rules and regulations. This can make changes in committees or service positions occur quite often and confuse things for a while. But we need the freedom that voting and communicating ideas brings.

I seek patience and understanding when working with others, remembering that I am responsible to the addict who still suffers.

July 19

DÉJÀ VU

The feverish pitch [of acting out reached the point at which I began my story, where I felt once again like I had to end it all. It was all too familiar. The patterns were tiresome. – S.L.A.A. Basic Text, Page 204

I believe sex and love addicts have a unique form of déjà vu in that they keep repeating the same patterns and are unable to stop. They repeatedly ask themselves, "How did I get in this situation again?" Or they repeat familial patterns even though they always said they would never be like their parents. When that familiar feeling stops being a vague sense of "having been here before" or I feel like I'm becoming my mother" and turns into, "How can I stop doing this?" we are lucky that S.L.A.A. is there for us. The tools of the program help us to stop the destructive patterns and makes the disease release its control over our behavior. We don't have to keep waking up in that depressingly familiar place of hating ourselves and being suicidal or homicidal. We can make choices about who we want to be and where we want to go instead of finding ourselves becoming people we don't want to be.

I use top-line behaviors and affirm myself with esteemable deeds.

July 20

HAPPINESS

The possibility that no durable happiness or fulfillment could ever come from living out this pointless pattern did not occur to me at all. In fact, the promise of the "next one" being the situation that would make me whole, or complete me in some way, was a carrot that seemed to be forever dangling in front of my nose coaxing me onward. – S.L.A.A. Basic Text, Page 8

In my disease, I never believed in durable happiness. Even if it did exist, it sounded boring. Over-the-top joy and revelry were my goal. But what goes up must come down. That frantic happiness always led to a crash. Sex addiction hides behind love addiction and makes me think that pointless pursuits will lead to wholeness and to fulfillment of promises. My goal was serenity, but reality always burst that bubble. When I tried to harvest happiness from magical thinking, I found only fool's gold. Living out a pattern of sex and love addiction seemed like the only way to live. I felt stuck in that vicious cycle of needing love, thinking I could get it through sex with a stranger and then finding out I was wrong. S.L.A.A. showed me the road to true lasting happiness. It's not over-the-top and not always there. But chasing that feeling and needing it all the time is what got me into trouble in the first place (an addiction to happiness).

I find fulfillment in life using the tools of S.L.A.A. and my Higher Power's guidance.

July 21

FINANCIAL DEPENDENCY

I chose to focus on the romance of supporting the "starving artist" both financially and emotionally. I loved being needed, and I thought that by filling that need we would be bonded for life. – S.L.A.A. Basic Text, Page 50

Romance and finance are usually intertwined. Every marriage article I've ever read focuses on what to do about finances and that it can cause relationship trouble. It's when we expect money in exchange for sex or love or flirt to make more money instead of relying on the merits of our work that we get into trouble. Sex and love addiction twists a normal problem into an upside-down way of looking at a relationship. When I'm fearful of not making enough money for my survival, I look for people to rescue me. Using my sex and love addict behaviors is an easy way out and I'm lazy. But in that case, my financial rescuer always has control. That made me feel insecure; I was on the whim of my rescuer, which is shaky ground. But if I am compensated for my talents and do a good job, it builds my self-esteem and I stand on solid ground, knowing that I can work someplace else if I don't like the conditions of my workplace.

I rely on my Higher Power and talents to take care of financial fear today.

July 22

MONOGAMY

The cumulative effect of this continued questioning of our sexual myths and motivations was that a climate of trust and emotional intimacy began to evolve. – S.L.A.A. Basic Text, Page 158

I always said, "How boring that some people stay with one person for the rest of their lives," and, "Everybody cheats so why not beat them to the punch?" I used this as an excuse to steal husbands and boyfriends and to cheat on my lovers. Addiction twisted my ideals and perceptions. I believed the more sexual partners I had, the more self-esteem I would gain. Having multiple partners would give me the power in all my relationships. It ended up creating the opposite scenario. I was spiritually sick. S.L.A.A. showed me how to stop searching for love in empty relationships. Finding a Higher Power's guidance and unconditional love has allowed me to stop my endless search for attention and affection. But when I finally was able to find and commit to my true partner in life, all of the scary intimacy issues came up. Responsibility, honesty and openness were never my strong suits. Doing a Tenth and Eleventh Step every day helped me maintain a level of emotional intimacy of which I never thought myself capable. The Twelve Steps and Higher Power gave me the humility and gratitude to be able to maintain a healthy monogamous relationship for more than a decade so far.

I am monogamous today, knowing that my Higher Power gives me strength.

July 23

SPONSOR DIRECTION

With our sponsor, we begin to address recurring problems. Our sponsor helps guide us through the rough passages many of us experience as a result of letting go of our addiction...[and] shares his or her own experience and feelings from having been in situations similar to ours, taking care not to give advice.
– from the "Sponsorship: A Return from Isolation" pamphlet

I've always thought of sponsor direction as following the path in the program that my sponsor took. She said to me, "This is my experience and my opinion. You can always do it your way but this is what I see in this situation." She was able to see reality much more clearly than I could with my addict eyes. Because of her guidance, I never said to my sponsees, "Do this or I'll fire you." I've heard of people doing that and maybe that's what they needed at the time. I believe we find the sponsor we need. Our sponsor guides us through the Steps,tells us how they stayed sober through tough times, and how they handled breaking their bottom lines. Listening and learning from their experience can help us avoid the pain of making the same mistakes. Some people listen, but their addiction is so strong they do it anyway. That's when the sponsor guides them to the Steps and actions that will help them get back to sobriety.

I listen to my sponsor today and draw from their experience, strength and hope.

July 24

PARADOX

Minus the guilt, our experiences in addiction had been transformed into lessons for living of profound depth and durability...The paradox was that our usefulness as channels for healing was a direct result of our experiences in sickness as well as in recovery. – S.L.A.A. Basic Text, Page 102

It doesn't seem logical that hiding from people we love would help us. But taking a break from a qualifier can lead to sobriety. There are a lot of paradoxes in S.L.A.A.: Surrendering to Higher Power gives us freedom; withdrawal helps us have healthier relationships; pain helps us grow. The dictionary definition of a paradox is a self-contradictory or ridiculous statement that nevertheless proves to be true. I felt like my sponsor and people in meetings were making those kinds of statements all the time. Whenever I expressed that feeling to my sponsor, she cautioned me against contempt prior to investigation. I needed to stick around long enough to see that the statements were true. The Basic Text and my sponsor explained a lot and investigation led me to experiences that proved most of the paradoxes true. Usually, when I was thinking something sounded absurd in the program, I was just afraid of doing it or that I wasn't good enough for it to come true for me. S.L.A.A. and trust in a Higher Power helped me find the self-esteem to have hope that the paradoxes would come true—and they did.

S.L.A.A. members and my Higher Power guide me through life's paradoxes.

July 25

HEALTHY RISK-TAKING

I described the pain brought about by these addictive patterns of compulsive sexual activity and emotional intrigue...Sharing these things, regardless of whether I was met with sympathy, envy, or vilification, helped me immensely. It was by taking these risks that I continued to develop perspective on much that had happened to me. – S.L.A.A. Basic Text, Page 34

There are many healthy risks to take in sobriety: Asking someone we're attracted to out on a date, following a dating plan even though we risk ridicule or losing someone, sharing at meetings, being completely honest and vulnerable, trusting a partner, etc. It is when we take the risk and let the chips fall where they may that we know we truly trust a Higher Power and have found self-esteem. When we show our true selves, it's possible that people will dislike us and walk away. S.L.A.A. tools give us the strength to be honest anyway. We know it's a healthy risk if we're in self-care as we take it. Reaching out to fellows and our sponsor and doing inventories around the risk are all actions to ensure we aren't doing something unhealthy. Ensuring our emotional, physical and spiritual well-being isn't about hiding out in anorexia; it's about living in the world. That involves risks. As long as we continue to do Twelve Step work, we will be able to handle it.

I identify and take healthy risks today knowing that my Higher Power is with me.

July 26

THE TWELFTH SIGN OF RECOVERY

We are restored to sanity, on a daily basis, by participating in the process of recovery. – S.L.A.A. Core Documents, "S.L.A.A. Signs of Recovery"

I hear it all the time in meetings—insane sex and love addict behavior that could get us locked up or sent to a mental hospital. But the greatest insanity was in my mind when I was alone, trying to control this disease. When I participate in the process of recovery, I am no longer alone with the crazy voices in my head. It's the things that my addict voices tell me will fix the situation that I battle every day. Those voices are only my disease trying to keep me sick. The Twelfth Sign of Recovery says "daily basis" because every morning I need to start anew and keep working my program. Morning meditation, writing in my journal, reading recovery books or calling a fellow starts my day off right. When confronted with difficult situations, I need to take my character defects out of it to the best of my ability. I try to recognize my part as quickly as possible. If I allow myself to get mired in the mud of fantasy, the addict voices find a way in. Higher Power and fellows can clear them out for me.

I participate in my life today by working the process of recovery.

July 27

ALCOHOLICS ANONYMOUS

Since the beginning of Alcoholics Anonymous in 1935, the Twelve Steps of that fellowship's program of recovery have been adapted to a wide variety of human problems. Among these are gambling, overeating, smoking, narcotics abuse and child abuse. – S.L.A.A. Basic Text, Page vii

Our program is based on the Steps, Traditions, and Concepts of A.A. Our founder, Rich, was a sober member of A.A. That's where he found many prospects to grow this Fellowship. Whenever we have a problem in S.L.A.A. Conference committees, it's not uncommon that someone will ask, "How does A.A. do it?" The introduction of Chapter 4 in the S.L.A.A. Basic Text explains the adaptation of the program of A.A. to sex and love addiction. A.A. literature is recommended with the suggestion that we "substitute the words 'our addiction' or 'sex and love addiction' for the direct references to alcoholism in those books." I struggled for four years to get sober in S.L.A.A. I was also sober in A.A. My sponsor told me I should let my sponsee go because I was acting out in S.L.A.A. She refused. So, we met each week and read the Big Book of A.A. One alcoholic's story about burning down a barn revealed to me in stark reality the seriousness of my own sex and love addiction. I burned down the barn of my life over and over again because of this disease. I was able to get and stay sober immediately after that.

I benefit from other Twelve Step Programs to enrich my S.L.A.A. recovery.

July 28

SEXUAL ABUSE

Like other people, we had been life's victims in many respects. Many of us had memories of emotional deprivation or of being physically or even sexually abused...our feelings about these events had hardened into a great bitterness which we held for those people who had mistreated us. – S.L.A.A. Basic Text, Page 90

I spent a lifetime hating my abusers and using the abuse to explain why God didn't exist. I was angry and distrustful of the world. Why live in a world where abuse exists? I couldn't face the pain. I numbed it with drugs and dangerous sex. It didn't matter that I was putting my life at risk; I didn't want to be here anyway. I wasted my life on that excuse. I didn't have to work towards goals or even happiness because I had the monolith of abuse blocking my path. Every time I tried to change, I was plunged into depression. I thought the hole was too large to climb out of. I couldn't see that recovery could work for my particular brand of problems. When I entered the rooms of S.L.A.A., I kept seeing a fellow who had been sexually abused by her grandfather her entire childhood. She cried and raged at every meeting for years. But one day I saw her start to change. She attributed it to working the Steps and the help of S.L.A.A. fellows. Today, I see her in the rooms and she is always smiling and sharing about how S.L.A.A. gave her a life that she enjoys. I started to believe it could work for me and it has.

Higher Power, help me recover from my past and live in the now.

July 29

MIXED MESSAGES

As much as she had invested in her fantasy of me and the super-human role I was supposed to fill in her life, she was nevertheless starting to be aware of my emotional inconsistency...The commitment marriage would require was impossible, but so was doing without her. – S.L.A.A. Basic Text, Page 8

It's difficult to avoid mixed messages when sex and love addiction has got us by the throat. We want to be consistent and clear, but the addiction won't allow it. One day we profess undying love and the next refuse to answer any calls. Most addicts may attempt commitment or fidelity but get stopped in their tracks by fears of withdrawal. It can feel like death to an addict to abstain from indulgence. Fantasies take over and we think we want one thing and then reality kicks in and we realize the error in thinking. Vulnerability and intimacy get shut down and the ones we love are left dazed and confused. Sometimes we play a role to try and have strength and mask how we are really feeling. We act like we don't care when inside we're full of insecurity and doubt. The Steps of S.L.A.A., in combination with prayer and meditation, help us calm the stormy emotions. We can be consistent instead of acting like we are. The program helps us see our true emotions and stick to our values. We are finally able to make and keep commitments and be emotionally consistent.

I am conscious of mixed messages today and pray for balance.

July 30

ACTING OUT DREAMS

In this dream I fought a gorilla, my addiction, for possession of a very nice and precious pocketknife. The gorilla was tremendously strong, and clenched this knife in his fist. I had never been without this knife and was incensed that this brute could have taken it from me. – S.L.A.A. Basic Text, Page 33

When we first go through the process of withdrawal, it's likely that our addiction will try to reach us in our dreams. We may wake up feeling terrified at having acted out in our subconscious, or we may feel a strong urge to carry these acts out in real life. When we put a sudden stop to a long pattern of addictive behavior, it's going to take our body and mind a little while to catch up. Acting out dreams can feel very real and leave us feeling off balance. As time goes on, we may experience a variety of dreams, including those in which recovery seeps through and we resist the urge. However our dreams may manifest themselves, they are not a reflection of our progress in recovery. The true measure is how we handle ourselves once we've woken up. If we feel triggered, we can talk to someone in the program or share about it in a meeting. Talking about the experience can take away some of its power. The dream, just like any trigger, will fade from memory with time.

I accept my dreams as part of life and act on them appropriately.

July 31

TOLERANCE

There were good moments together and some actually intimate sharing, but neither of us was healthy or mature enough to survive the disagreements, to work through our differences and to engage in a true partnership. – S.L.A.A. Basic Text, Page 207

True partnership requires the willingness to tolerate another person's ideas, opinions, and behavior even if I don't agree with it. In my toxic sex and love addict relationships, this was impossible to do. Regardless of the fact I didn't have the patience to tolerate anything, the partners I chose always had outrageous or dangerous behavior. Tolerance worked against me. For some reason, I could tolerate bad behavior better than a simple difference of opinion on something fairly irrelevant. If a potential partner wanted to have an intimate conversation, I ran. Working through differences in a relationship usually involved violence. My work in S.L.A.A. changed all of that for me. The Traditions were there to support me in my service work. The idea of following group conscience even when I disagreed helped me keep commitments. I was no longer alone with my thoughts, thinking I was the only person with any good ideas. My sponsor pointed out to me that my good ideas got me into trouble anyway, so why not give other people's ideas a try? I've found that a Higher Power is always there to catch us if we fall.

I practice tolerance today and appreciate differences of opinion.

August 1

SELF-AWARENESS

I could become capable of making some decisions about how to live my life. This would now be based on the discovery of who and what I really was, which might emerge during my time alone, in full awareness of my addictive past. – S.L.A.A. Basic Text, Page 23

It's difficult to be self-aware when all I do is think about myself. Sounds contradictory, but it's true. When ego gets in the way and makes us use sex and love addiction to get our needs met, it clouds our judgment. Is it really a need or only a desire that might hurt us in the long run? Being aware, for me, meant looking at both my character assets and defects in my Fourth Step. I had to take time alone in withdrawal to do some self-reflection and meditation and prayer. People would mention things in meetings that resonated with me and I'd ask myself if I had the same behaviors or characteristics. They would usually give good strategies for dealing with problems, even if it was simply the act of sharing with the group in that moment. Working with sponsees revealed my own areas to work on in my character. After withdrawal and a period of sobriety and a lot of work getting to know myself, I found that self-awareness could only be maintained by listening to others and not putting up a wall of self-defense and taking things personally. If I truly look at a criticism and level-headedly decide if it's true or not, I can glean insight about myself. Being able to humbly admit my errors is key.

Higher Power, direct my thinking and keep me humble today.

August 2

SEX DRIVE

This loss of one's soul could only be all the more poignant if the body in which it lived continued to exist, unanimated spiritually from within, and monstrously driven by imperious instinctual drives which would now have become its masters.
S.L.A.A. Basic Text, Page 70

Instinctual drives are the masters of an unanimated body. Being a slave to my sex drive was not something I signed up for in my fantasies, which were dressed up as romance. I didn't know that because of my sex and love addiction I would end up a shell of a human being. I lost my soul to addiction. No wonder I turned to suicide as an alternative. But the instinctual drives still kept me searching for one-night stands, rationalizing that I was looking for "the one." This situation was not poignant to me at the time because I didn't think God existed. But after my spiritual experience in S.L.A.A., I look back at the young me with compassion. The words I learned in S.L.A.A. ring true for me now: S.L.A.A. and God can save me if I put them first before my sex drive and my need for love. I believe that all my needs will be met if I practice a spiritual approach to life.

I put my Higher Power first today and am grateful to be whole.

August 3

THE EIGHTH STEP

Made a list of all persons we had harmed, and became willing to make amends to them all. – S.L.A.A. Core Documents, "The Twelve Steps of S.L.A.A."

Some believe this Step is just a shadow of the Ninth. But this is a very important Step that requires caution and thoroughness. I had a friend who made the list and ran right out to make her amends before talking to her sponsor. She ended up acting out. My sponsor had me create three lists, people I would: make amends to now, make amends to later, and never want to make amends to. We discussed each one in depth. The people in my "never" category were my blocks to willingness. I feared letting them go or was holding on to resentments and felt they needed to pay for their crimes. Why should I apologize to these horrible human beings? It helped to pray for the well-being of those I resented as well as the ones I couldn't let go. It hurt to pray for my married qualifier to have a happy family life without me, but it helped me let go of the fantasy. It didn't seem right to pray for the person whom I had a horrible resentment against to get what they wanted, but it made them more human and made me realize there was enough in God's world for everyone. I prayed for them to get recovery, which makes the world a better place when spiritually sick people get better.

I overcome fear today and make amends to those I have harmed.

August 4

SOCIAL PRESSURE

I never wanted to have children at all, just as I had never anted to be married. Such situations represented bondage to e. Increasing responsibility could only impinge on my ability o pursue sexual and romantic adventure. It was society that as sick, I thought, trying to force bondage upon me. – S.L.A.A. asic Text, Page 11

Social pressure is difficult for a sex and love addict to live up o. We have so many excuses for why we should be different and/ r can't do it society's way. We don't want to conform. We want o be special—to stand out from the crowd. Social pressure can otivate people to achieve. But it only gets in the way of a sex nd love addict's acting-out "adventures." That's why so many ddict behaviors are in the shadows. I looked at social pressure s a negative thing, making me hide. But in sobriety I look at it s a system of checks and balances to see if I'm on the right track. ask myself, "If society would look down on me for doing this, hould I be doing it?" I write a pros-and-cons list, check with my ponsor and fellows and pray. If the answer is yes, I should do it nyway, then I do it. Sometimes social pressure is bad, trying to ake us do things we shouldn't do (that don't fit for us). But now at I have a Higher Power's guidance in my life, I can see what's ight for me.

I do what is right for me, asking daily for my Higher Power's uidance.

August 5

POETIC LOVE

Engaging in romantic obsession distorts our perceptions. I the height of our obsession, we may: see the object of our obsessio as someone other than who s/he really is; project qualities onto th person that s/he doesn't have. – from the "Romantic Obsessio pamphlet

Sounds a lot like poetry, doesn't it? The classical poets ofte wrote about people who were dead. Love at first sight or overl romantic love can happen. I see it in the movies all the time. Bu that's not real. Maintaining communication with another huma being who has their own thoughts and feelings is hard wor Especially for a self-centered addict like me. Lovers in the page of a book or on the movie screen are much easier to handle (or s I thought). Movies looked much different to me when I watche them in sobriety. I get into trouble when I believe in the fantasy o someone and start to obsess. I need realistic expectations to kee me rooted in reality and sobriety. If I allow myself to go flying o into the clouds, I'm lost. Prayer, meditation and contact with sobe S.L.A.A. members keeps me tethered and sane.

I am grounded to a world of truth.

August 6

VALIDATION

Affirming signs of growing self-esteem: Replacing feelings of self-loathing with an appreciation of self; being able to be with ourselves in solitude with a degree of comfort; being able to accept a compliment or kind word; being able to recognize and acknowledge our accomplishments. – from the "Measuring Progress" pamphlet

Parking in my city is horrible. I have a friend in recovery who would wander around whenever he got a parking ticket stub saying, "I am seeking validation." We both knew what that really meant. Seeking validation isn't bad unless we're addicted to it and will do anything (including high-risk behavior) in order to get it—especially from unavailable people. When we learn to give ourselves validation, we have a much stronger foundation for self-acceptance. My disease loves to tell me I am unworthy. In early recovery, when people complimented me, I explained to them all the reasons they were wrong. If I did something good, my perfectionism would step in to point out all the mistakes I made. Validation used to come through how much sexual attention I would get. But that didn't allow me to feel comfortable in solitude. When I wasn't getting constant outside validation, I felt like a desperate fraud. When I was in a relationship, if my partner even hinted at a problem, there was big drama. The program taught me the difference between validation for ego and for healthy self-esteem. In recovery, I look for opportunities for the latter.

I seek internal validation today and choose esteemable actions for myself.

August 7

COMMUNICATION

I recall no greater loneliness than that of being with someone I supposedly loved without any deep, positive communication going on, or even being possible, between us! It's far lonelier than being by oneself. – S.L.A.A. Basic Text, Page 8

Some of the loneliest times of my life were when someone was sitting right there beside me. I couldn't turn to them and say what I was truly feeling because I was afraid they would run away in horror. When I felt anger, I suppressed it as long as I could and eventually had to express it in huge dramatic scenes. I couldn't let my childhood stuff come up because no one wants to deal with that baggage. Communication was difficult at first. I would immediately hate the rooms of S.L.A.A. after sharing openly about my pain. I would get paranoid that everyone disliked me and was plotting to kick me out. I wanted to punch my therapist for making me remember trauma. When I found it particularly difficult to communicate with someone, my sponsor in S.L.A.A. told me to write down everything I wanted to say and read it to her first and then the other person. I could read my thoughts right off the paper. That was a novel idea to me. I always thought you had to look someone in the eye and talk spontaneously in order to communicate. In that case, I could never get the words out. Communicating in this way was awkward but the only way I could deal with difficult issues at first. It became easier with practice and now I can look people in the eye and tell them how I feel.

Today, I am open, honest and direct with others.

August 8

THE NINTH CHARACTERISTIC

We avoid responsibility for ourselves by attaching ourselves to people who are emotionally unavailable. – S.L.A.A. Core Documents, "Characteristics of Sex and Love Addiction"

When I was trying to fix my partner, I didn't have time to look at my childhood issues or fix the problems with my career, or even do the laundry. Trying to help an emotionally unavailable person feeds my addiction to drama. Situations can get very dramatic when confronting someone who doesn't want to deal with emotions. It's interesting that this characteristic uses the word "attaching." The unavailable person doesn't want me insinuating myself in his or her life. In this ninth characteristic situation, I wasted a lot of valuable time investigating and chasing my partner around. I might as well admit I was stalking. When I came to S.L.A.A. I didn't want to admit that that was a characteristic of my addiction. That's just a normal relationship, right? But there it was in black and white in the characteristics. One meeting that I went to even printed each characteristic in a huge font on a sheet of paper and had everyone share on it. I couldn't ignore it anymore. I had to start looking at myself instead of my partner's faults. No one allowed me to just sit there and complain; I had to get into action with the steps.

Today, I focus on myself and my recovery.

August 9

EMOTIONAL ABUSE

Using film heroes as my models, I decided that if I never showed my feelings, I'd get what I wanted, that if I was abusive towards women they would be secretly smitten. Adoring me for abusing them, they would cling to me and never leave – S.L.A.A. Basic Text, Page 2

One day after hearing my mom yell at my dad ceaselessly, I asked her why she was so mean to him. Her reply was, "I always thought being mean made him stay." My parents were together since they were 14 and my dad would do anything for my mom. But they were miserable. I felt sorry for my dad. That way of going about relationships never worked for me anyway. I kept finding myself in situations where I was being physically and emotionally abused. I ignored emotional abuse, because at least they weren't hitting me. I was so desperate for them to stay that I felt I needed to put up with anything. I was so used to self-abuse in my addictions that it seemed okay if I was with a partner who lashed out in anger or told me I was fat when he saw me eating fast food. Listening to people share in the rooms of S.L.A.A. and working the Steps made me realize I needed to get out of any relationship that wasn't loving and that included my relationship with myself. I needed to stop the emotional abuse in my mind first.

Today, I set healthy boundaries with people, places and things.

August 10

TABOO

The brave new worlds of morality where "anything goes" because "nothing matters" boomeranged leaving us grasping for some residual meaning or reality in life. – S.L.A.A. Basic Text, Page 69

Is society intolerant, or are people who break taboos acting out of a psychological compulsion? When engaging in so-called illicit behavior, sometimes the lines of morality are blurred because of society's ever-changing view toward sex and love. The sharp differences of sexually accepted modes of expression can be cultural, generational, even historical. What might be taboo behavior for one society may be permissible for another. I don't have to know what's right for others, but I can define what's right for me. I don't have to continually chase the forbidden just because it entices me. I no longer feel the need to engage in illegal or antisocial behavior in order to look cool in the eyes of a potential lover. By turning it over to a Higher Power, talking with my sponsor and working the Steps, I can define healthy behavior that serves me. I might also realize actual ways to confront intolerance, ways that no longer disconnect me and create more intolerance. I no longer listen to the addict voice that tells me "nothing matters" knowing that my Higher Power has a plan for me.

I define what is right for me and live by my real values.

August 11

TAKING THINGS PERSONALLY

We still seemed unable to respond in kind, often coming up against our own inner blocks, which kept experiences of genuine trust and caring at arm's length... God's grace would give us freedom from the burden of our old self. – S.L.A.A. Basic Text Page 86

I had a friend who told me I "needed to get a thicker skin." I would fly off the handle at every little thing. "This person is doing this to me," was my mantra. Everyone was out to get me in this world because I thought it was all about me—and in a negative way. Sometimes people aren't even thinking about me. I used to even think people in S.L.A.A. meetings were sharing "at" me. My sponsor had to repeatedly tell me that I wasn't the center of the universe. I needed to get over myself and look for ways to be of service. Being of service at the Intergroup and Conference committee levels taught me to stop taking things personally. I saw people listening to the group conscience and making amends if their behavior negatively affected the group. They stuck around and continued to be of service in situations where I would have run. They had a sense of themselves as important in God's world but still part of the team. Seeking my Higher Power's will in every situation helps me to realize that I am a small part of a plan and I don't need to control everything.

I am open to genuine feedback.

August 12

MEETINGS

A meeting can...serve as a focal point for sharing experience, strength and hope concerning recovery from sex and love addiction, a place to which new people can be directed...Working with others was the best way to thwart that erosion of consciousness which... was such a characteristic of the disease. – S.L.A.A. Basic Text, Page 121

I used to go to three Twelve Step meetings a day. That was the only place I felt relief from my various addictions. I gathered strength to continue in my recovery from the small group of people in those cramped meeting rooms. I would complain about the coffee or the uncomfortable seats at first. But as the meeting went on, all those concerns melted away. I heard stories of strength and courage. I usually heard exactly what I needed to hear to help me in that moment with whatever I was going through. I saw people with light in their eyes who no longer walked around in the fog of addiction. Most of them had service commitments at the meeting. There were treasurers, greeters, secretaries and S.L.A.A. literature sales commitments. Working as a team, they made sure there was a place for newcomers and old-timers to go and help each other recover. I am grateful that there are meetings available in my area. That wasn't the case in previous years. I had to struggle to get to a meeting. But it taught me more discipline than I ever had before. When I really needed a meeting, I had to do the work. Like my sponsor used to say, "If your pants are on fire, don't debate it, just jump in the river."

I attend S.L.A.A. meetings regularly and am grateful for collective wisdom that I find there.

August 13

SITTING WITH FEELINGS

When the pain comes now, I don't automatically resort to a sexual thought or solution. I have time to process the feelings and to realize they can't overwhelm me, by going to either my higher Power or a member of the S.L.A.A. Fellowship for help. – S.L.A.A. Basic Text, Page 205

I was addicted to drama, adrenaline and busyness. Sitting with feelings meant boredom and pain (or at least discomfort)—things I avoided at all costs. I really did think I would die from overwhelming feelings. Early in recovery, I had panic attacks that would blind me. I had swirling lights in my eyes and if it caught me on the freeway I would drive blindly until it passed (thank God for bumper-to-bumper traffic). I found a co-worker who was willing to walk with me until I was able to cry and able to see again. All the feelings that I avoided with addiction were coming up and I had to just let them. I didn't go back to my old behaviors. One day at a time, I got better by turning my feelings over to God and trusting I was in a safe place. Because the Twelve Step process helped bring these feelings to the surface and replaced unhealthy behaviors with recovery, the feelings that I sit with today are much easier to deal with.

My Higher Power and S.L.A.A. support me through changing feelings.

August 14

AFTER WITHDRAWAL

We had seen that it was possible for us to live through the pain of withdrawal without returning to our old patterns, and we sensed that the Power to do this was coming from outside ourselves. – S.L.A.A. Basic Text, Page 76

When will I get through withdrawal? When can I start dating again? When can I have sex again? These are some of the questions we may ask ourselves when going through the necessary pain of withdrawal. The answer to all of them will come when we are able to stop asking them. There are no definite timelines where withdrawal is concerned. As the S.L.A.A. Basic Text suggests, when we are no longer obsessed with these questions then we are through the process of withdrawal and perhaps healthy enough to begin an intimate relationship. Once the pain of withdrawal lessens, do we come out into the sunlight thinking we are cured? Do we think, **Well, I'll never do that again, I've learned my lesson**, and give ourselves permission to rest? It's good to be grateful for getting through withdrawal but it's not time to retire. Meetings where we can share our experience will help newcomers see the light at the end of the tunnel. There is hope for coming out of withdrawal a whole person. Hearing newcomers in the pain of withdrawal reminds us that we never want to or have to go back to that if we stay on the path of recovery.

Higher Power, guide me through withdrawal, and let me support others through theirs.

August 15

STALKING

Engaging in romantic obsession distorts our perceptions, obscures reality, promotes self-destructive behaviors and stops us from fully engaging in life. – from the "Romantic Obsession" pamphlet

"No. You can't drive by his house just to see if his car is there," said my sponsor. "That's stalking." How could she use such a harsh word? It may be harsh, but it woke me up. I had a distorted perception that it wasn't hurting anyone. What if my boyfriend had found out that I was doing that? He would think I was crazy, would be mad that I didn't trust him and would stop trusting me as a consequence. The obsession with him was obscuring reality. It was creating a fantasy world where he was probably cheating on me when I already knew him to be a trustworthy person. How could I go so quickly from believing I chose the right partner to convinced he's a cheater? Love addiction. Control. Living in fantasyland. I get so bored with reality and being kind to myself that I need to stir up trouble. Stalking takes up all my time so that I don't have to fully engage in life. The distorted thinking is that if I'm trying my best and fail in life's achievements, then I'm a failure. But if I have the excuse of love addiction, then it's not my fault. I had to let it be what it was and be okay with even failure before I could get and stay sober.

I create my own experience today, knowing that I choose the right path for me.

August 16

THE SECOND TRADITION

For our group purpose there is but one ultimate authority—a loving God as this Power may be expressed through our group conscience. Our leaders are but trusted servants; they do not govern. – S.L.A.A. Core Documents, "The Twelve Traditions"

When I started doing service at the Conference committee and Annual Business Meeting level, I wanted to take charge and change everything to make it more "efficient." I thought, **If people would only see that my way is better, we'd get things done.** My sponsor reminded me that other people are not me and they have their own ways of doing things. Everyone has an opinion, that doesn't mean it's right for everyone. That's why we pray and meditate about choices. The group votes on anything that is brought to a motion. I need to listen to what the group decides, whether I like it or not. If I don't like it, I know it can change because of rotation of service. When the secretary of a meeting could be voted out in six months, they don't accrue too much power. I think it's interesting that this Tradition says a "loving God" is the ultimate authority. My Higher Power used to be some all-powerful, all-knowing, heavy-handed, punishing God. But the groups in S.L.A.A. were always loving. Even during arguments in a group conscience, someone could call thirty seconds of silence to get us to meditate on our Higher Power's intent. Usually, people came out of the silence with a better perspective.

Today, I am a trusted servant of the Program.

August 17

MEDITATION

Meditation could be a formal time set aside for that purpose, or simply a moment of quiet listening, stilling our own thoughts to allow God's ideas to slip into awareness. The style or amount of time devoted to this was unimportant, as long as it was frequent enough to be a regular part of our day. – S.L.A.A. Basic Text, Page 100

Before S.L.A.A., meditation seemed like some magical thing that only transcendent beings participated in. I was too tough for that. So, when my meeting added 10 minutes of silent meditation, I would sit and make lists of what to do later that day. Sometimes I would have conversations with people in my mind. My thoughts were screaming two-year-olds running around in my head. Whenever I could quiet my thoughts, there was a block to allowing God's ideas to slip into awareness. Maybe it was insecurity—thinking that I wasn't good enough for God to ever speak to. Or maybe it was not trusting God enough to help me. I spent a lot of time debating whether people could tell the difference between God's will and their own. I needed to remember that I couldn't put my intellect to work on spiritual matters. The slogan "Don't debate it, you'll lose" helped me put thoughts aside and concentrate on stilling my mind. The more practice I got, the easier it became. Today, I concentrate on my breathing during meditation and imagine myself pushing thoughts out. I ask for God's will and pause to listen.

I practice quiet listening today and ask for my Higher Power's guidance.

August 18

CLOSURE

[The] wish to clean up the messy, incomplete feelings, which were so common in our addictive relationships...could only result in "falling under the ether" of our addiction once again. Of course, it was often necessary to break off some relationships, or otherwise set some situations involving others right, early in sobriety. In such cases we found that writing a simple letter to these people was safest. – S.L.A.A. Basic Text, Page 92

I told my sponsor I needed to speak to my qualifier one last time to get closure. He said, "It's over. There's your closure." I don't need to go back to my disease one last time for any reason. Life is unpredictable. The only way to get closure on a relationship sometimes is to do the inventories and Steps around it and give it to Higher Power. I can give myself a firm answer when doubts creep in about ending a relationship. But no matter what I say or do to end a relationship, the longing can stick around for years and crop up when least expected. S.L.A.A. takes the strength out of the memories and gives us the tools to stay away when necessary. I try not to get into the "what ifs." That fantasy makes me open the door to a situation that is best kept shut. Buying into the delusion that I could have made it work is just self-will run riot. If I seek God's will, I can stay away from a destructive relationship one day at a time.

My Higher Power has my best interests at heart and provides me with all the direction I need.

August 19

PROJECTION

I tried to deal with [the fear of her having sex or intrigue with others] by rationalizing it as being the projection onto her of my own wayward behavior and attitudes. – S.L.A.A. Basic Text, Page 17

It's come to my attention recently that every time I find fault with anyone, I have the same characteristics. I've chosen people in my life that have big character defects that I can hide behind and point at them. I feel such indignation that I need to endure their grievous character defects. I have a friend who I think is a showoff. Lately I've realized I have the same issue. My Higher Power, sponsor and meetings are helping me see that in every single case I have those very shortcomings. The reason the person is in my life is probably to bring to light aspects of my character that I'm not capable of acknowledging. Sometimes I think it's okay for me to express my defects the way that I do, because I'm not as bad as the other people in my life. I'm coming to a whole other level of accountability and realizing how I've impacted other people's lives. I always projected that it was someone else's fault. As the saying goes, "You spot it, you got it." I'm finally able to look at my defects and surrender them to my Higher Power.

One day at a time through the Steps, prayer and meditation, my defects of character are being removed.

August 20

PATIENCE

We might have asked to have the shortcoming of impatience removed, only to find that we did not need to practice patience. Instead, we had to get honest about our self-centered willfulness. As we practiced thoughtfulness towards others, really giving without holding onto the expectation of reward, impatience slipped away. – S.L.A.A. Basic Text, Page 88

I used to say, "Patience is not my strong suit." I thought that would get me off the hook for a lot of self-centered behavior. In my mind, patience was really laziness or weakness. If I'm not constantly going after what I want, I'll never get it. As a child, it was just a way for my parents to tell me, "No." If they told me to be patient, I knew I wouldn't get what I wanted. I usually threw a fit instead. That's understandable for a child, but it kept happening into my thirties. Those dramatic scenes killed whatever building blocks to intimacy I had created. Had I stepped back, listened and waited, I might have been able to make that connection with another human being that I so desperately craved. But the addict voices and cravings made that impossible. Feeding the addictive urges took precedence over all sober virtues. It was only because I went through withdrawal and started practicing service that I was able to gain any patience. Today, when I find myself getting impatient, I choose prayer and meditation instead of something outside of myself to calm the cravings.

I practice patience today, knowing that everything happens in my Higher Power's time.

August 21

"NOT MY TYPE"

There is great therapeutic value to being around a wide spectrum of people…Being around very attractive people within S.L.A.A. has forced us, within this sanctuary, to begin to learn how to interact more humanly with those who would have been cast as "types," on the outside. – S.L.A.A. Basic Text, Page 132

After doing the Twelve Steps in S.L.A.A. and working a rigorous program, I married a man who was not my type. In my disease, I chose dangerous and emotionally unstable men. Trying to fix them was a challenge. I felt too insecure to even consider chasing after a successful, self-sufficient or self-confident man. I would complain constantly and play the victim. When I discovered that I had value as a human being in the rooms of S.L.A.A., I began healing from objectification. Not knowing what other S.L.A.A. members did for a living helped me with that. I could relate to others on an emotional level instead of looking at their price tag. Outside success didn't matter. It was about serenity not ambition. Sobriety and connection with a Higher Power gave me dignity and community. I no longer felt superior or inferior and could explore relationships outside of my type. Thank God I did. My partner isn't perfect, but he's perfect for me.

I am open to meeting new people and accepting them as they are.

August 22

GATHERING INFORMATION

While in the program for six weeks and out of the last relationship for eight weeks, I was still not convinced I was a sex and love addict. I went out for what I hope will be the last time... [and] had an affair...It was during this exciting, ecstatic two-week affair that I realized I was powerless, truly powerless over the sex and love that this woman was offering me. – S.L.A.A. Basic Text, Page 189

Sometimes listening in meetings is not enough to convince newcomers that they are sex and love addicts. They need to gather more information. Many of us have to truly see and feel our powerlessness before we can stay in the rooms of S.L.A.A. and do the work it takes to recover. Gathering information in recovery may refer to someone who sits in the back of the room and listens, still undecided about whether they need to do the Steps or not. I was this person for years in the program. I didn't need to do the Steps until the people in S.L.A.A. were able to convince me that I was truly a sex and love addict. But no one even tried to convince me, saying, "Why don't you go do some more research? We're here when you figure it out." That research was painful but eye-opening. Finally convinced, I crawled back into S.L.A.A. ready to do whatever work was required to get and stay sober.

My Higher Power and S.L.A.A. are always there for me.

August 23

DELUSION

We learned not to worry about the inability of the blind to comprehend the concept of "color." Our affirming experiences in sobriety would later fall on more receptive and appreciative ears, once the new prospects had themselves faced and lived through the rigors of withdrawal and apparent deprivation. – S.L.A.A. Basic Text, Page 119

Delusion is self-will saying, "My way is right and naysayers are wrong." In my first few years of S.L.A.A., I told my sponsor I was moving in with the married man that I had been trying to break up with for months. We put a deposit down on an apartment, so it must have been reality that he was leaving his spouse, right? My sponsor said I was heading for a brick wall and it was going to hurt when I hit it, but she just had to let me do it, and it did hurt. I thought the pain would kill me when I realized he would never leave his spouse. My addiction tells me when I see a rainbow, that's a sign from God that my relationship was meant to be. My realistic fellows tell me it's just refracted light. The addict voice speaks to me, telling me that sex is love. It's difficult to stay out of delusion when the addict voice is constantly telling me things that aren't true but seem reasonable in the moment. The healthy voice may be hard to hear over the roar of the addict voice, but it's the one I need to hear.

Today, I empower myself by listening to my healthy voice.

August 24

SHOWING UP

If there was something there between Kate and me, I felt that I could now be available to work on it. The "success" of this, for me, would hinge on my ability to be emotionally "available" to her and to myself on a consistent basis. – S.L.A.A. Basic Text, Page 38

In my addiction, I would show up for commitments some of the time. If I didn't have a good excuse to get out of an event, my body would be there but my mind would be somewhere else. I never truly showed up for anything because that involves being emotionally present. Everything was all about me and getting my needs met. Because of all of the work I've done in S.L.A.A. and a healthy practice of prayer and meditation, I show up for my life today. I am more able to listen and get out of ego and fear. The ten-minute meditation in my home group meeting helped the most. I had to force my mind to quiet down because everyone else in the room was doing it. Practicing it every week helped me open the door to letting God calm the negative voices in my head. My sponsor told me to show up to commitments no matter what my addict voice said. I had to clear those voices out to avoid the numbing-out behaviors that kept me checked out of life. I'm so glad S.L.A.A. taught me how to suit up and show up.

Today, I am responsible; I keep my commitments.

August 25

FANTASY

Through mutual sharing, we had come to know [triggering individuals] as human beings, and their stories had exploded many a fantasy we could have trumped up about them. Myths about their addictive desirability had been dispelled before our very eyes. Our interactions with others were becoming more authentic and mutual. – S.L.A.A. Basic Text, Page 146

Unicorns, Martians and talking lions filled the pages of all my childhood books. I hid out in them to escape the scary reality of my life. My thoughts were full of wild hopes and dreams of a better, drastically different world. Children are supposed to dream. But when these thoughts carry into adulthood and distract us from having any real purpose in life, they cross over into addiction. Obsessing about unavailable people is living in fantasyland. I can't have an authentic relationship with a figment of my imagination. I need to listen to the other person and hear what they are saying instead of idealizing them and overlooking bad behavior. I must watch out for playing mind-reader, too. A mutual exchange of ideas is the only way for me to live in reality. Fear of conflict can keep me in fantasyland for years. One day at a time, I need to confront problems as they come and clear them out before they become full-blown fantasy worlds in my head and I'm paralyzed by the fantasy. Fantasyland can be a warm, comfortable place. So who would choose harsh reality? The only way out for me is to realize that my addiction can get to me more easily there and will pull me out into an even more harsh reality.

I have clarity and purpose in my life today.

August 26

INHIBITIONS

When I was dieting and thin, I got very sexy and ran from bar to bar, and bed to bed, inhibitions released by the booze, drinking to forget, then waking with still more to regret. - S.L.A.A. Basic Text, Page 165

For me, sex and love and drugs and alcohol quickly got all mixed up together. Unable to relate to others in a healthy way, I turned to drinking and drugs to allow me to break through my inhibitions. Like Cinderella, however, the next morning I was stuck with those same inhibitions and lack of true, lasting intimacy. Guilt pervaded my consciousness in a hangover brought on by intoxicating chemicals and the violation of my personal boundaries. If drugs or alcohol serve as a gateway for me to act out, it may be time to reevaluate how and when I use these substances, or whether I should use them at all. When I lose my inhibitions, the desire to stay sexually and emotionally sober drowns beneath intoxicating waves. Am I willing to break my bottom line just to have a drink or two? Many recovering sex and love addicts are engaged in other Twelve Step programs, some joining before becoming a member of S.L.A.A., and some joining after. We must decide if we want to add another addiction to our list, or if we need to.

I make careful choices today and live a full life.

August 27

CRIME OF PASSION

[In] a closed-energy-system relationship...Each participant walks around feeling as if his or her nervous system is being consumed from within. A kind of half-alive stupor is punctuated with attacks of murderous rage or child-like deification of the other. Clearly the "crimes of passion" are an increasing possibility as this situation continues. Each person in the relationship needs to "live," to have a life of his/her own. – S.L.A.A. Basic Text, Page 144

When nothing else mattered in my life except the relationship the murderous rage I felt when things went wrong was unbearable. I had no support group or Higher Power to take it to. I had no one to help me through it and no way to let it go like working with my sponsor and the Steps do for me now. Crimes of passion are committed because of a sudden strong impulse. I could never control my impulses in my disease. A closed-energy relationship is a setup to create such strong impulses. When I walk around in high anxiety every minute of every day, obsessing about what my partner is doing, I'm inevitably going to snap. With the help of S.L.A.A., I can take a step back from the relationship and go to a meeting or fellowship, forget about what my partner is doing for a little while and focus on me, others and my Higher Power. Those are much more life-enriching ventures than where my partner went to lunch that day.

I let go and let God.

August 28

DISCLOSURE

Our awkwardness around those to whom we felt susceptible forced us to talk about [our identity as sex and love addicts] openly, in spite of the likelihood that doing so would end any further opportunity for an addictive indulgence. – S.L.A.A. Basic Text, Page 116

I read an S.L.A.A. **the Journal** story that described a situation where an S.L.A.A. member disclosed her membership in our fellowship inappropriately and lost her dream job. She said we must choose carefully when and where to disclose. I've always given too much information too soon, hoping to bond people to me quickly. It usually ended up backfiring and pushing people away. When I first started going to meetings, I told everyone around me about S.L.A.A. I was lucky that most of them were also in Twelve Step programs and understood. If my family had objections, they kept it to themselves. In sobriety, I check my motives before opening my mouth. Am I trying to find a rescuer? Do I want to quickly explain away bad behavior instead of making amends? If disclosure will help another person or keep my bottom lines safe, I'm on solid ground to proceed. If not, I think and pray about it and pause to talk to my sponsor.

I protect my anonymity, remembering that self-care is an important part of the program.

August 29

"TRUE LOVE"

It is our belief that all along we were trying to derive something more meaningful from our addictive activities. Perhaps we confused sex and romantic intrigue with love, but in the final analysis it was authentic love we were, on a deeper level, seeking
– S.L.A.A. Basic Text, Page 141

Before recovery efforts in S.L.A.A., I had a big issue with jealousy in all relationships. I took hostages, as they say. But from doing a deeper dive into my motivations and through talking with fellows and praying and researching, I can now say that the battle is all but won. Whenever I start to get those jealous feelings within a relationship, I remember that this life is one of abundance and not scarcity. People have the capacity to love you, me, their other friends, their family members—all. There is not a finite amount of love. The more love one gives, the more one has the capacity to give and knows how to do it and it just keeps on coming. I take their love and let it grow through me and I don't hoard it. I pass it on and watch it expand to others. What a beautiful and freeing realization that was for me in this program. I no longer drain love out of people. I seek to give love and to be loving. That is when I felt the most loved in my life.

I look for opportunities to be loving today, expecting nothing in return.

August 30

RIGHT ACTION

My criterion for my actions used to be, "What can I get away with?" That is changing: now the criterion for my actions is, "What can I do that is going to help me in my spiritual recovery and in the maintenance of my serenity?" – S.L.A.A. Basic Text, Page 184

Before recovery, taking the right action meant whatever would make life easier, or would be socially acceptable to my co-addicted friends and family. I'd heard the phrase "right action' in a spiritual context, but it seemed more like an intangible, unattainable motto than anything at the time. During my Fourth Step, it became very evident that having been raped twice as a teen and sexually harassed (and then fired) at several jobs, I never considered reporting these incidents to authorities to be the right action. Each time, I thought I could handle it myself. The rest of my Fourth Step showed me how I couldn't handle it myself. Today, "right action" means recognizing my real needs through meditation and outreach calls, and asking how and where I can get those needs met before they turn into acting out on resentments. Burying my feelings under acting out won't solve anything and will only make matters worse. Taking right action and building self-esteem eventually leads to serenity.

I take the next right action today with the help of my Higher Power and fellows.

August 31

THE FOURTH SIGN OF RECOVERY

We learn to avoid situations that may put us at risk physically, morally, psychologically or spiritually. – S.L.A.A. Core Documents, "S.L.A.A. Signs of Recovery"

Avoid risk? Why would I want to do that? In my acting-out days, I lived for the adrenaline rush of risk. That's why people jump out of airplanes, right? They don't know that their parachute will definitely open. When the situations involved reducing the risk with my intellect, I got the added bonus of an ego boost. It felt good to pat myself on the back for avoiding consequences with lies. But when the risk of physical death became a real consequence of my acting out, I had to admit I had a problem. It was only when I went to S.L.A.A. meetings that I realized the risky moral, psychological and spiritual situations could kill me too. Morality and spirituality seemed to go together, and I wasn't having any of that "God stuff." I wanted to say I was a free, independent spirit. But in reality, I was lonely, miserable and beating myself up. The risky situations always involved the one who (in my fantasies) was going to save me. S.L.A.A. taught me how to separate fantasy from reality and to run the other direction if a situation would harm me. It took years of work and a lot of support, but I was finally able to put down the drug of adrenaline and ego and avoid risky situations.

Today, I look for healthy situations that feed my spirituality.

September 1

CELEBRITY CRUSH

Romantic obsession is...an unhealthy fixation on another person with whom we may or may not have a relationship or even have met...The addictive nature of obsession can distort our thinking and behavior and can lead us in a direction that violates our dignity and personal integrity. – from the "Romantic Obsession" pamphlet

"Crush" sounds so harmless. I always told myself that's all it was. I wasn't obsessed with the celebrity, it was just a crush (infatuation). But my addiction twists everything and made this thirty-year-old scream like a teenager when she saw a picture in a magazine. It's not healthy to sit around for hours fantasizing about what life would be like with a certain celebrity instead of doing the dishes. If I can enjoy their work and be entertained by it instead of going into fantasy, then I know it's an innocent crush. As long as I'm honest with myself if it starts to turn into obsession, I won't have to cross any boundaries and harm myself or others. I don't have to let the addiction lead me down a path of destruction. I can keep my dignity and personal integrity if I tell on myself to sponsors and fellows, pray and let go. A harmless little crush can stay a crush if I realize I'm slipping into fantasy. I can bring myself back to reality with the help of others.

Today, I live in the present, free of obsession.

September 2

ILLEGAL ACTIVITY

As we are all governed by our own conscience, we do encourage members to study and understand the Traditions of our program to assist in group conscience / individual decisions on matters associated with crimes / illegal activity. – from "Anonymity, The Law and S.L.A.A."

People commit crimes in pursuit of love and sex. This prevented me from feeling like I was worthy of recovery. I felt isolated and alienated from the world. This emotional atmosphere of self-loathing and shame can perpetuate more of the same behavior as a means of relieving pain. The amends-making process can help heal the pain so we don't have to act out over it. Illegal activity can be defined differently in different countries. It is not up to me to decide whether these laws are fair. I seek freedom from the addiction, and freedom to live in society, and that means that I refrain from engaging in behavior contradictory to the law of the land. I set appropriate boundaries regarding incriminating information. I determine when it is safe to share information about my past illegal activity. I don't assume or prevail upon others to keep secrets for me which may compromise that person's own moral integrity. The possibility to recover from sex and love addiction by working the Twelve Steps is real and exists for all individuals, regardless of their past behavior. We can attain sobriety, while being mindful of the safety of ourselves and others.

I accept my past. I am worthy of recovery.

September 3

SHADOW SELVES

What came to pass is that as we refrained from seeking to escape from ourselves through acting out on our sex and love addiction, we began to become intimate to ourselves. – S.L.A.A. Basic Text, Page 113

Sometimes what we're doing through romance is seeking to grow, to expand our own horizons. We want to learn what our lovers know, and become what they are, acquiring their skills, style, social status or culture. This is not bad in itself. However, a payoff of that kind may blind us to our own real needs, abilities and limitations, which we may fail to address in our attempt to lead the other person's life. When I did the Steps and went through withdrawal in S.L.A.A., I was finally able to meet the real me. I didn't have to live in the shadows anymore. I found out that I'm good with computers. I can pursue that career without depending on my lover to show me the way or to provide me with contacts. I can be self-supporting. I look to myself and my abilities instead of enviously concentrating on someone else's life and career. My sponsor told me to stick to my side of the street and that has helped me grow.

Concentrating on myself today, I pursue my own hopes and dreams.

September 4

CHANGE AND GROWTH

The old emotional habits...had subtle payoffs which made them difficult to surrender. We now moved...toward surrender to a life-long process which would refine the qualities we carried within and contributed to life. Underlying this whole shift in our attitude was increasing reliance on the God of our understanding. – S.L.A.A. Basic Text, Pages 85-7

If we can't surrender our old way of doing things to the Twelve Step process, we can't change. Most addicts hate change. My ego is so big that it tells me my way is best and I should keep doing it, even if it's killing me. Emotional habits (like making a partner jealous to see if they love me or watching porn so I don't feel lonely) have payoffs that make them difficult to give up. It's much easier to manipulate a reaction from a partner than to confront problems in a relationship. Watching porn is much easier than interacting with live human beings that have their own thoughts and feelings. Change means I have to first see myself for who I am, get rid of my ego and then give everything over to my Higher Power. Letting God be in charge is scary to me because sometimes I wonder if he wants to punish me for my past. But the Ninth Step helped me clear away that fear enough to let God in. The other Steps helped me get a better (non-punishing) God. I have definitely changed and grown in my years in S.L.A.A.

I seek growth today and allow my Higher Power to change me for the better.

September 5

ENABLING THE ADDICT

He...began drinking again and after not hearing from him for two weeks, I responded to his "rescue" call and re-entered the enabling behavior that Al-Anon had taught me to leave behind. - S.L.A.A. Basic Text, Page 208

In this chapter of the Basic Text, the writer explains that before she discovered the addict was drinking, she had been meeting with him weekly for superficial sex and was not happy with the relationship. When she realized she was in Al-Anon behavior, her sponsor convinced her to stick to a no-contact rule. She rationalized her pain and obsession as "loving him so much," and she remained reluctant to label herself an addict. Many of us love addicts set up a system of rescuing and enabling the addict in order to ensure that our love interest will never leave us. We hide addiction behind love. I always chose addicts and tried to rescue them because I thought that would make me an indispensable saint. Everyone would admire my attempts to make my partner better and my partner wouldn't be able to survive without me. But all it was doing was feeding my own sex and love addiction, enabling me to stay sick and enabling my partner to keep acting out. Without me there to pick him up, he might have hit bottom and gotten help sooner. In sobriety, I am no longer caught in this vicious cycle. My partner and I each have our own spiritual practice and self-care. We can stand on our own and respect each other.

Today, my number one priority is my health and well-being.

September 6

JUDGMENTAL

One day I ran into Rich. I had known him from A.A. but had judged him pretty harshly. I thought he had shown bad taste and judgment by moving on an A.A. newcomer while his wife was pregnant. – S.L.A.A. Basic Text, Page 248

I am grateful that the fear of judgment didn't keep me from sharing and being honest when I was a newcomer. I had fellows who told me, "Screw them if they judge you. Look where they are. My sponsor said if I was holding back because of fear of judgment "look at the people you are trying to impress." We're all just a group of sex and love addicts trying to get better. Judging people sets us above them, where we're too far away to be useful to them or ourselves. Whenever I start judging someone in a meeting it's usually because I've had the same bad behavior in the past and I'm afraid of going back to it in the future. It isn't a disease that I can catch. If someone shares about acting out constantly and being unable to stop, instead of thinking they're horrible, I remember how painful it was for me to act out. I try not to share judgment with fellows in these cases, only love and kindness because that was what was shown to me.

I am kind, gentle and loving today and treat others as I wish to be treated.

September 7

MARRIAGE VOWS

Kate and I got married when I was about eight months sober. I made an inner resolve to be "faithful"—although the notion that I could or would never romance or screw around again was incredible. Despite these misgivings, my engagement, wedding and honeymoon went off well. – S.L.A.A. Basic Text, Page 9

In this chapter of the Basic Text, Rich reveals that he found out he had contracted a sexually transmitted disease six weeks after the honeymoon. We may stand before our friends and family and make a public vow to be faithful during a marriage ceremony, but sometimes our addiction makes those empty words. S.L.A.A. helps us mean what we say in our marriage vows. Many of us never would have thought of marriage before getting sober in S.L.A.A. But if we work a rigorous program and keep conscious contact with a Higher Power, we can see the value in making and keeping commitments. I didn't want to say traditional marriage vows when I got married for the first time at the age of 40, because I didn't want to pledge to obey my spouse. But I do obey him as he does me. We care about what the other person wants. We each have authority in the relationship. Vows are not about the words we say, but about our intention and actions. This sex and love addict intends to love, obey and honor her commitment. What a change from my addictive past.

I honor my spoken and unspoken marriage vows today.

September 8

THE NINTH STEP

Made direct amends to such people whenever possible, except when to do so would injure them or others. – S.L.A.A. Core Documents, "The Twelve Steps of S.L.A.A."

It can be a terrifying idea to think of contacting someone from the past and admitting to them that we behaved badly. The shame around our actions may have been brewing for years. It's painful to admit face-to-face that we were wrong. They might not believe us, or worse, they might try to get revenge and harm us in some way. But confronting shame that we tried to bury with numbing-out behaviors helps us to be humble and clear away the wreckage of the past. We have to confront ourselves when we listen to the person, we are making amends to. They may lovingly understand, or they may tell us a list of grievances. We should hear them and consider where we can improve ourselves from their feedback. If they are wrong in their assessment, we can realize that we have changed. We don't argue with them. We quietly listen and later take any resentments to our Higher Power and fellows. I used to take the "except when to do so would injure them or others" part of this step as an excuse not to contact people. So, I let my sponsor decide each case. For some, I had to just let go and write a letter to them that I would never send. I've had emotional miracles happen with amends-making, mending relationships that had been broken for years. Thank God I got over the fear and did the work.

I am willing to make amends today, knowing that my Higher Power is there.

September 9

RESCUING

I was smitten with her enshrining me as her knight in shining armor mounted on a white steed. It seemed, for me, a realization of the heroic role in which I had cast myself...I could not let her down. The cause was holy. – S.L.A.A. Basic Text, Page 4

Rescuing, for this sex and love addict, has never been about the person I'm "helping." It's about wanting to feel needed, feeling superior, needing attention and having someone in my debt that I can control. Sad to admit, but when I'm saying someone needs rescuing, I'm saying they're not capable. That hurts me as well as the other person when we both play our roles. When I first started dating, fellows told me that "water seeks its own level." In a rescuing relationship, two people are always at different levels, feeling "better than" or "lesser than." If I stick to fixing myself, healthier people come into my life. The more I avoid rescuing, the more I allow others to have their Higher Power and self-esteem. My relationships are more mutually respectful today because of this. When I find myself wanting to rescue, I discuss the situation with my fellows and check my motives. If I'm helping with no motive to get something in return, I can take the action, as long as I'm not hurting anyone.

When being of service today, I am clear about my motive to help another.

September 10

ATTENTION AND FOCUS

Many of us were so numbed that only a blast of physical and emotional intensity from a sexual or romantic "hit" could penetrate and animate our progressively deadened, dissipated beings. Like a cattle prod jabbed into someone who is exhausted and dazed, an addictive hit jolted us into a temporary illusion that we were alive and really living. – S.L.A.A. Basic Text, Page 69

If I put the focus on my career, my finances and my spirituality that I put into intriguing with other people and trying to get sexual and emotional hits, then I would be a superstar billionaire Buddha by now. The good news and the bad news is that my recovery is really all about where and when I put my attention. When my finances, career or friends need my time and energy, I focus on that. When I need validation or my spirituality is lacking, I put my focus there. The truth is that I'm not always interested in that. I have fought for so long to avoid my life by checking out. That's what my sex and love addiction looks like. When I divide my energy appropriately, I don't have that desperate need, and I don't have to behave like a vampire, sucking all the attention out of the room. I no longer feel that desperation because the stuff that needs attending to is being taken care of.

I focus on my emotional and spiritual needs today.

September 11

DISTORTED THINKING

It was not that our logic, motives or intents were wrong. Rather, our very ability to see the problem clearly, and our wishes to change ourselves, were themselves systematically distorted by the addiction. That part of our mind which at least intermittently recognized our sickness was itself not immune, and could not be solely relied upon to guide us to health. – S.L.A.A. Basic Text, Page 74

My mind makes up all kinds of excuses to rationalize irrational behavior. I want what I want, when I want it. So, if someone tells me I'm going to get it, I believe them no matter how far they stretch the truth. If I listen to the addict voice when it tells me to do crazy or dangerous things, I get an idea in my head that seems logical and I run with it. There may be a nagging doubt in the back of my mind (the sane part), but I squash that by chalking it up to fear. I can't rely on my own thoughts because they are distorted by the addiction. If I had told my sponsor that I wanted to chase my cat around the apartment with an electric shaver because I thought getting rid of the pet dander would make my cat-allergic married qualifier come back, she might have pointed out the fallacy in my thinking. Today, I don't solely rely upon my mind to guide me to health. I tell fellows, my sponsor, God, and I share at meetings. All of this clears my mind, so I can focus on reality.

Sharing with my Higher Power and fellows helps clarify my thinking.

September 12

DESTRUCTIVE BEHAVIOR

We felt new depths of humility, as we saw what damage had been done, and how much of it could never be undone. As we concentrated on our own part in this, we came to a new understanding of our motives, so often a poignant mix of normal human needs for love and a meaningful life, twisted by the addiction into something ugly and harmful to ourselves and others. – S.L.A.A. Basic Text, Page 91

Whether my destructive behavior was to feed my image to the world of being cool and bulletproof or if it was a consequence of my enslavement to addiction, it was a high-risk vicious cycle that only S.L.A.A. could free me from. Destructive behavior is addictive. I was so used to driving too fast, smoking, drinking and eating too much in response to the difficulties of living, that I could only get glimpses of the misery and chaos it was creating in my life and that it was killing me. The adrenaline rush of high-risk behavior and the ego boost of surviving through dangerous, painful events can be alluring drugs. It was difficult to get used to a normal "boring" life in sobriety. But as my sponsor always said, "Boring is much less likely to get you killed." When I came to S.L.A.A., fellows taught me how to replace harmful behaviors with self-care. Prayer and meditation were a large part of that, even though I didn't believe in God at the time.

I seek life-affirming behaviors today. I value my well-being.

September 13

THE SIXTH CHARACTERISTIC

We sexualize stress, guilt, loneliness, anger, shame, fear and envy. We use sex or emotional dependence as substitutes for nurturing care, and support. – S.L.A.A. Core Documents, "Characteristics of Sex and Love Addiction"

Before sobriety, I initiated sex to avoid feeling guilty instead of talking about things I did wrong in my relationship. When I was stressed at work, sometimes I flirted with my boss or watched Internet porn to lessen anxiety. When I was lonely, I watched porn instead of going out in the world. When I was angry, I had revenge sex. Feelings of shame made me hunt for a conquest to try and boost my ego instead of talking about my feelings. I believed that if I had sex with enough people, I would be better than the people I envied. I used to think that everyone used sex to get what they wanted or to ease painful feelings. I didn't see any other way to make people stick around. What is nurturing care and support anyway? I never saw it growing up. I only saw rage and drama and narcissism. But I began to understand the meaning of those words when people listened without interrupting in S.L.A.A. meetings, when my sponsor met with me for free every week and when people took my phone calls and listened to my rantings. Practice with this helped me choose a partner who gave me support and pointed out when I was sexualizing instead of dealing with feelings. Today, I can give myself nurturing care instead of acting out to avoid painful feelings.

Experiencing the full range of feelings is an integral part of my recovery.

September 14

INTRIGUE

When I was still actively addicted, this network of potential intrigues had constituted a kind of safety net, or security, for me. These gestures of kissing and hugging and touching were the currency of my external personality, of the way in which I related to others. – S.L.A.A. Basic Text, Page 28

When I was a baby, my mother was very ill and did not come to my crib often. She told me later that I was the best baby ever; I never cried. Considering this now, through the eyes of recovery, I think I probably did cry, but learned my cries would not be answered. So, I stopped crying. I became a pretty self-sufficient little person. This pattern has been pervasive in my life. I crave touch, but I'm also repulsed by it. When someone hugs me, I get triggered. Before sobriety, I took it as a sign of potential intrigue. Whether I pursued it or not, I got high. Sometimes this was the only way for me to feel a part of the world. But I have a solution today—the steps are healing me in this area. Little by little, my Higher Power is restoring a healthy relationship to touch in me. When I am feeling touch-deprived, I put my arms around myself and imagine my Higher Power is hugging me. I find that I am much less triggered today by touch. By degrees, I am developing touch intimacy with my spouse as my Higher Power restores me.

Today, I relate to others from a place of abundance and know my Higher Power is present in each relationship.

September 15

TERMINAL UNIQUENESS

I realized that I could have been anyone else, that my seeming uniqueness as a "lover" was an illusion. I was trying to trump up a sense of my singular, irreplaceable qualities as a person through engaging in one of the great common denominators of mankind. Hardly unique, I was merely another player. – S.L.A.A. Basic Text, Page 22

Uniqueness sets me apart from others and isolation will set me on the path to self-destruction. All human beings want to be unique. I was always trying to be better than everyone in the room or did crazy things to stand out. I ended up hurting myself in the process. When I joined S.L.A.A., I needed to become part of the community. My sponsor told me to become a worker among workers. Trying to stick out and get noticed would send me running from the rooms. If I had run from the rooms, I never would have found recovery and I would surely have died. I had to identify instead of compete. I had to find humility and fellowship. I had to listen to old-timers and follow what worked for them. I couldn't do the Steps or program my way. Identifying with other sex and love addicts and becoming part of the program of recovery was difficult. I battled my ego every step of the way. Being of service and reaching out to others saves me.

I follow the program of action that has worked for others. I am part of a fellowship.

September 16

TRIGGERS

Circumstances which can trigger this erosion of our awareness of our sex and love addiction are so frequent and numerous that we need to be able to "ground" any sexual and emotional ambiguity which has started to undermine our stable functioning. No matter how far we have evolved in sobriety, we are never beyond reach of temptation's siren song. – S.L.A.A. Basic Text, Page 127

I used to watch a television program that was popular with everyone I knew. I started to identify with one of the main characters and wanted to live a "free" sexual life like she did. I realized it was opening the door to my disease and making me think I should leave S.L.A.A. I had to put that television series and any like it on my bottom lines. I was embarrassed to admit that after years of sobriety, I was unable to watch a popular TV show because of the way it triggered me. But anything that erodes my serenity has got to go. I don't need to become anorexic and cut everything out of my life, but I do need to recognize when something isn't necessary. We ground ambiguity by getting current in meetings and fellowship. We share our daily trials. Others can see if our disease is speaking to us. Like the Basic Text says, "from meeting to meeting we need to get current and stay open." If I am triggered, I can get support and much-needed tools to help pull me out of my addiction.

Going to a meeting and getting current helps me to stay safe.

September 17

DEATH

***Once the negative thinking is allowed a beachhead, my addictive nature is all too quick to respond. I mention this in order not to paint sobriety unrealistically. The rewards of sobriety are immense, however. Life is more beautiful than ever before, and the promise of a future with some peace of mind is real.* – S.L.A.A. Basic Text, Page 217**

A loved one died suddenly from a brain tumor this year. Even after years of sobriety, I indulged in "What's the point?" negative thinking. Grieving is painful. Excuses for numbing-out behavior seem valid. Peace of mind is shattered. I feel like there is no future if we're all going to die. But life in sobriety has been beautiful. I have had magical moments that I am so grateful for. My grandparents lived into their hundreds. Their lives mattered. Instead of concentrating on fatalistic thoughts and negativity, I try to be of service and make a difference in the lives of my S.L.A.A. fellows. It's easy to fall into depression when we're isolated. But when the S.L.A.A. community and our Higher Power surround us, we can get through anything. It's not about replacing loss or trying to outrun death, it's about making the time we have here count in the lives of others and enjoying life—difficult to do when mired in addiction, but a goal to work toward in sobriety. Hope can always be found if we look for it.

I celebrate the lives of deceased loved ones and make a difference in the lives of the living.

September 18

COURAGE

Courage to change the things I can – S.L.A.A. Basic Text, Page 77

My compulsive-addictive feelings always come up at the same time I experience pain. It is an act of courage to wait out my pain. I used to think I had courage when I would do mindless dangerous things. But most of my actions were really done out of fear. Courage in sobriety, for me, means being honest even when I'm fearful someone will abandon me if I do. It means that I share openly in a room of sex and love addicts even if I worry that someone will judge or hurt me. I sit with painful feelings even when I am afraid doing so will break me. I don't run or numb out anymore. Knowing I can rely on Higher Power gives me the strength to walk through the fear instead of acting out over it. I ran from my feelings in the past. It seems that I have a higher tolerance for physical pain than emotional pain. The fear of losing what I have or not getting something, I think I need doesn't cripple me anymore. With S.L.A.A. and my Higher Power I feel safe in the knowledge that I have everything I need.

I have the courage to change the things I can today.

September 19

FRIENDSHIP

We have found that if we do not find balance and meaning in our lives then we are all too easily drawn into non-sexual relationships that are not unlike the addictive ones. Our relationships... must be subject to the same principles which keep our sexual lives sober. – S.L.A.A. Basic Text, Page 142

Friendship is based on mutual knowledge of each other's personality and character that is acquired and deepened over time. Friendship involves a mutual commitment to be present for each other whenever possible, and supportive even when we can't be present in person. It isn't governed by the emotional uncertainties of lust, longing, fantasy or projection. Friends don't have to resemble each other or agree with each other all the time—we can stand by our friends regardless of our differences. We shouldn't expect others to give us everything we need at any and every moment. Trusting in the support of our loved ones is one way we can live out our faith in a power greater than ourselves, for our Higher Power works through the help and affection our friends give us. The experience we gain in our friendships can help us know what true sharing in a relationship can be.

Maintaining healthy boundaries with friends keeps me balanced.

September 20

PROSTITUTION

[I] soon began to find prostitutes to get what I desperately needed. These were my first experiences with prostitutes, and the guilt and growing sense of myself as a pervert resulted in my frantically going to the yellow pages to find a psychiatrist. – S.L.A.A. Basic Text, Page 200

I entered S.L.A.A. because my dishonesty with women in my life had driven me to conclude that professional sex workers were the only way to go. I knew on a deep level that rationale was twisted thinking. Still, I convinced myself on a daily basis that I was beyond hope and so I might as well indulge in whatever behavior I liked. I was sure that no woman would ever want to enter into a relationship with a pervert like me. I couldn't even convince myself that I could be in a relationship without acting out. It took dozens of S.L.A.A. meetings, sharing the deep shame of my actions and receiving encouragement and acceptance from my fellows before I began to recognize the faults in my thinking. By the grace of God and by working this program, I have been blessed with a willingness to abstain from commercial sexuality, the courage to live and speak honestly and have been given a genuine desire to be monogamous. I have been imparted greater humility, serenity and increased awareness, all of which allow me a healthier viewpoint regarding all aspects of life.

I am restored to sanity daily and worthy of love in a healthy relationship.

September 21

COMMON WELFARE

Our common welfare should come first; personal recovery depends upon S.L.A.A. unity. – S.L.A.A. Core Documents, "The Twelve Traditions"

If the group doesn't survive, I won't survive. I must compromise sometimes. I have many aspirations. But if those goals would harm the group, I need to abandon them. Tradition Two states our Higher Power and group conscience decide what is good for our common welfare. If we get caught up in long, drawn-out arguments over where our money should go or what the format of the meeting should be, people will get frustrated and leave. A group conscience vote doesn't always go the way I want it to. But I remain quiet, knowing the group has spoken and the future will tell if it was a mistake or not. If I just have faith that we can work it out together, I don't need to become combative. I need to rely on meditation and prayer to work with someone I don't like in Intergroup or at a meeting, for the good of the fellowship. If I can't do that, I can go to a different meeting or start my own. I don't have to create chaos.

I put my opinions aside today in favor of unity within the fellowship.

September 22

FLIRTING

The fear that we were not or could not be deserving of real love led us to make excessive sacrifices to parents or lovers, to flirt with everyone to prove we were attractive, and to lie to impress others. – S.L.A.A. Basic Text, Page 81

In addiction, flirting is usually about empty promises. We flirt to get craved attention or material things such as promotions at work or discounts at stores or bars. But the intended purpose of flirting should be to let someone else know of our interest in them. When done for any other reason, it can be considered acting out. We don't want to send the wrong message. It's better to abstain from flirting unless we want to pursue a relationship. If it is used to pursue a relationship, we need to be mindful of how we flirt. Before sobriety, my method of flirting was to use sexualizing language and tell a potential partner what I was capable of. My fellows in S.L.A.A. helped me curb that behavior. Healthy flirting during sober dating is different. It was a whole new experience for me. When my love interest took the conversation down a sexual path, I steered it back to everyday conversation. The kind of person who needed this kind of flirting was not for me anymore. This was scary for me. I had always been so insecure about my ability to find real love that I thought sexualizing was necessary to get and keep a partner. Refraining from this type of flirting helped me find true love and a healthy partnership.

Today, I express myself honestly in thoughts, words and actions.

September 23

ACCESSORY BEHAVIORS

We would engage in such solitary activities as masturbation, voyeurism, or exhibitionism and claim that they were improvements because we were no longer involving others directly in our disease. Such attempts were as futile as for an alcoholic to switch from beer to wine, or wine to beer, claiming either as an "improvement" over the other. – S.L.A.A. Basic Text, Page 72

After three years of sobriety from my bottom line, I moved into a place by myself for the first time. In less than a week, I was acting out. I told myself that as long as I didn't act out on my bottom line, I would be fine. But soon I found myself doing things that I had never done before, and the addiction was even stronger than I remembered it. I played down my acting-out behavior with others in the program or completely neglected to mention it. When I'd finally had enough, I laid it all out for my sponsor and started a policy of strict honesty with him and others in the meetings. I admitted every time I acted out, even if I planned to do it again later. Eventually, that honesty brought me back to sobriety. Engaging in accessory behavior is like playing with fire. I could have crossed my bottom line at any moment. If I'm getting an addictive hit off of my actions, then it's probably not something I should be doing. I may even need to add a few things to my bottom line.

Today, I commit to the behaviors that protect me and keeps me sober.

September 24

SELF-LOVE

Amidst all difficulties and uncertainties, a simple intimacy had come into being for us: we had met ourselves, and found ourselves worthy. We had become beloved to ourselves. – S.L.A.A. Basic Text, Page 115

Oh, to be beloved by someone...anyone. It never occurred to me that this someone could be me. In fact, before recovery, the thought of loving myself was dismaying. There were too many flaws, too many imperfections. The goal was to find the perfect mate who would love me despite my imperfections. Surely, I could find this person if I looked hard enough, worked hard enough on my appearance, acted right, and loved that person despite their imperfections. Who could help but love me then? Those insane thoughts kept me stuck in a never-ending search for someone that did not exist. Today, I realize I don't have to look any further than my own mirror and I find a person who will love me forever, flaws and all. When I make mistakes, I tell myself, "It's okay I still love you and I approve of you." I get to take care of myself today. I take her on long walks on the beach and listen to her thoughts and desires. I don't beat up on her for being different (an addict).

I am enough, I have enough, and I do enough.

September 25

JEALOUSY

Jealousy is not necessarily a mere egotistical desire to possess for one's very own, not just a selfish unwillingness to share. It is the anguish of despair; the wholeness one thought one had found with the loved one is shattered...One is overwhelmed with fear.* – *S.L.A.A. Basic Text, Page 55

Fear that my partner will abandon me or cheat on me, fear that I'm not enough—these are just a few of the fears that overwhelm me when jealousy hits. The anguish of despair is feeling like I'm not good enough to keep a relationship with a normal person. In the first year of my sober relationship, jealousy hit a lot. I kept praying for it to be removed because I knew it was fears left over from my previous relationship. I knew I had chosen a trustworthy partner this time. I tried not to let it show when I was jealous, but it overwhelmed me in social situations and my partner could tell. I was selfish of his time and attention. I had to prevent my negative, magnifying mind from believing he was cheating on me. I had so many signs that he was trustworthy, but my need for drama made me ignore them. It helped to remember that I was with a healthy person who wouldn't hurt me if he could avoid doing so. Even if he did, we have tools and God to deal with whatever comes. I can pray, let go of the outcome and trust that my Higher Power is taking care of me.

I see the positive and am grateful for what I have.

September 26

MASTURBATION

The experience was transcendental. I felt that I had tapped some secret, tabooed power which really ran the universe, but which was never acknowledged in the world...masturbation became a daily staple for me right away. – S.L.A.A. Basic Text, Page 3

Masturbation was never a problem for me, so I was surprised by the intense withdrawal when I gave it up for one month. Previously, I masturbated sometimes to help me sleep, sometimes to make myself feel better if I was upset or stressed out, and sometimes if I was feeling attracted to someone, which I always found exciting and ultimately very unsettling. Within the first month, I felt the difference. Masturbation wasn't a form of self-love for me, I only used it to avoid my feelings. I heard of other S.L.A.A. members doing an emotional check-in beforehand and being able to use it only to practice self-love. But for me, when the overwhelming craving hit, it was in reaction to personal conflict. So, I made it two months. At two months, my car broke down after buying groceries for an event I was hosting. My first thought wasn't to call a friend or a tow service. My immediate thought was, I need to masturbate now. Fortunately, I made an outreach call, prayed and got a tow. One year later, I decided to try masturbating again, but after three weeks of feeling foggy and not present, I put "no masturbation" on my list of bottom-line behaviors. Not everyone in S.L.A.A. needs to do this, but it is best for me.

With my Higher Power and sponsor's help, I set the bottom lines that are right for me.

September 27

RESPECTING OTHERS' PRIVACY

So it is that in a closed system each person comes to expend more and more energy riding herd on the other, even as less and less energy is received from a wider experiencing of life. To maintain their security this energy must be expended in riding herd on each other, making sure that neither will stray, so that no possible shortage of supply from each other will follow. - S.L.A.A. Basic Text, Page 143

It's normal to read my partner's journals to make sure he's not cheating on me, right? That's what my diseased mind told me about snooping. My sponsor told me that his business is none of my business and that I needed to stick to my side of the street. That didn't sound right to me. I thought partnership meant that if you weren't always in each other's business, you didn't care. That was just a rationalization for me to control the situation. I don't get to tell my partner how to live his life. He has his own Higher Power and gets to make his own decisions. If he chooses to tell me everything, that's great, but it's his choice. I get to experience my life with him by my side instead of ignoring what I need to do in order to follow him around. Following him around only leads to feeling desperate and insecure. Paying attention to my life builds self-esteem. My energy is best spent on improving the quality of my life and, as a consequence, our lives together.

I respect others' privacy today.

September 28

THE FIRST SIGN OF RECOVERY

We seek to develop a daily relationship with a Higher Power, knowing that we are not alone in our efforts to heal ourselves from our addiction. – S.L.A.A. Core Documents, "S.L.A.A. Signs of Recovery"

Why would I want to develop a daily relationship with something I didn't believe in? I came into the rooms of S.L.A.A., at the very least, agnostic. I went to meetings every day. I was also trying to quit smoking and drinking. That forced me to develop a relationship, because I had to say the prayers that everyone else was saying or risk looking stupid (horrible for a sex and love addict) or worse—to risk someone calling me out on it. So, I said the prayers, not believing them, and sometimes screaming rebellion in my thoughts. But the day I started to heal was when I started wondering if maybe my prayers could be heard by some kind of presence in the universe. Maybe all of these people holding hands and saying prayers together were a power that could heal. The person next to me was probably struggling with the God idea, too. I would talk to people after the prayer and get their methods of coming to believe in a Power greater than themselves. When I stuck around long enough, I finally got a relationship with a Higher Power and some sobriety.

I am healing through attending meetings, prayer and meditation.

September 29

SYNCHRONICITY

I continued to experience enticing situations which could have lured me back into the addictive quicksand. Among these was one more very serious trial concerning Sarah. The timing of this was so uncanny as to be particularly meaningful. - S.L.A.A. Basic Text, Page 36

Rich goes on to describe a situation where a friend of a qualifier asked for some assistance. He says, "The Devil himself could not have created a more tantalizing situation. Not only did it offer a chance for musical recognition, thus appealing to my professional ego, but [the friend] was beguilingly attractive." He found himself in a situation where it was a choice between staying sober and reconciling with his wife or trotting down the path of temptation and bad motives. One theory of synchronicity suggests that life is not made up of coincidences, but that a larger order governs even the most seemingly random events. If a triggering event was synchronous, I thought it meant I was supposed to stay in addiction. During withdrawal, I mistook running into my qualifier at the mall for synchronicity. My sponsor said, "There are no coincidences. God's got a plan. I don't need to understand it, I just need to say, thy will not mine be done.'" I need to pay attention to my Higher Power's will for me and ignore supposed signs that will lead me back to addictive behavior.

I live a life rooted in sobriety and rely on my Higher Power for continued clarity.

September 30

EMOTIONAL AFFAIRS

Sensing the danger of involvement, I tried to keep control by not sleeping with her. In spite of this, I became increasingly obsessed until the prospect of not seeing her was torment...I went into a state bordering on paralysis. The hook was already set very deeply. – S.L.A.A. Basic Text, Page 11

Sometimes our primary relationships have difficulties or we get bored. There may be that coworker who understands and is fun to be around. Society tells us in movies and television that it's okay, even exciting, to have that push-pull of an emotional affair. I used to think it was okay if we weren't getting physical, but emotional ties feed craving. Sex and love addicts in their disease crave attention. If we get it from the wrong source, it feeds shame and fear. Quite often this makes us lose control and cross the line into a physical affair. It's like the alcoholic putting a little whiskey in his milk at lunch. Just a little flirting couldn't hurt, right? Before you know it, we're drunk on love and acting out in sex addiction We may think, **I can control it because it's harmless,** but that's just the addict voice. We need to let our Higher Power in to guide us in our emotional lives. If there are difficulties in our relationship we should take them to our sponsor or fellows in S.L.A.A. instead of turning to the understanding, attractive person outside the relationship. Sobriety hangs in the balance.

My sponsor, fellows and my Higher Power guide me in my relationships today. I am not alone.

October 1

TRAUMA AND TRAGEDY

Frequently overcome with grief, loss and feelings of abandonment, I had few experiences which gave me a feeling that I was O.K., that I had value as the creature God had created.* – *S.L.A.A. Basic Text, Page 1

When life gets difficult, it can be hard to believe that a Higher Power exists and has our best interests at heart. For years in my addiction, I used the trauma of my boyfriend killing my best friend as an excuse to act out. Feelings of grief had to be numbed, not dealt with in a healthy way. God couldn't be relied upon if he would allow such a beautiful human being to be taken from this world. This created an anger at God that was hard to recover from. If I couldn't live the way I wanted to live, I didn't want to live. So, I became self-destructive in response to the tragedy. S.L.A.A. helped me realize that it wasn't God who killed my best friend, it was the guy I had chosen as my partner in life (for nine years). They taught me to pray and meditate to improve my conscious contact with my Higher Power. This made me more willing to believe that God didn't cause tragedy and he would help me through it.

Higher Power, support me through difficult times.

October 2

the JOURNAL

My story has been shared not purely for its ending but for its process. The writing of it is to let you know you are not alone and that there is hope. – S.L.A.A. Basic Text, Page 63

When I got sober, I had writer's block for ten years. In my childhood, I had big dreams of becoming a world-famous author. That didn't happen. But when I discovered ***the Journal*** (our "meeting in print"), I found new creativity and a sense of community. We weren't writing ***the Journal*** stories to impress some publisher, because the writing is anonymous. Writing to be of service and help other people by telling our stories is very healing. There are stories of sex and love addiction from all over the world. We see that everyone can have the same feelings that we have no matter where they live. Sometimes the stories tell us how to deal with problems that we are facing. Sometimes they remind us of where we've been and how far we've come in recovery. When traveling or unable to attend a meeting, I find words of wisdom and help within the pages of ***the Journal***.

Today, I heal by sharing my story with others.

October 3

SUPERSTITION

External challenges, especially those with psychic overtones, did occur, and we felt ourselves thrown back into having to devote all our energy, once again, to abstaining from addictive behavior...Yet we must say that, tenacious as the psychic hold may appear, it, too, does respond to the withdrawal process.* - *S.L.A.A. Basic Text, Page 111

This passage goes on to say, "Many of us have found, in S.L.A.A., that we needed to accept the possibility that psychic occurrences can happen, in order to make sense of some of these situations which seemed so uncanny. Even when we felt far removed from actual contact with a former addictive lover, such things happened as unexpected letters, or finding ourselves in settings with special meaning in the past relationship. These things could serve to catalyze, or charge up, a feeling of being psychically connected to our former addictive lover. Eventually we came to expect that we would continue to encounter a barrage of such experiences." My disease will grab ahold of anything to say my addictive lover and I were meant to be. The feeling that God put him in my path can be an opportunity for growth or an excuse that my disease uses to keep me sick. Part of living with sex and love addiction means accepting that triggers are all around us. The withdrawal process brings me back to reality and I realize that seeing my qualifier doesn't mean we're psychically linked, we just happen to be at the same place at the same time. I don't need to go back to the misery. Superstition is not my friend unless it prevents me from going back to my addiction.

Higher Power, allow me to see clearly today.

October 4

THE TENTH STEP

Continued to take personal inventory, and when we were wrong promptly admitted it. – S.L.A.A. Core Documents, "The Twelve Steps of S.L.A.A."

It's humiliating to promptly admit I'm wrong. I want to hide out for a few days and mutter an apology under my breath. But if I'm taking personal inventory every night, I can't avoid it like I used to. Writing down all of my anger and fears on paper forces me to take a realistic look at my behavior. Also, included in the writing is a list of my assets and things I'm grateful for. Funny how quickly I forget these things. But it wouldn't be a thorough personal inventory without them. I think "continued" is an important word here. I must make self-searching a regular habit. I promptly admit my faults keeping me honest and humble. This Step takes patience and persistence and understanding. If I can't understand my writing, I can take it to my sponsor to interpret. I usually find the right path to take to clean up my mess. Sometimes I find out that I handled something fairly well. Taking this Step helps me avoid the emotional hangover. If I clear out my fears and anger before they become too huge, I don't become physically ill over them. That alone makes this Step worthwhile to practice.

My daily inventory keeps me honest and humble.

October 5

PLAYING THE VICTIM

Whether we were victims or victimizers (and most of us were both), we had used the disturbed relationships about us for our own purposes, for obtaining the addictive payoff. Regardless of what others had done or failed to do, our own part in these relationships was riddled with dishonesty and manipulation of others, with willfulness and pride. – S.L.A.A. Basic Text, Page 90

I get attached to the story of my life, and a lot of that has to do with early abuse in my family. I hold onto that and I don't move on because I'm constantly reverting back to that victim. When I focus on that I'm in my disease and I'm not progressing. The more I do this, the more I leave myself open to being victimized by others. When I'm a victim, I'm isolated. I want sympathy but I don't want to do anything about it. I don't want to get into the solution and that keeps me in my addiction. When I know that I'm connected to a Power greater than me, I don't have to be a victim. I don't have to manipulate people or seek pity. I can be in the solution and I don't have to be alone. Sharing at meetings keeps me connected to other people who have been through the same experiences. To not play the victim, for me, is to live my life from a place of freedom and joy.

I take responsibility and concentrate on my recovery.

October 6

EXPLOITATION

As we looked at our current lives and at our past, we saw that virtually everything we did and everyone we knew was exploited to satisfy our addictive needs. – S.L.A.A. Basic Text, Page 80

If I were clearly exploiting someone and they stayed with me anyway, this fed my ego. I thought I was so important that people couldn't leave me even if I mistreated them. My addictive needs took over everything in my life. It was necessary to take advantage of whomever I could in order to get those needs met. In my twisted mind, I believed ill treatment made people stay. My mom used to say, "All men are dogs. That's why you have to treat them badly to get what you want." But when the tables turned and my love addiction forced me to take abuse, I finally saw how destructive exploitation is. It is an empty victory. When I got sober and started being of service to others, that huge ball of needs went away. I found it was more satisfying to treat people with respect and look for ways to help than to get everything I could and then throw them away. I stopped looking at people for what they could give me and saw them as human beings. The intimate honest partnership that I have today is much better than anything I gained from exploitation in the past.

I accept myself today without shame and choose personal growth.

October 7

SOCIAL STIGMA

We knew that our 'condition' of sex and love addiction was no less stigmatizable, in contemporary society, than alcoholism had been in the 1930's and 40's. – S.L.A.A. Basic Text, Page 122

I don't like the special stigma that is attached to sex and love addiction. It brings forth fear when a meeting is kicked out of a church because of our name. We even took on a pseudonym (Augustine Fellowship) to help out well-meaning members of society who wanted to rent meeting rooms to us but were afraid of the potential backlash. The fellows who wrote the Basic Text decided to do this "after considering that this would be a problem wherever [they] went." But in the 1930s, alcoholics were just as misunderstood and feared. Over the years, society learned more about alcoholism and saw people recover in A.A. I believe there will be the same kind of learning curve with S.L.A.A. And the more the membership grows, the less mystery is attached to the program. The more people who know someone who has "attended one of those meetings," the more the fear dissipates. Public outreach efforts will integrate S.L.A.A. into society the way it has done with Alcoholics Anonymous. Once people see how much S.L.A.A. has changed lives and brought families back together, they will want to support (or at least tolerate) the effort.

Today, I am responsible for deciding how, when and where I share about my disease.

October 8

MIDDLE GROUND

I had long since learned that for me one-night stands, pick-up bars, prostitutes and the like were all bummers, but I still hoped there was a happy middle ground in a liaison of a few months duration with no real commitment. – S.L.A.A. Basic Text, Page 262

My friends who were acting out either died or got into recovery. They realized how it affected their lives. I had a friend who thought he might be a sex and love addict. He was still going to bars even after he had been sober in A.A. for over six years, mainly to find partners to have sex. He got picked up in a bar and was murdered. That brought it home to me—my friend could still be living today if he'd gotten into recovery. This is a deadly disease; it does kill. I have to commit myself to my recovery. I have to turn it over to my Higher Power. I choose to be vulnerable. I have to open up and know that God is in my life and there's a plan for my life without addiction. When it comes to recovery, I'm either in it or I'm out. I could be on the edge for a long time, and this takes me to a jumping off place where I'm either going to work the Steps or die. I choose to stay in the rooms of S.L.A.A. and stop thinking there could be a middle ground.

I am silent when needed and feel comfortable in solitude.

October 9

NEUROPLASTICITY

I began working at my art again; I felt my brain returning...I took up jogging...I took formal instruction in Transcendental Meditation...Compulsion for somebody in my life to fix the pain has been lifted. And the pain underneath has been bearable. It is a healing pain that I endure because of the gift I have received from God – the first partnership I have ever formed. – S.L.A.A. Basic Text, Page 223

Neuroplasticity is a big word for the brain rewiring itself over a lifetime—it deletes the connections that are no longer necessary or useful and strengthens the ones that are. The brain decides this depending on life experiences and how recently connections have been used. Neurons can grow weak from underuse and die off. When we suffer trauma or injury, an uninjured part of the brain takes over for the damaged part. Depression and addiction make my brain work too hard. When I practice self-care every day, my brain will start rewiring itself for healthy actions instead of addictive ones. I remember drinking whiskey as a teenager and saying, "Whoops, killed another brain cell." I never realized that traumatic, dramatic relationships work the same way, only slower. I want to function to the best of my ability. Self-care and seeking God's will (in other words, sobriety) instead of mind-numbing behaviors, will help my brain learn to heal itself from all these years of addictive damage.

I practice self-care daily healing my mind, body and spirit.

October 10

ADVERSITY

Some of us suspected that God had been the architect of many a painful, growth-fostering situation we had encountered along the course of our sobriety, or at least had allowed these to occur. Only gradually did we see that in God's scheme of things, these difficulties might have been permitted in order to spur our awareness of our own finite nature, thereby rendering us ready to further our relationship with God. – S.L.A.A. Basic Text, Page 99

Sobriety doesn't necessarily help me avoid problems or prevent them (although I don't find myself in nearly as many dangerous situations as I used to), but it does help me walk through adversity with grace instead of numbing out in addiction to escape problems. My reaction to adversity in the past was to run from it (usually to the arms of a dangerous man) and to feel that I'm doomed. Fate was never my friend before sobriety. Whenever problems arose I went straight to negative thinking. If the kitchen sink backed up, "See, God really does hate me" was my immediate response. Today, I realize that my Higher Power loves me and as long as I stay close, together we can handle anything that happens. I never liked the idea that God would allow difficulties in my life in order to help me grow. Suffering should not be part of my God's plan. But getting through suffering with God's help has given me more faith and hope than I had in the days of my addiction. Adversity has helped me grow. I may never understand God's reasoning, all I know is that I am now stronger and more able to handle situations that used to baffle me.

Higher Power, help me face life's adversities.

October 11

RIGHT-SIZED

We often found ourselves feeling entitled to being treated in a particular way and trying to coerce others to meet our own exalted standards. Or we were aroused by what seemed to be the machinations of others, feeling that we were being victimized. The simple truth was that when our own spiritual condition was less than solid, everyone around us seemed to be "sick" with a malaise which, upon reflection, was remarkably like our own! – S.L.A.A. Basic Text, Page 97

I spent a lot of time before recovery trying to get "adoring fans," but knowing in my heart that I didn't deserve them. Whenever things didn't go my way, I wallowed in my victimhood. S.L.A.A. taught me how to be right-sized. People would laugh at my insane ideas when I shared at a meeting. I would get flustered and angry and feel like the meetings weren't for me. But, over time, I realized I was being delusional and that others were identifying. When I took my ego out of it, I gained a level of humility. Trying to coerce others to meet our own exalted standards takes a lot of time and mental energy., and it's not real anyway. Today, I let the chips fall where they may. This is saying that I have trust and faith in God's will above my own. When I concentrate on finding God's will instead of my paranoid perception of the machinations of others, I stay right-sized according to reality, rather than the drama going on in my head.

With humility, I remain right-sized in body, mind and spirit.

October 12

EMOTIONALLY UNAVAILABLE

All my life I either seduced people with my intellect or seduced them with my body. I never seemed to know what real emotional intimacy was...I was so emotionally dishonest I could not admit even to myself what I really felt. – S.L.A.A. Basic Text, Page 164

I felt like I was outside of my body, floating around the room in social or stressful situations. If there's danger ahead, it can be a good thing to be able to get lost in fantasy. But if you're at an intimate dinner and you're constantly checking the door to see who comes in next, it's putting up emotional barriers. I told myself that I just needed to know what was going on. If my partner complained, I quickly jumped into bed. Seduction was my go-to tool. But this just allowed me to run from my feelings. I couldn't live in the moment and be present and vulnerable. I was predicting the future or trying to fix the past. I thought feelings would overwhelm and kill me. Whenever anyone tried to drag feelings out of me, anger would well up inside. I had thoughts of hitting and screaming at my therapist in the beginning of my recovery. I finally had to confront my emotional unavailability in my Fourth Step. The Fifth Step forced me to become vulnerable and admit everything to my sponsor and God. The rest of the Steps helped clear out many of the barriers to emotional availability.

I live in the present, allowing myself to be vulnerable and trustworthy.

October 13

THE EIGHTH CHARACTERISTIC

We become immobilized or seriously distracted by romantic or sexual obsessions or fantasies. – S.L.A.A. Core Documents, "Characteristics of Sex and Love Addiction"

I felt like I was paralyzed. I remember staring at my computer screen at work, on the phone with my qualifier, unable to leave my desk. He kept me on the phone for an hour. The plan was to visit my sister for the weekend, but he didn't want me to go. I knew it was his disease making him unable to breathe without me, without his "fix." He was a sex addict in the program also. My disease told me to stay with him in town. I had enough recovery to leave for my sister's. I was so distracted, that when I backed out of my parking space, I got into a car accident. "She came out of nowhere and was going too fast" didn't cut it with the insurance company. Later, when my qualifier and I broke up, I got in another car accident because I thought I saw him standing on the street. When I ran into him at a meeting years later, I was proud of myself for not talking to him, but as soon as I left the meeting, I got a traffic ticket for not paying attention to the road signs. Recovery has helped my concentration. As long as I don't swing the door open for obsessions and fantasies, I can lead a fairly responsible, happy life.

I live my life one day at a time.

October 14

SPIRITUALITY

The possibility of finding some form of faith, based not on any specific conception of "God" but rather on a need to find such a faith, was the beginning of spiritual healing. – S.L.A.A. Basic Text, Page 75

Spirituality focuses on personal growth with a Power greater than ourselves. I like that S.L.A.A. suggested finding spirituality rather than saying, "You need a specific religion." People like me run from religion all the time. My addict intellect will grab at any excuse to run from hard work or pain. Growth is painful. But finding spirituality helped me stay in S.L.A.A. and grow. It's a daily practice. I see others in meetings who used to be atheist or agnostic and I believe them when they say a spiritual life works for them. I hear people say that prayer and meditation got them through some really difficult experiences without losing their sobriety. We see proof in the rooms of people who lived insane lives before S.L.A.A. and have now found happy and healthy lives. They credit the Twelve Steps and finding a faith that works for them. Prayer and meditation transform my life—a life I wouldn't have without S.L.A.A. and a daily practice to keep me in faith.

Through daily practice, my spirituality is growing.

October 15

CONFUSION

I couldn't tell anyone who I REALLY was, and was confused behind the façade. Sex was a way of "stopping the clock," a place to go when the rest of the world was too much. - S.L.A.A. Basic Text, Page 245

Addictive distractions and being an actor on the stage of life, presenting who we wanted to be in the world instead of showing our true selves, creates confusion that is difficult to break free of. When I hid out in sex, it may have "stopped the clock" for a little while, but ended up creating more confusion because I was with unavailable partners. Hearing him say, "I have to get back to my partner," after just having sex is hard to reconcile in this addict's mind. Caught between relief and guilt, I can't see the reality of the situation. In my acting-out days, I walked around trying to understand my predicament. Why did I keep acting this way when it brought me so much pain? The distraction of "I want that now" makes it impossible for me to stay present to myself and my responsibilities. Without a Higher Power to give my troubles to and to ask for answers, I float around the world on the wind. I can't pin down any idea that will make my life peaceful and give me serenity and sobriety. S.L.A.A. and Higher Power showed me the way out of my confusion and I have chosen to stay there ever since.

Today, I take my thoughts to my Higher Power and ask for understanding and patience.

October 16

RETREATS AND WORKSHOPS

In new sobriety we found that along with the task of staying away from addictive activities, we had the equally difficult task of filling up all that free time. We needed to have a lot of time alone, to give feelings a chance to surface, but we also needed to keep busy. – S.L.A.A. Basic Text, Page 140

Retreats and workshops were a great chance to let feelings surface while keeping busy. Our Intergroup's workshops were always held at a gorgeous retreat center in the hills. It had a reflection pool, fountains, an olive garden and lots of places to meditate. Going to an S.L.A.A. workshop all day on a Saturday was not my favorite idea for filling up free time. I rarely looked forward to delving into the S.L.A.A. topics that the workshops were based on. This was just contempt prior to investigation. But sitting and looking out over a beautiful landscape while I thought and wrote about my S.L.A.A. issues really helped me get to know myself and my disease. There was a sense of spirituality in that environment. Bringing my writing back to the group solidified my place in the program and helped me get and stay sober. Retreats were a longer period of time to get to know other members of S.L.A.A. as well as spend time in reflection and meditation.

I spend my time today on healthy, top-line activities.

October 17

THREE-SECOND RULE

We were working at standing still, at freeing ourselves from the tentacled clasp of a frightful addiction which had driven us to such a pitch of self-destroying activity. Simply not doing it took tremendous effort. We were suspending, for the moment, our very real fears concerning the outcome of all this...we were discovering that there was a joy to be had in successfully negotiating our way through each twenty-four hour period.* - *S.L.A.A. Basic Text, Page 109

I implemented and used the three-second rule right away in early withdrawal. It was the only way that I could relieve myself of the obsessive thoughts. It was a great tool to use again and again. I still use this tool when needed, and it has been one of the most useful tools of recovery for me. Once the thoughts start and I notice them, I allow the thoughts for a maximum of three seconds and then move on to other thoughts or tasks. When obsessive thoughts come booming into my mind, I visualize throwing them into the trash can right away because they are garbage thoughts. Sometimes, this tool needs to be used over and over in a day, especially during early withdrawal. This is one of my favorite tools and helps me to maintain my sanity, and allows me to not obsess about others and keep the focus on myself and my own recovery.

I am powerless over this disease and look for my Higher Power's guidance.

October 18

EMOTIONAL ANOREXIA

We endeavor to stop acting out a pattern of sex and love anorexia...We have found, no matter how different or alone we feel, that reaching out to others—to give help and to ask for it—helps us to recover from our anorexia. - from the "Anorexia: Social, Sexual, Emotional" pamphlet

We anorexics often view the world in extremes. Extreme fear. Extreme pain. Excruciating loneliness. We want so much to connect with people, but are so afraid that we are going to be deeply hurt. So, we isolate and end up hurting ourselves repeatedly. We have walled ourselves off and it feels like there is no escaping this prison in which we find ourselves. But as we share, little by little, in the rooms, a crack starts to appear in our insurmountable walls. We peer through the crack and see our fellow travelers in S.L.A.A. smiling and accepting us. How can that be? We were vulnerable. We brace for the rejection and hurt, but we are not rejected. People talk to us after the meeting. They encourage us. Ever so slowly we risk a little more at each meeting. Our walls start to crumble and the slivers of sunlight come streaming through, warming us and beckoning us to venture out. We start to feel a growing confidence that even if someone did hurt us, we could turn to our new friends for support. We now feel safe surrounded by people who love us unconditionally and let us love them back. Finally, we are free to be who we always wanted to be.

Today, I am courageously loving and find fellowship among others.

October 19

REJECTION

B. was trapped by his sex and love addiction into thinking that if only he were reunited with his lover, his world would be alright. When she rejected him, he shot himself in such a way that he would be propelled out a window on the top floor of a ten-story building. – S.L.A.A. Basic Text, Page 219

Rejection is God's protection. When my qualifier rejected me after all that I had done to be with him, I felt my mind snap. I ran around doing crazy things to try to make him stay. If I hadn't had the years of working the S.L.A.A. Program of recovery and my fellows who supported me and pulled me out of that insanity, I would have killed myself. I thought my qualifier's love was the only thing that would save me in this world. Higher Power had a better plan for my life. That is what rejection is. Before the program, I could never date soberly and take it slow because of the fear of rejection. When I finally got sober and started attempting to date, and people said, "No," I shut down and didn't want to ask anyone else out. I cried for two days. No one else seemed to have this reaction. I took it personally, when it really wasn't. It's not about the other person. It's about how I feel toward myself. I reject myself and continually beat myself up. My Higher Power accepts me for who I am, and I don't have to be or do anything. When people reject me, it's not necessarily a bad thing. If someone doesn't want to engage with me then maybe we aren't right for each other and I can avoid a harmful situation. I can spend more time with friends who know and like the real me rather than wasting time pursuing people who aren't interested.

My Higher Power accepts me unconditionally.

October 20

OBJECTIFICATION

The objects of my passion were seen entirely in terms of their ability to fulfill my NEEDS. They were defined by how well they functioned in this way. They were functions, not human beings. – S.L.A.A. Basic Text, Page 47

I have a friend who reminds me that people are not vending machines. Ah, if they were. If we could only arrange them on stage and produce the show the way we want to. There would be no need for my anorexia. I remember how shocked I was when I heard men share in S.L.A.A. and realized that they had pain to deal with just like me. Or my partner would express feelings and I would realize that he's a lot like me. My sponsor tells me that people have their own thoughts and ideas and they may not do things the way I would do them. Agreeing to disagree was never good enough for me. I had to twist everything to fit my idea of perfection. If I couldn't do that easily, I moved on to the next person who I thought would give it to me. I rationalized bad behavior with an attitude of "Why not have multiple partners if one can't give me everything I need?" My addict needs were always unrealistic and exaggerated. Even a robot couldn't fulfill them. How could I expect a human being to? People are not objects to be used or abused. We all suffer, selling ourselves short, when reducing sexual love to a spiritually disconnected state of supply and demand.

I respect myself as I am, and I respect others as they are.

October 21

PEER PRESSURE

As we read our own version of what had happened [our 5th Step] we could often see through our excuses and our need to blame others; we clearly saw the progression of our spiritual malady and how "convenient" our memories could be in seeking to minimize our roles in our more painful debacles. - S.L.A.A. Basic Text, Page 79

The day that peer pressure changed for me was when I walked into a meeting of S.L.A.A. and saw that the "cool" people were the ones with sobriety. They weren't running around doing crazy stuff to impress others. People admired them because they refrained from acting out. They ran from peers who would pressure them into going to a strip club or picking up a one-night stand. I used to blame peer pressure for my acting out. "They made me do it" used to be a good excuse in my mind, but is a clear sign of my sex and love addiction. If I'm harming myself to impress others, then my love addiction is out of control. Today, I avoid anyone who glamorizes acting out and gravitate toward those who have serenity. If I find they have a hidden motive to find an acting-out partner or someone to justify their addictive behavior, I run. My Fourth and Fifth Steps revealed that I can't continue to blame these people if I'm just as sick as them and I continue to stick around for diseased behavior (mine and theirs). It helps us both if I walk away from the situation and seek sobriety.

Today, I lift myself up with positive energy, while engaging in sober behaviors.

October 22

REALITY

During our active addiction, we had been the embodiment of sickness, tainting reality for all those who came in contact with us. Our spiritual, emotional, mental, and sometimes physical disease had contaminated even those relationships which could otherwise have been healthy. – S.L.A.A. Basic Text, Page 92

Addiction can be a futile attempt to escape the pain of our lives—that pain being reality. I would twist reality with lies that I told myself and others. In recovery, we learn that reality will not kill us, but it can be the source of a lot of suffering. Addiction is a self-centered attempt to escape. However, walking through pain is essential to moving beyond an addictive lifestyle. Accepting reality is the first step to dealing with the pain. Making amends brings our addict behavior into reality. We no longer get lost in fantasies or rationalization. Trusting our Higher Power to carry us through our struggles in life becomes our reality. Although real life is not free from suffering and problems, recovery gives us the tools we need to deal with the pain and live in the solution. Whenever there is tension and unhappiness, we are either given relief or we come to acceptance. One essential tool is honesty with ourselves and others which helps us find the truth. That truth is a bridge to a new freedom, a life free from addiction, a life of sobriety.

Truth is a bridge to freedom.

October 23

THE TENTH TRADITION

S.L.A.A. has no opinion on outside issues; hence the S.L.A.A. name ought never be drawn into public controversy.
- S.L.A.A. Core Documents, "The Twelve Traditions"

I might really hate the candidate for president who isn't in my party but I keep that to myself when sharing at a meeting. If a newcomer came in and heard me ranting about politics they might run from the conflict or use it as an excuse to say no one in the program has recovery. Or I might make a fellow sufferer worry about the state of the nation and they might use that as an excuse to act out. I try to focus my shares on experience, strength and hope. If I can't do that, I get current. I avoid wasting my time on global issues that I can't fix in a three-minute share (the courage to change the things I can). We don't have specialty groups that have any outside affiliation (Tradition Three). A.A. learned from its predecessors' mistakes that if you associate your groups with a movement and that movement fails, the fellowship fails. If we take sides on an issue, we waste our time mired in controversy instead of going about the business of recovery.

I maintain a pillar of dignity for myself and others.

October 24

ROMANTIC CLICHÉS

This condition of being relatively unencumbered by the left-over repercussions of our active sex and love addiction meant that any new sexual or romantic situation could carry a lot of novelty along with it. We had to be careful not to get carried away with this. Beyond the unavoidable and exciting "newness" in a beginning relationship, especially those carrying the possibility of physical and emotional intimacy, we could not build a partnership on novelty. – S.L.A.A. Basic Text, Page 155

The simple definition of cliché is something that has been used so often that it is no longer effective or interesting. That's what happened with my love life living as a homosexual. All my relationships were the same—just different faces. A new face always held promise for a better relationship but would soon fall flat. Romance was always the central focus of my life, so how could it avoid becoming a cliché? I dreamed of having the life of the romance novel or romantic movies, but ended up with abusive partners. The clichés became a way of escaping into fantasy, a way of coping with the misery of life and my shame. The bad clichés like "we are all promiscuous" found their way into my life, too. Jumping around to so many different relationships left me vulnerable to this. I turned into a person that I never wanted to be. S.L.A.A. helped me see reality and throw away the clichés for an open, honest and therefore intimate relationship that teaches me new things every day and helps me grow.

Higher Power, help me cultivate self-honesty by paying attention to my thoughts and actions.

October 25

HOME GROUP

The formality of having a regularly scheduled S.L.A.A. meeting, even if only two are present, can lead to a deepening sense of personal commitment in furthering the recognition of sex and love addiction by others who need to withdraw from it. – S.L.A.A. Basic Text, Page 121

What is the most comfortable environment you can think of? What makes it comfortable to you? Do you prefer the presence of many friends, or a small circle of close confidants? Do you prefer to be in a setting where people meet your comments with skepticism, or where your opinions are valued and respected? When we set out to find the right Twelve Step group for us, these may be important factors to consider. It's important that the group we end up at meets our needs. We might not have much choice in where we attend if there is only one group in our area. We may have to adjust to slightly uncomfortable circumstances in the interest of our recovery. If we place personalities before principles, it may be part of our Higher Power's plan for us to learn how to communicate and understand others. Eventually, we become more comfortable and identify with our fellows more than we notice the differences. One day, we may find that we are able to more freely express ourselves when at meetings. It is at that moment that we realize we are home.

I grow my sobriety when I express my true self among peers.

October 26

HEREDITARY PATTERNS

I was raised in a relatively "normal" family. There was no substance abuse, no physical abuse, no sexual abuse. Yet the feelings I grew up with are very similar to those of the people I have heard in S.L.A.A. who grew up in a much more obviously troubled environment. – S.L.A.A. Basic Text, Page 210

The above share goes on to say, "My mother was a strong-willed, hot-tempered woman who found it easy to criticize but difficult to offer praise or reassurance." I'm not debating nature versus nurture. But through S.L.A.A. and years of therapy, I was able to see how my parents and their parents didn't have the tools to deal with emotions and feelings in a healthy way either. They had all the same stuff I had. What I had previously thought normal was well-hidden addiction and emotional problems. They were just more skilled at hiding it and swapping addictions than I was. Ways of approaching relationships can be handed down from generation to generation. We learn from our parents how to act in the world (or at least how we don't want to act). If we see them having affairs or unable to show affection, we are affected. We may replay these messages well into adulthood. We may believe their negative views on society and life. But we can change our lives with the help of a Higher Power, the Twelve Steps and S.L.A.A.

Working the Twelve Steps keeps me sober and consistently helps me create new, healthy relationships.

October 27

THE EIGHTH SIGN OF RECOVERY

We begin to accept our imperfections and mistakes as part of being human, healing our shame and perfectionism while working on our character defects. – S.L.A.A. Core Documents, "S.L.A.A. Signs of Recovery"

A character of the typical addict has often been described as an "egomaniac with an inferiority complex." Some of us grow up with a skewed perspective of our own personal worth, while putting on a show for the people around us, trying to appear as though we have it all put together. In reality, we may hold ourselves to impossible standards, and then beat ourselves up when we fall short of our expectations. It is only a matter of time before the façade crumbles around us. With the Twelve Step process, our perspective can be realigned. Our fellows in the program can help us to take an objective view of ourselves and others. When we recognize that people are flawed, we can forgive our own imperfections and even come to love ourselves for them. This is where the healing process can begin. We no longer need be ashamed of who we are. We can take pride in our imperfection, knowing we are exactly who we are supposed to be.

Higher Power, help me recognize myself and others as perfectly imperfect.

October 28

DISHONESTY

I could not be honest because, love her or not, I really needed her. She was the security on which I depended for my ability to function. Being honest about the true scope of my feelings was not, and could not be, an option. – S.L.A.A. Basic Text, Page 87

Sex and love addiction made me lie to myself and others for most of my life. I believed that song that said, "All I need is the air that I breathe and to love you." To this addict, their love was the air that I needed to stay alive. In a closed relationship like that, it's impossible to state one's needs or to gamble on letting the chips fall where they may when we make mistakes. I spent a lot of time trying to cover up mistakes, lying, and hiding the real me. I wanted to stay in the immaturity of avoiding responsibility and never deal with the consequences of my actions. My constant need for "good sex" and adoration made me make a lot of mistakes. It was difficult for me to have any sense of self-esteem when I was changing myself to fit what other people wanted instead of standing up and being real. I even did it for years in S.L.A.A. But when I finally started opening up and sharing honestly and consequently falling apart in a meeting, I began to build a strong foundation for dignity and sobriety.

I am authentic today and take responsibility for the consequences of my actions.

October 29

ESTRANGEMENT

One by one such things as satisfaction in our work, friends and social activities dropped away…We had lost control over the rate or frequency (or both) at which we would seek the romantic or sexual "solution" to life's ills. – S.L.A.A. Basic Text, Page 69

Most addicts are no stranger to isolation. Estrangement takes it a step further. We are no longer on friendly terms with the social group that we built with our partner. Our former lover wants nothing to do with us. If estrangement occurred because of our acting out, we carry a heavy burden of guilt as well. In recovery, we clear away the wreckage of the past. We ask ourselves, what was my part in the dissolution of the partnership? What can I now do differently? It takes time, but if we do the Twelve Steps and stick to the principles of the program, people see the changes in us and some let us back into their social circle. Sometimes reconciliation with a former spouse or lover occurs. If we stick to our side of the street and are careful to stay on solid spiritual ground, we find our lives opening up in ways we never imagined. We regain the respect of ourselves and others. We no longer have to hide out in addiction. We have a community in S.L.A.A. that helps us have a community in the world.

I connect with others in my recovery community today.

October 30

GRIEVING

I was caught in a swirl of unrelenting grief. Weight loss, lack of sleep, loss of appetite, vomiting, and thoughts of suicide were my constant companions. – S.L.A.A. Basic Text, Page 5

Anything can be a loss—a death, losing a relationship or losing a job. As addicts, we often run from the pain of grief. Numbing-out behaviors are more easily rationalized when someone indispensable dies or leaves. If we have no sense of self (as is the case with most sex and love addicts), grieving can be catastrophic. Instead of a healthy process of letting go, for active addicts it can be self-destructive and narcissistic. I used loss as an excuse to plunge into negative thinking and desperation. I ran from the painful stages of grieving by acting out and so I never reached the final stage, acceptance. It was never acceptable that anyone would leave, even if it wasn't their fault. My first instinct was to replace the loss. I found another lover or someone special. But that was a fantasy—they could never live up to my expectations. Without processing my feelings, no one would ever be able to bring me out of my depression. In S.L.A.A., I can share about my grief and get support. I can avoid the mistake of trying to replace the loss or numb out over it. I can feel my pain and come to acceptance eventually.

I allow myself to grieve when I experience a loss.

October 31

GUILT

Now we were truly feeling some sense of deep release from the past! We were free of much guilt for our misdeeds, from the shame of having fallen short of our inner values. [We allowed] our own personal wholeness to take root and grow. – S.L.A.A. Basic Text, Page 95

Reflecting on the past was not serene before S.L.A.A. I was too busy beating myself up for what I had done. No one would forgive me, so why even try to apologize? I would end up doing something I regretted and beat myself up even more. I was caught in a vicious cycle of guilt and shame. When I tried to bury or ignore the feelings, they would come up at inconvenient times whenever a memory was triggered. Through many long and thorough Fourth and Fifth Steps and much sharing with fellows, I have cleared out enough of the guilt to experience a release from the chokehold of the past. The Eighth and Ninth Steps helped me realize that some of what I thought unforgivable can be forgiven. S.L.A.A. helped me realize that instead of being uniquely flawed, I was pretty much human and others had made similar mistakes. Guilt didn't have to haunt me forever unless I chose to stay in it. Now that I know the truth, the only reason I would choose to stay in it would be because my addict wants to put me in a position to act out. This idea reminds me to work through and release regretful feelings as soon as possible.

My Fourth Step Inventory reminds me that I am wonderfully human.

November 1

THE ELEVENTH STEP

Sought through prayer and meditation to improve our conscious contact with a Power greater than ourselves, praying only for knowledge of God's will for us and the power to carry that out. – S.L.A.A. Core Documents, "The Twelve Steps of S.L.A.A."

Prayer and meditation were difficult for me. I said the prayers that others in the program told me to say. But I didn't believe them. I must have said the Serenity Prayer a thousand times before I even thought any part of it could come true for me. Meditation was less about asking God than it was about asking myself what I was going to do later that day. But with practice and faith, I was able to gain a conscious contact with a Power greater than myself. It wasn't so conscious at first. It was more like a kid asking Santa Claus for presents. But the more I read about the Eleventh Step and listened in meetings, the more I knew that it had to be about humility. What does God want for me? If I discover that, what can I do to help it happen? At first I resisted, fearing that a Higher Power would take away my fun or that I wouldn't have the strength to maintain a sober lifestyle. But constant prayer and meditation give me the strength and insight to handle whatever comes.

Higher Power, give me the strength to carry out your will.

November 2

PERFECTIONISM

Two prevailing defects which many of us experienced were perfectionism and pride. Even as we failed to control our petty selfishness or chronic procrastination day after day—were less than "perfect"—we saw that we were learning how to accept progress, rather than perfection! If we could not always be proud of the results of our efforts to change, at least we had earned the right to respect ourselves for the efforts themselves. – S.L.A.A. Basic Text, Page 89

I was a competitive gymnast as a child and if I couldn't get the gold medal every time, I didn't want to participate. Depression took over and I wouldn't practice. Most people want to do their best but my perfectionism made me chase after it to the detriment of my sanity. I would try to do everything perfectly and if I fell short I would beat up on myself mercilessly. Progress is slow and steady. Perfectionism is quick and easy, at least in theory. No one really is perfect. It's an impossible goal to attain. I had to accept that I'm a human being with faults and I will make mistakes. I only get to be perfect in God's eyes, even with my mistakes. With the help of S.L.A.A., I found the unconditional love that I had always been seeking and realized that I could be me, flaws and all.

I am patient with my progress today, accepting my gifts of imperfection.

November 3

VALUES

The brave new worlds of morality where "anything goes" because "nothing matters" boomeranged, leaving us grasping for some residual sense of meaning or reality in life. – S.L.A.A. Basic Text, Page 69

Values and self-respect were characteristics I didn't possess when I was in the depths of my addiction. My outside appearance gave the impression I had them, but when I was acting out or planning in my fantasies to act out, then my values and self-respect went out the window. There was no sense of meaning or purpose to my life. Seeking the next high was empty and the emotional hangovers cut into my self-respect. Walking into the rooms of S.L.A.A., getting a sponsor and doing the Steps changed all of that. Today, I have values and decency inside and out. I have learned to match my insides and outsides through S.L.A.A. Doing the right thing and the next right thing is a way of life for me today.

Higher Power, give me keen perception and understanding that responsibility starts within.

November 4

HUMAN NEEDS

After we were sober a while, we began to name this need which drove us into more and more desperate and hopeless sexual/romantic situations: the need for our lives to have meaning. Having a steady income could be important, having a creative outlet was a pleasure, having mutually supportive friendships was essential. But none of these things gave our lives meaning the way we craved meaning. – S.L.A.A. Basic Text, Page 141

Acting out can often feel (and be rationalized) as if driven by a powerful, unconscious urge for basic human needs: the need for freedom, the right to feel, the right to experience, the right to love. These basic human rights have been denied, and still are denied to many people in many ways, in many families and in many cultures. In reality, my right to practice free love or seek unadulterated pleasure will not save the world. In my active addiction, my deeply driven need for sexual and emotional freedom was a fantasy that justified a lot of selfish behavior. It was destroying everything good and supportive in my life. People didn't trust me and I almost lost my job from acting out. I do have the right to sobriety and recovery from the inhumane oppression of my internal addiction. My more human needs like shelter, dignity and love are met in recovery.

It is okay to express my genuine needs and wants.

November 5

GENDER ROLES

We needed to see the motives behind the roles we played and the image we presented, to understand the payoffs we had derived from our addiction. – S.L.A.A. Basic Text, Page 79

I was such a tomboy growing up. My parents would get frustrated because I wanted the toys that "only boys should play with." I wouldn't go near my sister's dolls or makeup. Always the rebel, I refused to fit into the pretty little girl role they tried to assign me. I saw women being mistreated and I refused the partner and mother role as soon as I was able. Refusing to fit into the gender roles that society assigned made me feel like an outsider. When I came to S.L.A.A. and found others like me, I realized I didn't have to feel so alone anymore. That allowed me to look at my motives behind rejecting society's gender roles. I didn't want to be abused and I thought if I "acted like a man" I could have the power in relationships. But I kept choosing abusive men. My addict kept me in that addictive cycle. Today, after working all Twelve Steps, I know I don't have to fit into a role to be accepted by my fellows in S.L.A.A. I have many feminine ***and*** masculine aspects to my personality and can accept myself as I am. If others are uncomfortable that I don't fit into society's mold, that's their issue to deal with and God be with them.

I embrace and unconditionally accept my new normal.

November 6

FAMILY DISAPPROVAL

I was therefore determined to be the super kid; I would do no wrong. But occasionally my frustration at not being able to earn my father's approval would be unleashed in explosive temper tantrums. When I left home and tried to function on my own, I discovered how handicapped I was by this deep emotional dependence. – S.L.A.A. Basic Text, Page 196

It's natural for children to seek the approval of those closest to them. As a child, family disapproval can mean we won't get our basic needs met (being sent to bed without dinner for example). If disapproval makes me numb out in addict behaviors, especially as an adult, instead of helping me find a sense of myself, then I need help sorting through the mess of feelings. S.L.A.A. helped me do that. My sponsor saw that I was enmeshed, so the next stage to freedom from the need for my family's approval was to separate from them for thirty days. I had to rely on my own thoughts and feelings to see what I really wanted in my life instead of using them as a gauge for my behavior. These actions helped me see that if I was doing something good for myself, I needed to keep doing it, even if my family disapproved. Disapproval does not mean death. They still loved me anyway. If they didn't, that was an issue for them to work out, not me. When I stay sober, my family approves of me more and more.

I develop a greater sense of self-worth daily, while letting go of seeking approval.

November 7

SELF-SEEKING

We were right that a meaningful life is one filled with love but we had distorted that meaning with selfishness, seeking only to "get" rather than to "give," to "rip off" rather than to contribute. There could be no enduring meaning in "love" that was a rapid consumption commodity on an open market
– S.L.A.A. Basic Text, Page 141

We are often self-seeking because we are so fearful. In trying to protect ourselves from being hurt, that inward focus on ourselves made us lose perspective and consequently connection with others In trying to get our needs met, our self-seeking was so blind, that we ended up driving others away. This left us even more lonely and desperate. Self-seeking is a lonely pursuit. We can feel so damaged and worthless that we have to aggressively seek to have our needs met. The only seeking we need to do is to seek our Higher Power God loves us unconditionally. All we have to do is ask for help We soon realize that when we seek our Higher Power, our self is taken care of much better than we could ever do alone. We can ask God and others to help us be more useful in doing God's will Self-seeking does slip away when we strengthen our conscious contact with a Higher Power.

Higher Power, enlarge my spiritual life through prayer and meditation.

November 8

JOURNALING

Another defense against these unnerving onslaughts was sustaining awareness by starting and keeping a list of very short observations of exactly how we were feeling...we did not edit out any negative sentiments. – S.L.A.A. Basic Text, Page 111

Journaling started for me with my Fourth Step and inventories. But today, I read a part of a meditation book or some literature from S.L.A.A. or other Twelve Step literature—I write summaries and read them to my sponsor and I talk about how it applies to my life. It's helped me to grow in recovery and feel closer to my Higher Power and my sponsor. Sometimes I just write resentment inventories or fear inventories or whatever's on my mind. Getting the swirling thoughts down on paper makes them stand still so I can look at them. When they're loose in my head I can't shine the light of reality on them. If I'm dealing with a particular problem I write about that. It's been key to my recovery to journal every day. When I don't do it, I feel the difference. I start to get moody or depressed or worried.

I journal daily, shining the light of awareness on any dark corners of my mind.

November 9

THE TWELFTH CHARACTERISTIC

We assign magical qualities to others. We idealize and pursue them, then blame them for not fulfilling our fantasies and expectations. – S.L.A.A. Core Documents, "Characteristics of Sex and Love Addiction"

As soon as I began the withdrawal process from my sex addiction, I discovered something called love addiction. One person in particular, a married coworker, was my primary source of emotional stability. I told her on a regular basis how perfect she was. I relied on her to make me feel good about myself. This dependence was just as dangerous as my addiction to sex. I was greatly disillusioned when, inevitably, the flaws began to appear in the idol I had constructed. One careless, drunken night, I wrote her a letter detailing how emotionally destroyed I was when she did not live up to my expectations. In return, she said, "I am not responsible for, nor am I capable of, making you feel better." It was a harsh but true statement. I cannot rely on any one individual to get my needs met. No one is capable of being anything and everything to me. Today, I see people for what they truly are: flawed individuals just like me. To acknowledge this is to take one more step out of fantasy and into reality.

Today, I forgive the mistakes made by myself and others.

November 10

PREDATORY BEHAVIOR

Accessory behaviors include the strategies I have used to obtain partners or materials for acting out. They are warning signs, obsessions and rituals that may precede an episode of acting out or "acting in." – S.L.A.A. Basic Text, Page 108

My sponsor told me to write "watch predatory behavior and flirting" on my bottom lines list. I thought my behavior was normal. These are behaviors that may not necessarily be a slip, but ones that I need to be very careful around. Predatory behavior can sneak up on me and I'm doing it before I'm aware of it. When I have the thought that I'm attracted to a newcomer, I might approach them to be helpful, not knowing that my ulterior motive is to steal attention from them to feed my ego. This is dangerous ground that could eventually lead to Thirteenth-Stepping if I don't stay aware of my motives. Flirting is similar. I must be sure I'm doing it with an available person for the purpose of dating and not to obtain some kind of self-serving reward. In the beginning of my recovery, there were many other predatory behaviors that I engaged in. I drove by the neighborhood, dressed in provocative clothing, had conversations with an erotic subtext, etc. This kept me acting out for years. I started writing down a list of these behaviors and this kept me vigilant. Finally, the tide started to turn and I was able to stay sober.

I grow daily in personal awareness, looking objectively at my thoughts and behaviors.

November 11

LUST

The depression lifted, as the excitement and deception and intrigue took over my life. It was a rollercoaster of fear and lust, but the thrill of secret adventure and new lovers was somehow satisfying, and I did not want to stop. – S.L.A.A. Basic Text, Page 165

In my acting-out days, my fellows viewed lust as a good thing. We had a "lust for life." It had the reputation in my religion as a grave sin and that was just another reason for me to avoid religion altogether. Why not just call it desire? It's defined as sexual desire. When it reaches a certain level, it receives the status of lust. That level is the point where we're consumed by the search for lovers (or the need to have sex with a particular person). The point at which it reaches addiction is when it blows up everything in our lives and we just can't stop obsessing. I rationalized that I didn't want to stop because the excitement eased my depression and I still had a job so it didn't completely blow up my life. Yet with sex and love addicts we hide this character defect even from ourselves. We profess to love someone (and may even believe it on some level) so we can hide lust in a dark corner of our minds. S.L.A.A. helps us get honest and prevents lust from lurking.

I explore the world through the lens of healthy sexuality that supports my sobriety.

November 12

GROWING UP

I'm a kid at thirty-seven, finally learning to grow up! But also like a kid, I'm experiencing life in a new way. The challenges are exciting. The learning is painful but not nearly as painful as all that guilt and acting out. – S.L.A.A. Basic Text, Page 206

At 13, when my mom told me that painful experiences were a part of growing up, I remember crying for days. I didn't want to grow up—especially if it involved pain. I liked my stuffed animals, naps and being in my own little make-believe world. I wanted everyone else to take care of me. I was given very few responsibilities. Chores could be easily managed with a fantasy world. Living in the real world was to be avoided at any cost. I held onto that philosophy until I walked into the rooms of S.L.A.A. and started working the Steps. Running errands, promptly admitting when we're wrong, being of service and a worker among workers may not be glamorous but can be exciting because it builds self-esteem. I started focusing more on contributing at work and I made more money as a result. Knowing that I was earning as a result of my abilities instead of asking someone else for money (and therefore being under their control), was self-esteem building. I was able to stop looking for partners who would rescue me. Finally growing up made all areas of my life better.

Today, I welcome the pain and privilege of growing up in the fellowship.

November 13

MUTUALITY

We began to notice those daily phone calls, or other overtures which we habitually made to those who never responded in kind. We came to regard the energy needed to maintain these meager relationships as an unacceptable expenditure. – S.L.A.A. Basic Text, Page 114

"Am I having the relationship with you that you are having with me?" I must ask myself this question constantly. As a love addict, I want to fantasize and idealize every relationship. As a sex addict, I need to do everything I can to manipulate relationships to get what I want. I heard in a meeting that serenity is another word for clarity and honesty. If I'm spending a lot of time and energy on someone who ignores me or doesn't seem to like me very much, I need to be honest with myself and investigate my motives. If I'm doing anything I can just to make someone stay because I'm afraid to be alone, I can use the tools of the S.L.A.A. Program to learn to feel comfortable in solitude. I can pray and meditate and take myself out on a date and appreciate myself. If I'm not given loving kindness in my relationships, I can find it in a meeting or in meditation. I can stop going to the "hardware store for milk" and realize when someone is not capable of giving me what I need.

I am interdependent in my relationships, putting my well-being first.

November 14

PROGRESS

From the surrender to our powerlessness over sex and love addiction and then over ourselves, we had come to know ourselves more as we really were, and had entered into partnership with a Power that could free us from the addiction and lead us into a new life. We had begun to develop spiritual qualities which we had never had, or had allowed to go unused during our active addiction. – S.L.A.A. Basic Text, Page 89

"Progress, not perfection." I heard that phrase all the time when I was going to S.L.A.A. meetings and still acted out for years. I couldn't understand why progress in recovery was so slow when the progression of the disease could be so quick. Why didn't God just take it away without all this work from me? It's a long journey from being an active addict to a spiritual recovering person. Progress is difficult to see when you're still acting out. At first, I needed fellows to point out how much better my life was than it was in the days when I was acting out. Eventually, the tools of S.L.A.A. helped me know myself and to see reality enough to see my own progress. The Steps helped me transform my life into a better version of myself through partnership with my Higher Power. The spiritual qualities like patience and serenity which were never available to me in my addiction, became available with my progress in the program.

I am happy and patient with the daily progress of my recovery.

November 15

EUPHORIC RECALL

Often a life pattern that seemed, to me, to have been as grim as anything I had experienced myself would simply be lost to the person's conscious awareness as soon as the current crisis was over... He or she would leave us, ready to go out and repeat the pattern of self-destruction once again. – S.L.A.A. Basic Text, Page 39

Euphoric recall kept me stuck in abusive relationships and bad situations my whole life. For some reason, no matter how bad a situation was, after a week or sometimes a couple of days away from the person, I would remember only the good things about them. He was kind to me once, forgetting about all the times he put me down. He came to see me when it was inconvenient for him—forgetting about all the special occasions he missed. Overlooking negative experiences usually meant that I wanted to continue to have sex with the person. If I set boundaries or pointed out bad behavior, I risked losing what I so desperately wanted to survive. S.L.A.A. sharing dragged me out of that denial. I had to let go of the fantasy that my magical thinking could change a bad relationship into a fulfilling one. Fellows made me remember how miserable I was in the past addictive relationships. Listening to sponsees reminded me of what I used to put up with. Realizing I could rely on a Higher Power instead of sexual acting out helped me to stay out of fantasy. I trained my brain to get out of euphoric recall as soon as possible.

Higher Power, help me stay present and recognize euphoric recall when it occurs.

November 16

TOOLS OF RECOVERY

What are some of the tools we have found which can help us hold up and behave with consistency in spite of external challenges? Clearly we needed some ways to counterbalance the erosion of our awareness and resolve. – S.L.A.A. Basic Text, Page 111

The Basic Text answers this question with some suggestions in Chapter 5, "The Withdrawal Experience," such as, "Sustaining awareness by starting and keeping a list of very short observations of exactly how we were feeling in withdrawal...daily prayer and S.L.A.A. related activities...regular contact with other members of S.L.A.A., or others who were trustworthy and knew what we were trying to accomplish...abstain[ing] from sexual or romantic entanglements...In fact, every way we found that had awareness-sustaining power was important." I would add to the list of suggestions: self-care, meditation and, if necessary, attendance of other Twelve Step meetings. Therapy and recovery literature also helped keep me aware. Having non-triggering fun and positive thinking can help too. If I do at least one thing on my list every day, I guard against a slip. The tools of recovery help me stay in the program and learn how to avoid the things that drag me back to addiction.

The more I use the tools of my recovery, the sharper they become.

November 17

SHAME

I now know that there are others out there who are making their imperfect way through life as I am. I have nothing to be ashamed of. I have everything to look forward to. I have one day at a time. I have myself. – S.L.A.A. Basic Text, Page 176

From what I've learned about myself in recovery, guilt and shame seem to be the axis around which my disease comes alive So, when I come from a place of shame, and I'm not aware that I'm having these feelings—I want to act out on them. I go into romantic intrigue or romantic obsession. I try to find my next sexual fix, or I think about cheating on my partner, or I become interested in pornography. When I'm in a state of shame, I lose my relationship with my Higher Power and I start losing myself. The more that I've become aware of my shame and am able to make friends with the feelings, the more I'm able to know that the feelings won't consume me. I don't need to act on them and I can get a sense of freedom. Knowing that others in S.L.A.A. are trudging the same road with me helps. I try to remember that I wouldn't shame a fellow for doing the same things I am powerless over because of my addiction.

Today, my Higher Power is releasing me from shame.

November 18

THE FIFTH TRADITION

Each group has but one primary purpose—to carry its message to the sex and love addict who still suffers. – S.L.A.A. Core Documents, "The Twelve Traditions"

I try to keep my shares focused on sharing my experience, strength and hope. S.L.A.A. was the solution for me. It brought me to my spiritual experience. Without it, I was destined to a hopeless search for something that would cure me. Because of this idea, the Fifth Tradition was born. Our primary purpose is to carry the message. The only thing that matters is that each individual is a sex and love addict and can help other sex and love addicts heal like no one else can. Meetings focus on sobriety. Everyone laughs when the leader of a meeting says, "This is not a place to meet prospective partners." But that statement keeps the focus on our primary purpose for gathering together. Carrying the message is important because we can't keep the gift of sobriety unless we give it away. A hospitals and institutions program is important, as is speaking at meetings, public outreach, working with sponsees and being an example to people in the world who may also suffer from our disease and ask us how we are recovering.

Today, I carry the message of recovery and sobriety to others suffering from this disease.

November 19

COPING SKILLS

There was no judgment, no condemnation, no guilt, no punishment, no heaven, no hell, no purgatory, no penance: just the adult manifestations of the coping strategy of a small child trying to survive as best he could in the situation in which he found himself. – S.L.A.A. Basic Text, Page 264

Growing up, my coping skills were mostly addiction-based. They did not served me well. Usually they created more chaos to deal with. Today, after working the Twelve Steps, I rely on my Higher Power for everything, for every decision. I call my sponsor and fellows to help me clear away my emotional turmoil. Only then can I make a clear decision because that's when I am able to hear my Higher Power's voice. I can't hear it when I'm clouding over with fear, resentments, anger, excitement, emptiness, shame, guilt, etc. Before recovery, when I got in that place where I couldn't hear, I used to run and soothe my spinning head and physical being with some sort of acting out. Now instead of acting out, I pray, I write it out, and try to look at my behavior by doing a Fourth Step. Then I call my sponsor, do a Fifth Step, and talk to my Higher Power again. It's cool that I have some tools. This is what I've been looking for my entire life. S.L.A.A. recovery is a gift.

Today, I use the skills I've gained working the Twelve Steps to cope with my discomfort.

November 20

ABANDONMENT

The horror of this "death"—a death of my "love" relationship with Lenore—was that my whole self-concept, which had come from being part of her was also dying. My sense of "I" had come out of my sense of "We." I had no positive, personal, independent self-concept. - S.L.A.A. Basic Text, Page 5

I heard somebody say in a meeting, "I abandoned me not to be abandoned by you." I was so much of a love addict in those days that I would constantly check my messages and ignore my life. In looking back, I realized I was abandoning my needs so as not to be abandoned. It's been a long hard lesson. The truth is that I could never be present because if I was in a relationship, I was not with me. I spent a lot of time preparing myself, anything for someone to notice me. As soon as my partner wasn't around, I was lost in my head and not present for myself. For 21 years in S.L.A.A., I've worked very hard, and my relationships today with men, women and family are different. They're healthy and I can be content with a loving healthy phone call or interchange and not have to cling and grab. I don't have to fear abandonment anymore. I have myself, a Higher Power and S.L.A.A. to rely on. I no longer take it personally when someone needs to leave. I live my life and let them live theirs.

I face my fears daily knowing my Higher Power is with me.

November 21

GETTING HIGH

The addictive experience has been so mind altering for most of us that, once enmeshed in it, we have lost track of ever wanting to be out of it!...[Eventually] the novelty of each new romance or "reconciliation" no longer screened the truth from view: each new situation was just another hopeless episode, holding about as much promise of fulfillment as swapping bubble-gum cards. As this jaded feeling broke through, the addictive "high" was becoming harder and harder to achieve and maintain. – S.L.A.A. Basic Text, Page 106

As a sex and love addict, getting high is one of my most favorite ways to check out and live in fantasy. I get a physical hit from an attractive person, from a romantic story, from any fantasy relationship that I can create with a stranger or a good friend. But over time, I became like the crack addict searching the drug dens for salvation and finding only misery and degradation. In my recovery, I'm learning to recognize that high and make different choices. I can choose to stop talking to certain people. I can avoid triggering movies. I can remind myself that an intriguing person is just a friend and that I only feel high because I want to numb out and escape my life. I remind myself that usually what I feel and think has nothing to do with that person, our relationship or reality.

Today, I recognize intrigue and set the boundaries I need to recover.

November 22

NARCISSISM

Self-centeredness and pride seemed to be at the root of our difficulties. We had dressed and acted seductively, craving attention and more than our share of sexual intrigue. We spent money to impress people, and verbally abused those who did not give us the attention we thought we deserved, or tried to hurt those who would not give us our own way. We proved our power by seducing our friends' lovers or spouses, and responded with anger when the satiation of our self-centered needs was thwarted. – S.L.A.A. Basic Text, Page 80

My obsession with getting my needs met meant that no one else mattered. At times, I was like a caged animal wanting to stalk its prey. An animal has no concern for the object of its affection except to devour it for all it's worth. Even when I wasn't the most narcissistic person in the relationship, I was still participating in self-centeredness. Staying with that kind of unavailable person is a form of narcissism, because I think I'm powerful enough to change them into a person who can give me what I need. Wasting energy on those kinds of romantic pursuits is not giving back to the community or being of service to others. In sobriety, serving my own agenda finally was replaced with seeking God's will and my narcissism eased. It still pops up in many things I do, because I'm an addict. S.L.A.A. gives me the tools to recognize and combat it.

Today, I seek humility and connectedness. I am one person amongst many.

November 23

HAPPILY, EVER AFTER

The image of our relationship that comes to mind is that of a plant which got pruned at a certain point and then sprouted off in a newer, stronger direction. The roots of the plant are still there, only the growth they are nourishing is a healthy, vibrant one...just for today my story ends with a "happily ever after" by my own definition. – S.L.A.A. Basic Text, Page 63

Before my recovery, I thought the idea of happily ever after was some fantastic dream in which I would be with the perfect partner and everything would be magical. I would have all my dreams come true. I didn't realize that real happily ever after means balance in any healthy relationship. This means that sometimes things would be good, and sometimes things would be bad. It means that at times things would be exciting and sometimes things would just be boring. To achieve balance, I need to go inside myself and see who I am, and what I'm contributing to my relationship. The magical thinking of finding happily ever after and my corresponding fantasy of what I'll get out of a relationship is outside of me. I need to look within to find serenity through my Higher Power instead. That is the only thing that is enduring. The fantasy goes up in smoke when the relationship hits rocky waters. My Higher Power and the program of S.L.A.A. are rocks I can stand on through any storm and find safety.

My happily ever after is the gift of sobriety.

November 24

CONSENSUAL SEX

I am learning to eliminate abuse of all sorts from my life...I give all I can, in whatever way I can, so that when the time comes that I get the insane urge to throw myself away on an abusive sex or love partner, I will be saved. S.L.A.A. and God can save me if I put them first before my sex drive and my need for love. - S.L.A.A. Basic Text, Page 260

During written inventories, we often discover how much we used and manipulated others or indulged in mutually harmful activities. I used excuses, saying, "But hey, it was consensual." Just because a sexual relationship is consensual, doesn't mean it's morally healthy. Throughout my Fifth Step, my sponsor kept saying, "In this situation you both were consenting adults, but he was spiritually sick just like you. When you're doing something because you're powerless over an addiction it's not really giving consent. You're high and not in your right mind." When it comes to sex, I now need to pause and ask myself, "Is this for my greater good?" I need to think about the other person. I ask myself, "Is this for their greater good?" I can't always take people at their word because I have an addict in me that can misinterpret and manipulate the situation. To stay centered and on the path of sobriety, it's helpful for me to outwardly question my motives with the help of my program, my sponsor and outreach calls. Today, I make sure I get more than merely verbal consent before any sexual involvement. I seek the spiritual consent of my Higher Power through the feedback of my support network.

I check my motives and truthfully assess the situation before deciding to have sex.

November 25

THE THIRD SIGN OF RECOVERY

We surrender, one day at a time, our whole life strategy of, and our obsession with the pursuit of romantic and sexual intrigue and emotional dependency. – S.L.A.A. Core Documents, "S.L.A.A. Signs of Recovery"

The phrase "life strategy" sums up my entire essence of existence. When I read that line in the S.L.A.A. Signs of Recovery, I knew it was me to the core. I lived a life of "if not this one, then bring on the next one." My hunger and dissatisfaction were insatiable. I was never content "winning" the partner, the search then had to begin for the one to put on the back burner. It was exhausting headhunting for future victims while obsessing about the current lover. The object was never to be alone with the realization that my life strategy was insane and killing my soul. Twelve Step work helped me create a better life strategy and to pursue more appropriate relationships. Thank you, Higher Power, for S.L.A.A. and the last affair that brought me to my knees in surrender. Thank you for the people who show up to meetings week after week with their experience, strength and hope to show me the way.

I surrender my will and ask my Higher Power to heal me from emotional dependency.

November 26

WHITE-KNUCKLING

I had enough background in psychology to understand the danger of trying to force myself to believe I had no wanting or desire. I knew that if I did this the desire would not go away, but would gather force and probably ambush me at some particularly inopportune moment. – S.L.A.A. Basic Text, Page 29

An addict has been through it: the earnest pledges to stay away from our substance of choice, the electric tension coursing through our body as we lie in bed, mentally banishing triggering notions from our head. We hold on tight, blood forced away from protruding knuckles, hoping we won't lose our grip before the urge passes. How long can we hold out? How strong must we be to fight our addictive impulses? If we are working a program, we don't need to worry about personal strength. If our willpower alone could keep us from slipping, we wouldn't need the Steps to begin with. The First Step says that we are powerless over our addiction. We need something stronger than us in order to find sobriety. Our Higher Power can hold on tighter than we can ever hope to. No more wishing, or swearing oaths, or white-knuckling. By letting go and letting God, we surrender our will to the one who has all power. We no longer need to fight the addiction alone.

Today, my Higher Power and the fellowship give me the strength to maintain sobriety.

November 27

WORDS INTO ACTION

We had to put into action on a continuous basis the principles we had used in our inventories and amend-making. We had to concentrate on making frequent appraisals throughout the day of our own intentions and shortcomings, and to do as much as we could to make these right as they happened. – S.L.A.A. Basic Text, Page 97

I can't just sit around and talk about changing. If I say I'm sorry for something, I seek to try my best not to continue to harm anyone. My living amends is to make sure I don't re-engage in the behavior once hurt feelings have mended. I can talk all I want about spirituality, but if it doesn't show up in my actions, people will know that I'm deluding myself. Doing a Tenth Step every day and reading it to my sponsor or trusted fellow helps me do this. I can get input if my words and actions don't match up. Others can see if I am living in fantasyland. Getting current helps too. If people laugh at what I'm saying, I don't take it personally. I realize that my disease is clouding my thinking and I can take action to stay sober. I pray and meditate and turn my will and my life over to the care of my Higher Power. And then I take whatever steps I need to clean up the wreckage of my past and to live in dignity and grace.

Today, I am willing to go to any lengths to stay sober. I am fearless in my recovery.

November 28

BLESSINGS

We have received, and continue to receive, many blessings we would not have known how to ask for. Life is open-ended, and wonderful. New chapters in well-being await us. – S.L.A.A. Basic Text, Page 103

Since getting sober in S.L.A.A., I daily thank my Higher Power for the peace of mind that passes all understanding and for being blessed with loving relationships, worthy goals, ideals and purpose. Because of recovery, I have personal fulfillment in my work and play. I have been granted freedom from financial worry and blessed with high levels of health and energy—all of which my addiction would have never allowed or would have destroyed had I continued down the path I was on. Even today, after years of recovery, I still ask for my Higher Power's help to continue with all these blessings, to have an attitude of gratitude, and to serve at my highest level in my work with others. It's a blessing that I get to share my S.L.A.A. recovery and as a result become a channel for healing. The program has uncovered these blessings for me. I never would have been well enough to recognize them or participate in them before. Through my work here, I can feel the source of love which is of God flowing inside of me, through many challenges. I'm excited to see what new chapters of well-being await me.

Higher Power, I am grateful for the blessings of well-being today.

November 29

SELF-LOATHING

We had...turned this hatred inward, redirecting it against ourselves, using our self-loathing to justify our unworthiness to be loved by others, letting them off the hook! – S.L.A.A. Basic Text, Page 90

How far I was from loving myself when I came to S.L.A.A. I loathed myself and all I had done to harm others and to put myself at risk. I did not believe anyone could truly love me, because I saw nothing lovable about myself. After some time in S.L.A.A., I defined my bottom-line behavior. With the aid of my Higher Power, I have been sober from that behavior one day at a time for twelve years. My road to recovery has been full of challenges, and I have had to re-learn how to communicate and relate with others. My Higher Power has loved me through this process. Now I have come to love myself. By loving myself, I have room and experience to love others. My Higher Power has restored a family to me. My Higher Power gives me what I need. Because I know that a Higher Power loves me, I can love myself.

I practice self-love a day at a time.

November 30

OPPORTUNITY

Despite all the cultural and rational camouflage behind which our addiction could hide, it was impossible, short of suicide, to kill that innermost voice that whispered to us of life's opportunities for growth and wholeness that we were helplessly letting slip by. – S.L.A.A. Basic Text, Page 70

Opportunity can be a double-edged sword for addicts. Before sobriety, I looked for ways to create the opportunity to act out. If I was success-minded, it was only to find more addictive indulgences. It was more desperation than positive, creative energy. When my love addict took over, the right set of circumstances was a sign that it was meant to be. These opportunities were focused on romance. This allowed my addiction to hide behind cultural and rational camouflage. Everyone wants a relationship, right? I helplessly let everything else pass me by because my addiction was too powerful. Schoolwork, career pursuits, time for family and even time to enjoy nature were not on my radar. My only focus was on the "person" or the addictive high. S.L.A.A. helped me turn that into a more positive search for life-affirming activities. My Fourth and Fifth Steps opened my eyes to a whole new world. It widened my focus to include more than romantic pursuits. I run from opportunities to act out today. I look for ways to increase my conscious contact with my Higher Power. The beautiful things in life are open to me now because I'm not so focused on chasing a high.

I look for an opportunity or a lesson in life situations.

December 1

MIND-READING

We could clearly see that the inability of others to take us at our word gave evidence of how distorted their perceptions were. In truth, we could see, in their reactions, much of our own former, addiction-serving "misreading" of the intentions of others.* – *S.L.A.A. Basic Text, Page 116

Mind-reading is a form of fantasy. It's part of my objectification and sexualization of people. When I'm looking for potential partners, I make up stories in my head about complete strangers–who they are, where they're going in life and what their sexuality is. The reality is that I don't have a clue. The same thing happens when I'm in a relationship. I think my own brain will be more successful in determining my partner's intentions than I would be if I just asked. As a child, I was afraid to talk about my emotions or inquire about the emotions of others, so I assumed I would have to go on doing things that way for the rest of my life. In recovery, I practice sharing my feelings and thoughts with others so they may know the real me. When I'm unsure of someone else's intentions, I ask them for clarification. I won't get anywhere trying to read people's minds. If I engage with others and am willing to be vulnerable and open up about myself, then I get to live in reality. Through this process, little by little, fear fades away.

Today, when unsure what others are thinking, I ask.

December 2

COMMITMENT

Gaining sober perspectives in the areas of trust, sex and intimacy was difficult. True intimacy, we found, can not exist independent of commitment. – S.L.A.A. Basic Text, Page 103

Having experienced infidelity and multiple divorces between my parents, I learned early that commitment was unsafe and impossible. I did not see healthy commitment modeled for me so I did not learn how to be a reliable person. Not only did this early learning take a toll on my relationships, it took a toll on my work and my sense of self. I had little trust in others and less trust in myself. Even without these examples, trust is difficult. I had turned other human beings into my Higher Power and became fearful that their unreliability would turn my life upside down. Using the S.L.A.A. tools and Twelve Steps, I have come to see that faith in a Higher Power could restore my trust in life. I am no longer fearful that I will turn others into my Higher Power, and therefore my fear of commitment has lessened. But then the real work begins. Having sober perspectives in the area of trust was just the beginning. Sex in a committed, sober relationship has its challenges. I need my Higher Power and S.L.A.A. fellows to help me navigate relationship building.

I build healthy, intimate and committed relationships today.

December 3

SEX AS COMPETITION

For us, the sexual arena was loaded with treachery and a lot of defensive maneuvering. This caused us a lot of pain and a sense of futility. – S.L.A.A. Basic Text, Page 61

I was an athlete growing up and it was always like, "Let me show you how great I am. Ta-da. This is the show." I was often flying around the room. I was rarely present. In a crowded room I had to be one up on everybody. I felt that if I could get into the sport of any situation, I could feel safe, but it didn't usually work out that way. Having sex as a competitive sport doesn't allow for intimacy. It doesn't allow for me to be the real me. When I'm desperate to win, I do a lot of underhanded things. That doesn't build self-esteem. Being in S.L.A.A. helped me to learn how to become present and show my true self. I learned it doesn't have to be a competition, because in any competition someone is going to lose. In a relationship, if someone loses their footing, we both lose. Although people do come in and go out of our lives, we never stop relating to them. Relationships are like a balance—the goal is to be centered. If our partner loses and goes down, we may go up for a time and feel like we've won, but in doing so we've lost our center.

Today, I am an equal in all my relationships.

December 4

BELOVED

Our wealth of common experience, our deepening knowledge and understanding of each other, began to fulfill that promise of unfolding love which is what we had always been truly seeking in a relationship. We were now capable of loving and of being immensely loved, redeemed, and filled with grace, and we knew this. Our appreciation of this newfound wealth continues to grow, to this day. – S.L.A.A. Basic Text, Page 153

It's impossible to feel beloved when being abused or ignored. I could not reach that point of intimacy with a partner because of my alternating sex addiction and anorexia. Both are blocks to deepening knowledge and understanding of each other. I was too self-centered to bother trying to understand someone else (a fact that was revealed in stark reality in my Fourth and Fifth Steps). I kept choosing abusive or unavailable partners to continue the cycle of running away from scary intimacy. If someone really knew me, they would hate me, so why even start the process of really getting to know each other? S.L.A.A. restored my self-esteem and helped me find a Higher Power that I could slowly learn to trust more and more. I first felt beloved by my sponsor and fellows in S.L.A.A., then by my Higher Power and then myself. Only after I was given these gifts was I able to embark on sober dating and feel beloved by a partner.

Today, I am beloved to my Higher Power, myself and others.

December 5

UNREALISTIC EXPECTATIONS

One area in which we often experienced difficulty was in continuing to be open and forthright about our feelings and motives, and our expectations of others. We would hide disappointment, hurt, fear, or anger under a façade of acceptance... [We needed to concentrate] on our own faults and failures. We were coming to know that our own attitudes and actions were the only aspects of our lives which we stood any real chance of influencing. – S.L.A.A. Basic Text, Page 97

A character defect of unrealistic expectations was all over my Fourth Step writing. Sex and love addiction is rooted in fantasy. If I sit in the fantasy too long, I start to believe that life should be that way. I can't look at my attraction to a married man realistically and still try to steal him away from his family. Ego and pride make me have unrealistic expectations of life. This character defect makes it difficult to stay right sized with my feet on the ground. My sponsor taught me to stop the fantasy before it blew up to become unrealistic expectations. Talking to fellows and sharing at meetings can bring the expectations to light and help me see where I'm being unrealistic. True partnership can be in reach if I look at the other person as the human being that they are and not try to mold them in my mind into who I want them to be.

I place realistic expectations on myself and let go of controlling others.

December 6

THE TWELFTH STEP

Having had a spiritual awakening as the result of these Steps, we tried to carry this message to sex and love addicts, and to practice these principles in all areas of our lives.* - *S.L.A.A. Core Documents, "The Twelve Steps of S.L.A.A."

A key here is the spiritual awakening as the result of the Steps. If my therapist had been able to cure me of my addiction, I probably would have made her my Higher Power and eventually drifted away from the program. The Steps can bring about some kind of spiritual awakening, hopefully sufficient enough to help us stay sober and want to give back to the program. Spiritual awakenings can vary from little "aha" moments to lightning-bolt experiences. Any variety can be enough to help us try to carry the message and practice the principles. No one wants to work for free. In early recovery, when I was asked to speak on the other side of town or to clean up after a meeting, my first thought was, ***I should be getting paid for this.*** I came to realize that my payment is sobriety. Carrying the message can sometimes be payment itself. When people express gratitude for our service or when we see even hopeless cases recover, it can be self-gratifying (as long as we stay humble). Practicing the principles in all areas of our lives can be a difficult task. Attempting this sometimes brings out my perfectionism. But if I'm doing a thorough Tenth Step every night and practicing the Eleventh Step, it is possible.

It is my Higher Power's will for me to be of service to others today.

December 7

UNSTRUCTURED TIME

Even in the midst of withdrawal, we turned to hobbies or new pursuits that were engrossing and would consume some time and energy. As the addictive cravings lessened, we often found ourselves actively enjoying these new activities and the discovery, or re-discovery, of talents. We have, among S.L.A.A. members, new Ph.D.'s, new musicians, new marathon runners, new artists. – S.L.A.A. Basic Text, Page 140

When we were in our addiction, unstructured time was a terrifying concept. Mostly all we knew how to do was fill it with acting out and unhealthy behaviors. Acting out let us escape for an all too brief time, but the costs of that escape were great. So, we learned to fear unstructured time, as it triggered the insanity of our addiction. Now in recovery, we no longer fear it. We welcome it, as it gives us opportunities to work our program and nurture ourselves. We read and reflect on recovery literature. We pray and meditate. We call a program friend. Some of us have taken on new hobbies or gone back to school. A whole new world has opened up to us now that we aren't leaving time open just in case they call. In sobriety, unstructured time has become a gift that allows us to connect with ourselves, with God and with others. When we're thinking of God and others, no time is unstructured.

I fill open time slots today with thoughts of sobriety and how I can be of service.

December 8

KEEP COMING BACK

People found some grievance to serve as an apparent justification for leaving S.L.A.A. Some other S.L.A.A. member's personality traits, or some perceived S.L.A.A. "line" on a topic relating to sobriety, was often used as an excuse to have nothing further to do with the Fellowship. – S.L.A.A. Basic Text, Page 120

The Basic Text goes on to say that, "our group experiences seem to indicate that our difficulties with open, honest relationships with other human beings make us especially vulnerable to this kind of excuse to isolate ourselves from the Fellowship." Even though we say, "Keep coming back" to newcomers, they might not listen and they may leave. The Basic Text offers guidance on this: "We have neither resisted this type of strategy, nor have we encouraged it. After all, such individuals ultimately answer, as do we all, not to the S.L.A.A. Fellowship, but to the personal addictive pattern itself." I tried to talk myself out of meetings many times over the years. But I heard so many personal stories of people leaving and dying from our disease (or coming back and reporting great suffering) that I stuck around. The few times I did try to leave, I got so beaten up by my disease that I came crawling back, begging for help to ease my suffering. The fellowship saved a seat for me and welcomed me back with open arms. That helped me want to stick around. Staying in S.L.A.A. meetings saved my life and gave me a life worth living.

I remain committed to the program and the gifts of recovery.

December 9

THE THIRD CHARACTERISTIC

Fearing emotional and/or sexual deprivation, we compulsively pursue and involve ourselves in one relationship after another, sometimes having more than one sexual or emotional liaison at a time. – S.L.A.A. Core Documents, "Characteristics of Sex and Love Addiction"

Before joining S.L.A.A., I would get into relationship after relationship. Sometimes, I would have a partner who assumed I was monogamous with them, and then have someone on the side. I did this compulsively, repetitively, and without any self-awareness. Inside, I had such a deep feeling of loneliness and deprivation. After going to outside resources for help, talking to people in S.L.A.A., and talking with my sponsor, I realized it came from experiences in childhood in which I felt deprived. As an adult I was still carrying those feelings with me even though I wasn't experiencing deprivation in my life. I was self-medicating by getting into one sexual liaison after another. Even emotional and romantic liaisons that were non-sexual that were somehow intriguing or thrilling kept me from my feelings. It was a way to escape not unlike how an alcoholic or drug addict would escape using alcohol or drugs. Since I joined S.L.A.A., I can acknowledge and accept that sometimes I have feelings of deprivation and loneliness, but I don't have to act out on them. I can just have my feelings.

I am active in my recovery program and fully accept where I am today.

December 10

CONTRARY ACTION

Many members of the fellowship find it helpful to list behaviors that have a positive, personal element—behaviors that fulfill, nurture, bring healthy pleasure, growth and improve quality of life. Committing to do them can fill the time that we used to spend acting out and can help us grow along spiritual lines. – from the "Setting Bottom Lines" pamphlet

When the impulse to act out comes up, my sponsor tells me to take contrary action. Usually, this means actions of self-care: meditating, going to a meeting or taking myself out on a date. Sometimes, it can even be as simple as listening to classical music. Self-destruction was my default action in my acting out days. When I practice healthy habits, I'm less likely to unconsciously beat up on myself if I'm in the midst of triggers. When I encounter a person or situation that used to trigger me to act out in the past, I can stop, pray and decide the best action to take towards serenity. If I can't see what that action is, I can call my sponsor or a fellow. Thank God for cell phones. Outreach and prayer are great tools of the program. They stop my addict's voice of the past that says, "What can I get away with?" and turn it into, "What will help my spiritual recovery?"

My top-line behaviors support and sustain me.

December 11

SOCIAL MEDIA

I had thought that through time, the S.L.A.A. program, and... psychotherapy, I had let go of M., but I realize now that I had always been holding onto the shred of the fantasy that somehow sometime, we could reestablish an intimate relationship. – S.L.A.A. Basic Text, Pages 264-5

New forms of social media arise quicker than we can add them to our bottom lines. They make it easier to reach out and connect with an old flame, and allow us to keep tabs on or stalk ex-lovers. Every "like," every positive comment, every picture of our ex with someone new, has the power to lift our egos or smash them to pieces. Exchanges of emotional intrigue, that may have once taken months, may now take place in minutes. Yet it is not the medium that causes us pain, so much as our addictive impulses and our capacity to exploit any situation or environment to meet our addictive needs. Living in the modern world may require us as sex and love addicts to set limits on what media we consume or how we consume them. It doesn't mean we must cut ourselves off from technology completely. Working with a sponsor helps us determine what works best for us in our recovery. That may mean avoiding social media sites, unfriending past lovers, or unfollowing friends so we don't see their posts. If we are honest with our sponsors and others in the program, we can determine what methods work best to stay sober.

I focus on healthy behaviors and work with my sponsor to abstain from bottom-line behaviors.

December 12

CHAOS AND DRAMA

We were working at standing still, at freeing ourselves from the tentacled clasp of a frightful addiction which had driven us to such a pitch of self-destroying activity. Simply not doing it took tremendous effort. We were suspending, for the moment, our very real fears concerning the outcome of all this by attending to those tasks immediately at hand. – S.L.A.A. Basic Text, Page 109

Before S.L.A.A., I believed it was normal to bicker and constantly have fresh chaos and turmoil in intimate relationships. That's what I experienced as a child; that's what I created as an adult. I ran from it as a child and hid out in my fantasy world. As an adult, I thought life was boring without it. I had to create dramatic situations in order to test my partner's loyalty or gauge interest. The resulting chaos was always more than I could handle. It became like a snake that would move too quickly for me to catch it. Life as a snake-handler was stressful. It didn't allow for hopes and dreams. I had a sense that something was wrong in that I could not change it on my own. Through working the Steps in S.L.A.A. I have healed most of the long-term baggage that I thought I would carry around forever. The obsession to act out has been removed from me and I no longer compulsively create drama. I no longer inject chaos. I'm happy today. If I can do it, you can do it too.

I attend to tasks at hand promptly and face the daily challenges of life.

December 13

DECEPTION

Most of us were riddled with insecurity and feelings of inferiority. We were terrified that if we gave up the "con," and the defects which gave rise to and supported it, we would be viewed with contempt and would never find anyone to "love" us again. – S.L.A.A. Basic Text, Page 85

In active addiction, I thought defects were my friends. I thought it was natural and that everyone lied to get ahead. No one revealed their true selves at parties and in nightclubs. They had to have a con in order to find someone to go home with. My endless predatory search drew me to the places that I would most likely find sex. I had to live that life of percentages, because I was too insecure for the quiet, intimate, patient way of getting to know people and becoming intimate before having sex. Putting on the "con" was exciting. The risk of getting caught brought an adrenaline rush and feeling of superiority that was difficult to give up. Past experience taught me that whenever I revealed my true self, I was abandoned or viewed with contempt. No one wanted to deal with my problems (maybe because I met them in a bar). My sibling met the partner in a bar and lied to him about being a smoker. They've been married for twenty-five years now and have two kids. There was always proof in the world to rationalize my defects. S.L.A.A. taught me to let go of my rationalizations and defects and become vulnerable. Through working the Steps and following a dating plan, I was able to ease my insecurity and become intimate.

I am honest and authentic while practicing self-love.

December 14

SOCIAL ACCEPTANCE

In relationships with others we let go of self-serving power and prestige as driving motives. This left us open to the discovery of just what it is that makes any relationship with people, whether professional, personal or social, worthwhile. We found that in relationships with others we had only as much to gain as we had to share. – S.L.A.A. Basic Text, Page 102

I craved social acceptance but felt like an alien who was abandoned on this earth without a map. I also blamed my inability to connect on others: My parents moved me around the country too much; they didn't allow friends over to the house; my boyfriend was controlling and jealous so I couldn't go to social events. The list of excuses was long. But when I truly looked inside, I knew that I was only finding ways to hide out, because I felt that I would never be accepted for who I was. My way of hiding out was usually to numb out in fantasy about a relationship saving me and meeting all of my needs. I didn't need the social acceptance, because I had him. But that wasn't reality. He was almost never there for me. When I found S.L.A.A. and started going to fellowship and social functions, I found where I belonged. I was able to be a total nerd or to fall apart emotionally and people loved me through it and understood. When I reached sobriety and started giving back to the S.L.A.A. community, I started getting acceptance from the outside world, too.

I am happy with who I am today and accept how others may see me.

December 15

LIVING IN THE PAST

Our feelings about [love interests] often had taken on, during withdrawal, the rosy glow of sentimentality and idealism, especially in circumstances where the former spouse or lover had been living a considerable distance away from us. We were not thinking about the old, chronic, and perhaps only dimly recognized breakdowns in communication which had formerly crippled us. – S.L.A.A. Basic Text, Page 147

While it is good to learn from the past, as sex and love addicts, we learned some wrong things. Many of us still live in that time, trying to protect our inner child from being hurt and abandoned. But we are adults now, and we live in the present. The past is no longer our reality. We are not as powerless as we once were. We can nurture that hurt inner child and nurture our adult selves in the process. Now we deal with what is immediately in front of us. God takes care of the future, and he'll help us surrender the past, if we let him. The pain and abandonment of the past led us into addiction. By not letting go of it, we abandon ourselves. Others love us in the present. The past is but a small part of who we are.

My Higher Power changes me into a person who lives in the present and acts from my heart.

December 16

PRACTICE

We discovered that we needed to continue to live out the values which emerged in us through our recovery in S.L.A.A. in all areas of our lives. We had learned to work toward a high standard of honesty, openness, sharing, and responsibility, and to treasure the feeling of purpose and sense of belonging which accompanied these values. – S.L.A.A. Basic Text, Page 102

We strive to practice Twelve Step principles in all areas of our lives. Part of the five "S's" in the S.L.A.A. Preamble to the Basic Text is: "Our practice of the Twelve Step program of recovery to achieve sexual and emotional sobriety." We practice the Twelve Steps and then we get a spiritual practice. In Step Seven of the S.L.A.A. Basic Text there are clear instructions on spiritual practices: "This new partnership with God, in which we accepted direction about just what part of our spiritual being needed exercise, had amazing results. As we practiced thoughtfulness toward others, really giving without holding onto the expectation of reward, impatience slipped away." When we ask God to remove a defect, it doesn't just magically disappear. We may have a momentary reprieve or see what's hidden behind the defect. We need to practice "doing the next right thing." Even if we fail to change ourselves, we can use our mistakes to learn and improve our conscious contact with a Higher Power. I heard the old saying, "Practice makes perfect," my whole life. But the Twelve Step program emphasizes progress not perfection.

I practice the principles of the Twelve Steps in all areas of my life.

December 17

THE SIXTH TRADITION

An S.L.A.A. group or S.L.A.A. as a whole ought never to endorse, finance, or lend the S.L.A.A. name to any related facility or outside enterprise, lest problems of money, property, or prestige divert us from our primary purpose. – S.L.A.A. Core Documents "The Twelve Traditions"

When we have one goal and focus (Tradition Five—Each group has but one primary purpose—to carry the message to the sex and love addict who still suffers), the fellowship has more of a chance of survival and can help more people. Addicts (especially sex and love addicts) tend to want to be all things to all people. That's why we need boundaries that are clear. No matter how great the cause we don't endorse, finance or lend the S.L.A.A. name. Addicts often have a lot of bad ideas and waste a lot of time debating whether they are bad ideas or not. Even if we put our money and time into worthwhile endeavors, we are still taking resources away from our primary purpose. I have read nearly every book that a particular famous psychologist has written on sex and love addiction. But I wouldn't tell my home group to sell his books at our literature table or donate part of our rent to his foundation. If we did so and this man was found to be a fraud, people would lose faith in our group. Individually, I can buy his books and donate. But the group needs to take care of itself.

Today, my primary purpose in the program is to help others while ignoring outside influences.

December 18

FEAR

Deep-seated fear still lurked behind the scenes, prodding us into making unreasonable demands and attempts to extract absolute security from our personal relationships and endeavors. Only slowly and sometimes grudgingly had our provisional use of a Power greater than ourselves given way to a more regular reliance on this Power for guidance. – S.L.A.A. Basic Text, Page 98

Fear motivates nearly every action in an addict's life. It was instilled in us during childhood. Every time we witnessed what speaking up would lead to, every time we felt judged for sharing our feelings, every time we saw the model of what we wanted to be and realized that we fell short, fear was there to paralyze us. Most people are familiar with Franklin Roosevelt's famous quote, "We have nothing to fear but fear itself." Maybe it's a cliché, but it's true. It is only fear that holds us back and tells us we cannot be ourselves. It is only fear that leads us to cling to qualifiers or return to the computer for more acting out. If we are to combat this fear and live freely, we must remember that our Higher Power is in control. Faith in God erases fear. When we give our will and our lives over to our Higher Power, fear no longer runs our lives. We can live free, accepting life on life's terms and know serenity.

I convert fear to strength using my recovery tools.

December 19

QUICK TEMPER

The quick temper we asked God to remove was checked momentarily; we could suddenly feel the defensive fear that was hidden behind the anger, and find the courage to act on faith rather than fear. – S.L.A.A. Basic Text, Page 89

My dad was a rageaholic when I was growing up, so I tried to avoid lashing out in anger at anyone. I worry and find it difficult to manage the fear. When worrying reaches a boiling point, it comes out as anger, and I lose my sense of humor. I don't realize there are stages to a quick temper. First, the fear and worry, then the defensiveness, and then the anger. If I'm worried about losing my job for months at a time and someone makes a comment about my performance, I get defensive and explode in anger at them The program taught me to meditate and pray. I read in a recovery book on Step Two that I could take a year break from worrying. I don't know if I'll be able to do that for a year, but I'm mindful of the fear and practice every day. Today, when someone comments on my performance, I take a realistic look at my behavior. Are they right? I try to change where I can and if I can't, I have faith that my Higher Power will show me the way in each situation.

I accept anger as part of my emotions and allow myself to experience it.

December 20

EMPATHY

Yet here I was, not acting out addictively and actively reaching out for others with whom to share the awareness I had found about my addiction. There was a great sense of warmth in discovering, experiencing and sharing a common bond with...other people. – S.L.A.A. Basic Text, Page 36

It was difficult to understand or feel what another human being was experiencing in my acting-out days because I was so self-centered. I never even noticed or cared what another person felt unless it affected me. Being able to sit in a meeting and listen to everyone's open and honest sharing has helped immensely. I hear people talk about things that I've experienced before and I relate. Even if I haven't experienced what they're talking about, I usually have felt the same feelings. Sometimes I feel like my empathy goes too far and I'm depressed for the rest of the day or crying when I don't mean to (after all, I am trying to heal my co-dependency). But I've come to realize if that happens, it just means emotions are surfacing that I need to look at. There's a lot of supportive energy when sadness is shared in a room full of people who are capable of empathizing.

I empathize with others, being grateful that I can relate.

December 21

SELF-FORGIVENESS

Through the Fourth Step process, we realized that pride and willfulness had hidden the yearning of a lonely and fearful child, an emptiness that cried out to be filled. We did not cause it, and we could not control it. In this realization was the beginning of compassion, our first glimpse of self-forgiveness. – S.L.A.A. Basic Text, Page 81

Before the program, I couldn't deal with the shame that I felt over my acting-out behaviors. I tried to numb it out and blame it on alcohol. But in my heart, I knew I was broken. I thought I could deal with the yearning, loneliness and fear with my search for "the one" in, of all places, bars and nightclubs. But as most of us know, that's usually not a good strategy. It created more shame and emptiness, a feeling that there was no hope in the world. One-night stands and public liaisons with married men do not create good self-esteem opportunities. Hearing people share their experience in S.L.A.A. gave me hope. I brought all the shameful acts out in my Fourth Step and my sponsors said they had gone through the same experiences. I realized I was not alone. I didn't have to be that fearful child lashing out at the world anymore. I could be kind to myself and forgive my actions instead of engaging in self-destructive acts. S.L.A.A. gave me a new freedom and joy in fellowship and newly found respect of myself and from others.

I forgive my past self and give myself the time to heal.

December 22

GOSSIP

I became terribly disillusioned toward the end of ninth grade when I discovered that people were gossiping about me just as much as I gossiped about them...Emotionally, I had adopted [a "Lone Eagle"] stance to the world – I spoke to no one about my inner life. – S.L.A.A. Basic Text, Page 233

It doesn't say anywhere in our Twelve Traditions "thou shalt not gossip." It's human nature to talk about other people. I learned in the program that gossip mixed with anger is a polite form of murder by character assassination, feeding our ego by proclaiming our own righteousness and putting ourselves above the people we are talking about. We aren't trying to help them. Gossip, by definition, involves details that are not confirmed to be true. I always tempered my shares early in the program because I was so afraid of people talking about me. In my family, gossip is dangerous because it is character assassination and is used against me to make me feel shame. Over the years in the program, I've learned to forgive the people who gossip about me. I realize they are spiritually sick. I don't have to fear that their words will destroy me. The people who know me love me and know that the gossip is untrue. The people who don't know me will either get bored and focus on someone else or will come to see the truth. All I need to do is stick to my side of the street and focus on my life and the rest will resolve itself.

I choose restraint and respect when speaking of others.

December 23

MILESTONES IN S.L.A.A.

This shift in our attitude from need to hope brought us to another fundamental milestone in our recovery. We had laid the first foundation stone for the acquisition of faith. We had seen that it was possible for us to live through the pain of withdrawal without returning to our old patterns, and we sensed that the Power to do this was coming from outside ourselves. – S.L.A.A. Basic Text, Page 76

When the Fellowship-Wide Services store started selling Step chips, I thought it was strange. But when I gave my sponsee her Step One chip and realized what a milestone it was to work through the Steps with someone else, I realized the value. Admission of powerlessness, having a spiritual experience, letting go of long-held resentments, making amends, recognizing and letting go of character defects and being comfortable carrying the message are all milestones in recovery. The list goes on and on. If we stick around long enough, we get to experience them all. We constantly grow and change. When we get through pain without going back to our old patterns, we know the addiction doesn't have its power over us. The Steps are the blueprint and we are the architects. Our Higher Power doesn't change us without our help. Loved ones may not see each milestone as it happens, but they see the changes in us. We know that although S.L.A.A. is hard work, it's a much better way of life.

I recognize and celebrate the milestones in my recovery from sex and love addiction.

December 24

INDEPENDENT

I had never learned a sense of independent thought. All my responses to life were gauged in terms of what my parents would expect of me. While this is undoubtedly true of many people, I'm not sure it lasts well into most people's thirties. – S.L.A.A. Basic Text, Page 198

My need for dependence started with my parents. The message of my upbringing was, "You have no common sense, so let me control you." Independent thought was met with rage. How dare I speak out? Children are to be seen and not heard. I carried that into all my relationships. If I had my own thoughts or expressed some need, I would ruin the relationship. I desperately needed to avoid a dismal future. Those were my options. Not the vision of what I am today. S.L.A.A. taught me how to feel comfortable in solitude and take care of my own needs. It helped me discover new hobbies and find a purpose in life. I don't have to shut down my dreams in favor of preserving relationships anymore. If someone has an opposing thought, I discuss with them instead of plunging into paranoia that they will run screaming from me. When a task needs to be done, I don't search for the rescuer who will do it for me and then control me because of my inability to take care of myself. I can do my own tasks. I can be confident in my independence and sexual orientation because I rely on my Higher Power.

I honor my own thoughts and remain open to others.

December 25

LISTENING

Whatever decisions were to be made would have to be the result of really being able to hear the other's points of view—not just listen, tolerate, and dismiss the other. – S.L.A.A. Basic Text, Page 60

I read an article that said talking about ourselves releases dopamine. Some people get addicted to this and talk too much. We need to learn the art of listening. I think that's what S.L.A.A. teaches us. No crosstalk means that we sit and listen to a thirty-minute speaker or three-minute share without interrupting them with our self-centered thoughts. We may have those thoughts, but we don't say them out loud. We get to practice concentrating on what the speaker is saying instead of ourselves. Meditation teaches us to listen for God's will. I learned to listen to my sponsor when I hit enough brick walls because of my acting out. Only then did I realize maybe she had some experience, strength and hope to help me out of that kind of pain. I found my intuition in S.L.A.A. (something that was rarely present in my acting out days) and began to listen to myself. Listening takes patience and humility. The article also said that we get bored after thirty seconds of listening to someone else. The boredom is a lack of dopamine. With sobriety, we learn to get appropriate amounts of dopamine from healthy activities, instead of being addicted to getting more at all costs.

I improve my listening skills daily to build bridges of understanding and compassion.

December 26

SUPPORTING S.L.A.A.

The only qualification for S.L.A.A. membership is a desire to stop living out a pattern of sex and love addiction. S.L.A.A. is supported entirely through the contributions of its membership and is free to all who need it. – S.L.A.A. Preamble

When I dropped coins in the Seventh Tradition old-timers would say, "How much money did you spend on your addiction?" Thousands. It would have been hundreds of thousands if I had continued in my disease. But why should S.L.A.A. be supported entirely through contributions of its membership? Because of our Seventh Tradition. If I don't support S.L.A.A. monetarily and with service and attending meetings, it won't survive and I will consequently die in my disease. It can't be free to all who need it if we aren't doing volunteer service work and giving donations. I had thought of it as a one-way street. S.L.A.A. supports me. But after the program supported me for a while, I realized that the ones who stuck around and stayed sober were of service and cared about making sure S.L.A.A. had a future. When old-timers do the work "for fun and for free," newcomers realize the idea of humility. It helps us stay nonprofessional (Tradition Eight) and stick to our primary purpose (to carry the message). We don't have to be swayed by any one contributor's opinion out of fear of losing their support.

S.L.A.A. supports me and I, in turn, am happy to support S.L.A.A.

December 27

CASUAL SEX

I sedated my anxiety, sadness and emptiness with a lot of casual sex...going to bed with—the guy I met in the laundromat, the guy who worked in the liquor store, the guy who lived upstairs and his roommate, and the man I met when my car broke down. – S.L.A.A. Basic Text, Page 212

If you take the emotion out of the word casual, it means not permanent. I preferred sexual relationships this way (except when I couldn't get enough on demand). An agreed-upon casual attitude allowed my social and emotional anorexia an excuse to flourish, unnoticed by me. When emotions are involved, casual means relaxed and unconcerned. This has made me realize I have never had casual sex. It was never relaxed when I was on the hunt for the drug-of-choice to sedate my anxiety or uncomfortable feelings. Even though I acted unconcerned, I was secretly concerned all the time. I had all kinds of fears swirling around in my head that I never let out. Usually, numbed-out feelings came back full force or more the morning after an encounter. Being in a constant state of needing more just to feel even doesn't ease anxiety. After years of sobriety in S.L.A.A, I've come to find that many things in life can be casual, but for me, sex isn't one of them. I need some permanence and concern.

I approach sex from a state of wholeness and integrity before I connect with another.

December 28

THE SEVENTH SIGN OF RECOVERY

We allow ourselves to work through the pain of our low self-esteem and our fears of abandonment and responsibility. We learn to feel comfortable in solitude. – S.L.A.A. Core Documents, "S.L.A.A. Signs of Recovery"

Talk about low self-esteem. Putting myself down used to be one of my favorite things to do. A friend in S.L.A.A. broke me of that habit. Whenever I was around her, she would only allow me to say nice things about myself. Doing my Sixth and Seventh Steps also helped me realize that I am human and make mistakes. I don't have to let perfectionism rule my life and make me feel like I'm a piece of crap. My sponsor said, "To have self-esteem, do esteemable acts." Being of service accomplishes that. But even when we deal with all those feelings of low self-esteem, this Sign of Recovery can be difficult. Many of us have been abandoned our whole lives. We have been immature, refusing to take any responsibility for our lives. Through my work in S.L.A.A. I was able to stop going for the unavailable people who would surely abandon me, and instead choose the trustworthy, reliable person. I finally learned to feel comfortable in solitude. The person that I used to be was no fun to be around and it was dangerous to be alone with her crazy thoughts. But the person in long-term recovery is great. Who would have ever thought I would say that about myself?

I take a quiet moment for myself today and feel freedom in solitude.

December 29

JUDGMENT

Today I can compare that calm, centered feeling to a candle burning steadily. That small flame guided me on my path. When it burned steadily, I was usually on good spiritual ground. When it flickered or went out, I was headed for trouble. The process of stopping what no longer worked, and learning new ways to add things which did work, was pretty smooth. – S.L.A.A. Basic Text Page 249

Good judgment is not my strong suit. Making considered decisions was rarely appealing to me, much less within my reach I was so powerless over my addiction that I had to rush into everything without thinking about it. Getting it done now was imperative because so many things in my life tended to evaporate into the ether. In my chaotic, hurried existence there were no sensible conclusions. The things that made sense to my diseased mind were insane in reality. I did some crazy things thinking it would make my qualifier stay or come back. Whenever faced with the choice of two actions, I chose the easiest, which is not always the healthiest. The program helped me with judgment by teaching me to ask fellows, pray, meditate and write. Tenth Steps, pros-and-cons lists and journaling all help me consider a decision in depth. I still may choose the wrong path, but no one can say I didn't make an effort and I usually learn something useful. Out of it all, I can be proud of the fact that I'm more aware than I was in the days of my addiction. Seeking God's will keeps me centered.

I take time when contemplating a major decision by praying, meditating and journaling.

December 30

TURNING IT OVER

We came to understand that if we were unable to prescribe our own treatment for sex and love addiction, then we would be better off turning "our will and our lives over" to the God of our understanding, even if we did not know what might happen as a result. – S.L.A.A. Basic Text, Page 77

How do we turn over our will? Clear instructions to become ready to do this are given in Step Three. First, we look at where our beliefs have been faulty (relationships, personality traits and values). Then we stay clear of addictive entanglements and pray. We pray when we get up in the morning and say a thankful prayer when we go to bed at night. Once on the path of turning it over, we will often be attacked by doubt, fear and longing—voices telling us to go back to our old lives. We can stay on the path of conscious contact with a Higher Power of our understanding by sharing at an S.L.A.A. meeting, taking time for reflective solitude and gaining insight into ourselves and our addiction. Insight comes from a thorough Fourth Step. But it can also come from dreams, psychotherapy, meditation or sharing. Once we refuse to waste our energy on addiction, and instead turn to a Higher Power, the insights are able to come into view.

Higher Power, help me see and do your will, not mine, today.

December 31

EXPERIENCE

As we realized how helpful this network of support was, we sensed that a belief in any specific God or divinity was unnecessary. Our need for faith could be answered with an affirming hope, a sense of the possibility for spiritual guidance that was already apparent in the experience of the S.L.A.A. members who preceded us. – S.L.A.A. Basic Text, Page 75

Those in S.L.A.A. who have many years in the program and have sponsored many people can teach us a lot. They keep coming back and offer us examples of how to deal with life. Even if they have difficulties, they continue to show up and face their responsibilities. They keep the S.L.A.A. network of support going and are living proof that the program works and there is hope. Just the fact that they're in the rooms instead of out there creating havoc and demolishing lives is enough. Sometimes they say things that newcomers remember and it can give them hope. They share their experiences in sickness as well as in health, so we can see how far they've come. We can ask questions during fellowship and maybe get some insight into how to handle our problems. There weren't many problems that my sponsor hadn't come across. They shared their experience, strength and hope and that helped me come to an answer. If they hadn't experienced it, they had a group of other long-time sober people to ask. The fellowship helps me deal with life sanely and soberly.

I draw on the experience, strength and hope of others daily. I share what I have gained in the program and carry the message to other sex and love addicts in need.

The Twelve Steps of S.L.A.A.

1. We admitted we were powerless over sex and love addiction, that our lives had become unmanageable.
2. Came to believe that a Power greater than ourselves could restore us to sanity.
3. Made a decision to turn our will and our lives over to the care of God as we understood God.
4. Made a searching and fearless moral inventory of ourselves.
5. Admitted to God, to ourselves, and to another human being the exact nature of our wrongs.
6. Were entirely ready to have God remove all these defects of character.
7. Humbly asked God to remove our shortcomings.
8. Made a list of all persons we had harmed, and became willing to make amends to them all.
9. Made direct amends to such people wherever possible, except when to do so would injure them or others.
10. Continued to take personal inventory, and when we were wrong promptly admitted it.
11. Sought through prayer and meditation to improve our conscious contact with a Power greater than ourselves, praying only for knowledge of God's will for us and the power to carry that out.
12. Having had a spiritual awakening as the result of these steps, we tried to carry this message to sex and love addicts, and to practice these principles in all areas of our lives.

The Twelve Traditions of S.L.A.A.

1. Our common welfare should come first; personal recovery depends upon S.L.A.A. unity.
2. For our group purpose there is but one ultimate authority — a loving God as this Power may be expressed through our group conscience. Our leaders are but trusted servants; they do not govern.
3. The only requirement for S.L.A.A. membership is a desire to stop living out a pattern of sex and love addiction. Any two or more persons gathered together for mutual aid in recovering from sex and love addiction may call themselves an S.L.A.A. group, provided that as a group they have no other affiliation.
4. Each group should be autonomous except in matters affecting other groups or S.L.A.A. as a whole.
5. Each group has but one primary purpose — to carry its message to the sex and love addict who still suffers.
6. An S.L.A.A. group or S.L.A.A. as a whole ought never to endorse, finance, or lend the S.L.A.A. name to any related facility or outside enterprise, lest problems of money, property, or prestige divert us from our primary purpose.
7. Every S.L.A.A. group ought to be fully self-supporting, declining outside contributions.
8. S.L.A.A. should remain forever nonprofessional, but our service centers may employ special workers.
9. S.L.A.A. as such ought never to be organized; but we may create service boards or committees directly responsible to those they serve.
10. S.L.A.A. has no opinion on outside issues; hence the S.L.A.A. name ought never to be drawn into public controversy.
11. Our public relations policy is based on attraction rather than promotion; we need always maintain personal anonymity at the level of press, radio, TV, film, and other public media. We need guard with special care the anonymity of all fellow S.L.A.A. members.
12. Anonymity is the spiritual foundation of all our traditions, ever reminding us to place principles before personalities.

The Twelve Concepts of S.L.A.A.

1. Ultimate responsibility and authority for S.L.A.A. world services always reside in the collective conscience of our whole Fellowship.
2. The Annual Business Conference, by delegation, is the voice and conscience for our world services and of S.L.A.A. as a whole.
3. To insure effective leadership, each element of S.L.A.A. - the Conference, the Board of Trustees, staff, and committees - all possess the "Right of Decision."
4. The "Right of Participation" is maintained by allowing members the opportunity to cast one vote up to the level at which they are trusted servants.
5. The "Right of Appeal" prevails so that minority opinion is heard and personal grievances receive careful consideration.
6. The Conference recognizes that the chief initiative and active responsibility in most world service matters should be exercised by the trustee members of the Conference acting as the Board of Trustees.
7. The Articles of Incorporation and the By-Laws of the Fellowship are legal instruments, empowering the trustees to manage and conduct world service affairs. Although the Conference Charter is a legal document; it also relies on tradition and the power of the S.L.A.A. purse for final effectiveness.
8. The trustees are the principal planners and administrators of overall policy and finance. They have custodial oversight of the separately incorporated and constantly active services, including their ability to hire staff.
9. Good service leaders, together with sound and appropriate methods of choosing them, are at all levels indispensable for our future functioning and safety. The primary world service leadership must be assumed by the Board of Trustees.

10. Every service responsibility is matched by equal service authority – the scope of this authority is always well defined whether by tradition, by resolution, by specific job description or by appropriate charters and by-laws.
11. The trustees need the best possible committees, staff, and consultants. Composition, qualifications, induction procedures, systems of rotation, and rights and duties are always matters of serious concern.
12. The Conference observes the spirit of S.L.A.A. Tradition,
    a. taking care that it never becomes the seat of perilous wealth or power;
    b. that sufficient operating funds and reserve be its prudent financial principle;
    c. that it place none of its members in a position of unqualified authority over others;
    d. that it reach all important decisions by discussion, vote, and, whenever possible, by substantial unanimity;
    e. that its actions never be personally punitive nor an incitement to public controversy;
    f. that it never perform acts of government, and that, like the Fellowship it serves, it will always remain democratic in thought and action.

Notes

Notes

Notes

Notes

Notes

Notes

Notes